Love and Whisky

Betty Lee

Love and Whisky

The Story of the Dominion Drama Festival

 McClelland and Stewart Limited

The author and publisher gratefully acknowledge the assistance of the Canada Council. Acknowledgement is also made to Michael R. Booth for permission to quote an extract from his article "Pioneer Entertainment: Theatrical Taste in the Early Canadian West."

0-7710-5221-9

The Canadian Publishers
McClelland and Stewart Limited
25 Hollinger Road, Toronto

Printed and bound in Canada

To Marian M. Wilson,
archivist of the Dominion Drama Festival and Theatre Canada

"If this organization becomes a success, it will have
been founded on love and whisky."

Col. Henry E. Osborne,
Honorary Director of the Dominion Drama Festival,
1933–1939.

Contents

Foreword by Robertson Davies ix
Preface xii

PART ONE **Where Do We Go From Here?** 14

CHAPTER ONE **The Big Bash. Saskatoon, 1972.** 15

PART TWO **Beginnings** 42

CHAPTER TWO **The Way It Was** 43
1. From Neptune to the Road. 43
2. "Let's hit the road and clean up in Canada." 57

CHAPTER THREE **The Two Vice-Regal Schemes** 64
1. "With a view to encouraging the sister arts." 64
2. The amateurs are coming, the amateurs are coming. 76
3. The great idea. 83
4. "A red-letter day in the annals of Canadian drama." 94

CHAPTER FOUR **The First Years** 99
1. "Now we've got to get organized." 99
2. To be or not to be. 105
3. "The spirit of a nation." 114
4. And so, on to the next time. 122

PART THREE **The People and the Problems**   130

CHAPTER FIVE **Politics**   131
1.   The Road to the Top.   131
2.   And then there were the Incidents.   143
3.   The French are growing restless again.   161

CHAPTER SIX **Finances**   177
1.   "Well, we've created the thing, how will we
          pay for it?"   177
2.   It started all over again, but money migraines
          remained.   183
3.   Think commercial.   190
4.   Whisky and broadcasting.   197
5.   The nervous sixties.   204

CHAPTER SEVEN **Adjudicators**   213
1.   But where do we find the judges?   213
2.   Help!   229
3.   But did the adjudicators enjoy themselves?   236

CHAPTER EIGHT **The Social Side**   248
1.   "What do you do in the DDF besides putting on
          those plays?"   248
2.   Competition and awards are all part of the prestige. 258
3.   You mean it's old-fashioned to be dignified and
          socially acceptable?   269

CHAPTER NINE **Players, Plays, Photographers and Professionals** 274
1.   "I'll never forget the time I went to a DDF Final." 274
2.   "And look what the DDF did for me!"   281
3.   The play's the thing, but where are the
          Canadian playwrights?   287
4.   "And in this corner, the professionals."   299

CHAPTER TEN **Change**   304
1.   "We've got to keep moving with the times."   304
2.   So what happened to all those people in Saskatoon?   316

          Bibliography   321
          Index   324

Foreword

No one who was associated with the Dominion Drama Festival will read Betty Lee's pages unmoved, whether it be to astonishment, admiration, indignation or laughter. I was for many years a keen supporter and follower of the Festival and was even for a time one of its Governors, but I never knew that it was so rich and strange as this admirable book shows it to have been. I knew the toil and the heat of the regional preparations, rehearsals and Festival presentations, and for a time I was one of those who, Miss Lee assures us, looked so haughtily splendid, so demonstrably creatures of the *ancien régime*, at the Finals. But things were going on behind the scenes – the real scenes of the Great Theatre of Life, and not the *coulisses* of the many theatres in which the Festivals were held – which were dark to me. I knew, of course, of the perpetual anxiety about money, but even when I was a Governor I never knew how grave the financial situation was; the worst was veiled from all but a few. So, as I read Miss Lee's pages, the wonder of the DDF is presented to me in a new and more complete form than I had known while I was in the thick of it.

I congratulate Miss Lee on her achievement and am honoured to be asked to introduce her book. She has been both frank and kindly, revealing yet discreet. She has never been dull, which the Festivals themselves sometimes were. She has made an invaluable contribution to the history of the theatre in Canada, for which everyone who is interested in the development of the arts in this country will thank her. For the Dominion Drama Festival, from whatever angle we look at it, was an astounding achievement, and undoubtedly the most astonishing thing about it was that it was an artistic venture dedicated to destroying itself in the cause of art: whatever passions may have raged in the breasts of its patrons and competitors from time to time, it never lost sight of its desire to keep the art of the theatre alive in a country where it was greatly threatened, and in the end to bring about a better theatre, in the hands of professional artists, in which the amateurs would either have to relinquish their amateur status, or go back to seats among the audience. This is what it achieved. The foundation of our modern professional theatre rests on many stones, but the largest and the strongest is the achievement of the Dominion Drama Festival. The professionals may forget that, and it will do no harm if they do so, but the historians of art must never forget.

Into only one realm of Festival activity does Miss Lee fail to penetrate fully, and that is not her fault, for nobody could do so who had not been through the experience. That realm is the one which was inhabited by all those aspiring people who chose plays, rehearsed them and put them on the stage, won acceptance from a local audience and at last, tremulously, made their way to one of the Regional Festivals and submitted their work to the Rhadamanthine glare of the Adjudicator. There were, literally, thousands of us who did that, and we remember our misgivings, and the lifting of the spirit that followed a good adjudication. And we remember, alas, the terrible loss of face that followed a harsh adjudication.

We remember the adjudicators, in all their bewildering variety, from such great men of the theatre as Harley Granville-Barker and Michel St. Denis, and such admirable critics as Robert Speaight, down through a welter of judges of the lesser sort, ending in a few who played such tricks before high heaven as made the angels weep. When we recall the complete sway that these adjudicators exercised over the taste of so many otherwise independent people – an influence which varied little whether the adjudicator was plainly a man of great attainment or demonstrably a mountebank – we wonder why it was considered such very bad taste to adjudicate the adjudicator.

Best of all, perhaps, we remember the great progress from the presentation of one-act plays, often of trivial quality and played dowdily in curtains, to performances of classics and worthy plays from the modern repertoire, elegantly and imaginatively designed, dressed and lit. Though the DDF never succeeded in bringing a Canadian drama into being, it kept the whole country aware of what was being done in world theatre. And that was, in itself, a sufficient justification for its existence.

It is a fine thing to have a history of the Festival, and to have it so well done. As time passes, it will be realized more fully than is possible now what a great national effort that Festival was, and how it kept alight a flame which had been threatened with extinction. But thanks to the Dominion Drama Festival, Canada was never without a theatre.

Robertson Davies,
January 31, 1973

Preface

The room in which I have just finished writing the final draft of *Love and Whisky* is called the Locked Presses and it lies deep in the bowels of Massey College in the University of Toronto. For the past few months, I have locked myself daily in the Locked Presses, a prisoner of my assignment. The reason I am here at all, though, is that I was elected a 1972-73 Southam Fellow and Fellows are invited to use Massey College as their day or full-time headquarters during the academic year.

Despite repeated protests, it is hard to convince my colleagues that the two events that interrupted my journalistic career at *The Globe and Mail*, Toronto, were not planned to coincide. After all, this book was completed in the very building on which Vincent Massey – one of the founders of the Dominion Drama Festival – showered so much of his attention during the last years of his life. His papers and diaries are stacked in a vault not far from where I am now typing. His personal valet, Miroslav Stojanovich, is steward of the Massey College dining hall. Hart House – which once boasted the liveliest little theatre in Canada, thanks to Vincent Massey's patronage – is visible from the college gate house. Robertson Davies, a prominent DDF supporter in the corporation's early years, is Master of Massey. Dr. Pauline Mills McGibbon, a former DDF volunteer and president, is chancellor of the university itself.

The question I must ask myself, I suppose, is whether all of this somewhat eerie coincidence helped with the writing of *Love and Whisky*. It would be a romantic notion that a stroll in Vincent Massey's quiet quadrangle inspired me to get the job finally done. It would be equally sentimental to suppose that the sight of Miroslav Stojanovich standing to attention at the entrance of the Great Hall or Robertson Davies stalking to High Table in his Massey College gown spurred me back to the typewriter. More truthfully, it has been the individuals who have been close to the DDF and its controversial history — including Professor Davies, Dr. McGibbon, Librarian Douglas Lochhead of Massey College and countless others — rather than the coincidental atmosphere, which aided in shaping this book. As an outsider who was never there when it happened, I thank them all for their frankness and help.

Betty Lee,
Massey College,
November, 1972

PART ONE

Where Do We Go from Here?

CHAPTER ONE

The Big Bash:
Saskatoon, 1972

Ⅰt was somewhat of a jolt to members of Theatre Canada's national executive when they walked into their Saskatoon hotel rooms that Sunday, May 21, 1972, to find their annual festival had been upstaged by a Regina dog show.

Hotels in Saskatchewan distribute a provincial entertainment weekly called *Sight and Sound* to inform visitors of the province's current happenings. But instead of the 39-year-old celebration of Canadian theatre dominating the front cover of the magazine, the classy canines collected prime billing. It was annoyingly clear to those representing the national office, in fact, that the local festival committee had been dragging its heels and pinching its pennies as far as publicity was concerned. Even inside the book, Theatre Canada's week-long smorgasbord of cultural goodies was buried under a general listing headed *Theatre in Saskatoon.*

"Could it be Lassie?" joshed Theatre Canada's 1972 president, Helen Smith of British Columbia, straining to detect something theatrical about *Sight and Sound's* cover-pooch. As Mrs. Smith was aware, the presence of a Dominion Drama Festival was once enough of an occasion to set any Canadian town reeling on its ear. Who could forget the attentive press and broadcast coverage of everything from the DDF's visiting policy-makers, big-name adjudicators and ecstatic award-winners? The smiling attendance of Governors General, federal cabinet ministers and the upper-crust citizenry of that year's favoured host province . . . all-night parties in the homes of the great . . . white-tie balls and receptions. . . .

Mary Jane Scott, a Theatre Canada member-at-large who was sharing the presidential suite with Mrs. Smith at Saskatoon's Bessborough Hotel, grinned at her leader's comment, then launched into a cockney-accented suggestion that it might be as well to ignore the damned dog on the cover and order some food from room service. The president cheered up. Mrs. Scott was born in Edinburgh and is now president of the Victoria Theatre Guild. She is known in Theatre Canada circles as a dry wit, a tireless volunteer and a whiz at accents.

Despite the joshing, though, it was easy to note an aura of tension in the first hours of Theatre Canada's 1972 Big Bash in Saskatoon. This was just the second year since the Dominion Drama Festival changed its name and broke its traditional pattern of regional elimination contests leading to a Final Festival featuring adjudicators, Oscar-like trophies and cash prizes.

Adjudicators had now been replaced by animateurs (the name suggested by French-Canadians within the organization), professional persons who were expected to stimulate discussion among audience and participants. Competition and prizes had been abolished, to be replaced by pats on the back, encouragement and the democratic spirit of camaraderie. Festival was still basically Festival, but more important, it was also Showcase. In 1971, the first blueprint of the DDF's new look as Theatre Canada was unveiled at the National Arts Centre in Ottawa. Now, a year later, rumours were already flying that the restructured organization was panting for lack of financial oxygen and gnawing its nails over how to reduce its deficit of more than $20,000.

"You remember the time in 1969 when that group at the British Columbia regionals in Victoria lost their props?" asked Mrs. Smith. Mary Jane Scott nodded. "Sure I do. We hired a truck and drove all over town borrowing furniture and lamps and stuff. We lugged the whole load to the theatre, got the set fixed, then had fifteen minutes to skid back home and spray something under our arms in time for the evening's performance."

"We picked up a Vancouver newspaper on the way back," remembered Theatre Canada's president. "And there was this rotten headline about the DDF being just a lot of tea-drinking, mink-jacketed dilettantes. You know, the smoke just puffed out of my ears."

16

"I've never had a mink coat," said Mrs. Scott, preparing to order from room service. "Well, did you ever get your lamp back, Mary Jane?" asked Mrs. Smith. "No, I didn't, luv," replied Mrs. Scott. "Did they ever return your electric frying pan?"

Mrs. Smith flopped into a chair. "No, they never did. You know, I went to an executive meeting in Ottawa just after that crack about dilettantes. I was hopping mad about what people were saying and thinking. We'd been talking about changing the organization for some time. It had come up at meetings for years. But looking back now, I suppose 1969 was really the year we knew we had to do something about it."

Saskatoon's Centennial Auditorium is a $25,000,000 ramble of a complex which houses a 2,000 seat main auditorium, a cavernous basement, some conference rooms and acres of carpeted crush space. The auditorium is a fifteen-minute hike up Twenty-first Street from the Bessborough Hotel (which did better than *Sight and Sound* by hoisting a banner bearing the words *Welcome Theatre Canada*) and an even longer haul from the University of Saskatchewan where most of the 523 festival participants were being billeted at the expense of the Saskatoon committee. A Theatre Canada press release noted that seventeen groups – community, university and professional – would be involved in the week's non-competitive activities and would represent every province except Newfoundland and Prince Edward Island.

That first Sunday of the 1972 Festival, downtown Saskatoon was as empty as a prairie in a snowstorm. The Rexall Drug Store stared blankly at visitors who elected to walk to the Centennial Auditorium (most hitched rides as the week wore on) and so did Eaton's and the city's newest pride, an enclosed shopping mall. Over at the Auditorium, though, members of the local committee were trying out their registration techniques or sitting hopefully behind wickets waiting for local drama fans to storm the ramparts in search of tickets. The registration group looked nervous and harassed. The ticket sellers looked bored.

There was more festival activity upstairs. In one conference room a group of committeewomen from the national team was meeting with local volunteers about the makeup of a group to handle publicity. Nobody wanted to do Pictures. There was a lot of agitated talk about Pictures, then it was finally decided that if a photographer could be found who knew about theatrical subjects he could be left alone to do the job on his own.

Everyone seemed relieved at the decision and the entire group was positively beaming when Harry Hay, the tall, white-haired chairman of the local festival committee stalked into the room. Harry Hay, newcomers were whisperingly informed, was a Saskatoon optometrist who had an honorary doctorate of laws from the University of Saskatchewan. There were mixed reactions to the chairman's arrival among the group of national and local committeewomen.

Later, in another first-floor conference room, Dr. Hay sank into a chair and answered questions about how he became involved with Theatre Canada's 1972 Dramafest in the first place. "Well," he confessed with a small laugh, his teeth flashing, "Theatre Canada's regional representatives wanted the festival to come here and they needed someone to run the show. Actually, I did it because our former mayor, Sid Buckwold, asked me. Sid is a senator now, you know. An absolutely first-class fellow."

No, responded Dr. Hay. Strictly speaking, he didn't have much experience in the theatrical field though he had organized entertainment for the troops in Saskatchewan during the war. Concerts and things like that. Theatre Canada? Well, (again the small laugh), he had doubts about the organization's new image. The competitive aspects of former DDF festivals had drawing power, you know. He simply wasn't sure whether just a bunch of plays with discussions with "ana, ana, amateurs, sorry, *anamateurs*" was what the public really wanted. It wasn't that he was worried about the money involved, though the whole thing was going to cost Saskatoon plenty.

The budget? Oh, around $22,000. Out of that, the Saskatoon committee would have to fork over $5,000 to Theatre Canada's national office for its help in picking the plays, contacting the groups and its advice in organizing the festival. Saskatoon would also have to shell out part of the cost for feeding and sheltering participants and rental of auditorium and staff.

The local committee had managed to pry a grant out of the city and the Saskatchewan Arts Board and sure, there were other gifts from sundry sponsors. "But quite frankly," said Hay, shaking his grey head, "we'll have to sell a whole lot of tickets to break even. Thank goodness for the children's programs we've got together. They've been absolute sellouts."

He whipped off his glasses and got serious. "I'm going to be candid, now," he said, tapping the table. "I've been accused of being anti-French." He waited for reactions, then went on. "Anti-French! You know, there are four French plays in this festival. *Four!* I argued with the national committee. I wanted them to cut one or two of the French things because I *knew* they wouldn't sell in Saskatoon."

Now, continued Dr. Hay, box-office receipts showed he had been right on the ball. There was a French play about assassins or something from the University of Moncton scheduled for Monday night in the main auditorium. Just thirty-three dollars' worth of tickets had gone. He had suggested it might be a splendid idea to put on an Indian pow-wow for that night but the national people had been cool to *that* suggestion. On Tuesday at five o'clock there was another French play from Moncton which had sold only six dollars' worth of seats so far.

"It simply isn't fair to the performers who have come all this way," complained the festival chairman. "It's not that I'm anti-*French!* It's just that I'm concerned about those actors." Then there were other disappointments. Otto Lang, the federal justice minister and a local lad, had been invited to attend that night's festival kick-off, a musical called *Saskatchewan I'm Coming Home* performed by the Feehan High School. Lang had sent his regrets. "It's a pity," said Dr. Hay. "Otto is a Roman Catholic and Feehan is a Catholic school you know."

Other VIPs had also declined invitations. Secretary of State Gérard Pelletier had been invited for Monday night but had wired he had other commitments. The Premier of Saskatchewan, Allan Blakeney, was in Europe peddling local potash and so was Saskatoon's mayor, Harold Sears. Thank goodness the Lieutenant-Governor, Stephen Worobetz, was coming to the Thursday night performance. But both Roland Michener – who was Theatre Canada's patron, yet – and Prime Minister Pierre Trudeau had turned Saskatoon down.

But it had been pretty good fun, admitted Hay with another dazzling smile. Quite an experience, in fact. Perhaps, he

19

admitted cheerfully, he would think differently about the whole thing by the end of the week.

Back at the Bessborough hotel, Helen Smith was dispensing traditional executive hospitality in Theatre Canada's presidential suite. Until a few years back, white tie and tails and ball gowns were mandatory for top-echelon DDF brass at Festival. But in 1972 the men on the national executive wore tuxedos for Curtain Raiser night and most of the women wore informal gowns. One or two females actually arrived in pant-suits. "Don't you think it's wonderful," sighed Theatre Canada governor Barbara McIntyre of the University of Victoria, crossing her turquoise-panted legs, "that people can wear anything they want these days?"

"Were you at the 1969 Festival in Kelowna?" asked John MacPherson, Theatre Canada's first vice-president. Dr. McIntyre said yes, she had been going to Festival for a long, long time. Dr. MacPherson sipped impassively at a Scotch and water. "Bare feet," he said. "Girls with babies strapped to their backs. Amazing. It was lovely weather at Kelowna, though." He sipped again at his drink.

Members of the national executive – at least those who had turned up in Saskatoon – sat in two official boxes at the Centennial Auditorium that Sunday evening for the Feehan High School's performance of *Saskatchewan I'm Coming Home*. The boxes were suitably draped with Canadian flags. Harry Hay came on stage with a microphone to say the Saskatoon committee was having trouble selling tickets to the five o'clock performances and he wanted to announce that high school students could get in for just seventy-five cents. There was no reaction.

The festival chairman paused and cleared his throat, then told the audience that after the play, a group of ana, ana, amateurs – no, *anamateurs* ("We'll get used to that name after a while"), who used to be known as adjudicators – would come out and tell everyone how good or bad the performance was. There was some agitated whispering among the national office people that Harry was all confused about that. The animateurs were there to stimulate discussion after evening performances, not to *judge*. There would be in-depth sessions with cast-members next morning.

Dr. Hay plowed on. There would be quite an assessment of the play, in fact. Then the audience was invited to visit a downstairs lobby which had been christened the Green Room (no, ha ha, it wasn't really *green*) where there would be refreshments. Appreciative applause. The chairman laughed, then said people might be disappointed with the refreshments. Groans. However, everyone was invited to meet the cast and honoured guests and to make themselves thoroughly at home. All right? Then on with the play.

The musical from Feehan High School boasted a cast of almost 250 and was a repeat of a show written and produced to celebrate Saskatchewan's 1971 Centennial. It involved a gopher who had been commissioned by the Sun God to search around Canada and coax former residents of Saskatchewan back to their home province. After an hour and a half of singing, dancing and emoting, and just before the first intermission, quite a conga-line of cast members had been persuaded to head west. Several dog-tired festival visitors elected to head south to their rooms at the Bessborough Hotel.

After all, there were six days, twelve theatrical performances, two Theatre Canada meetings, three theatre conferences, a half-dozen early morning animateur post-mortems, a batch of workshops and twenty-seven children's shows to go before the 1972 Big Bash was over.

Feehan High School's *Saskatchewan I'm Coming Home* really got it in the neck at the 9:30 animateur session the following morning. The basement lobby of the Centennial Centre was jammed with members of the cast and other festival participants were curled up on the floor. Two Theatre Canada animateurs, Roland LaRoche, director, Centre d'Essai des Auteurs Dramatiques of Montreal, and Ken Kramer, artistic director of Regina's Globe Theatre, began the rap on a somewhat tentative key. Later, Yvon Dufour, Montreal actor and leader of the animateur team, wandered in and stood listening, his arms crossed on his ample chest.

LaRoche, a gaunt man who could easily double for Rasputin, chatted brightly about motivation and reasons for various techniques used in the production. "Yes, I liked that," he repeated, his intense eyes sweeping across the group. "I thought that was very nice, you know."

21

"Well, my main criticism of the play," decided Kramer, who is known as a non-traditionalist in the theatre, "is that the whole thing was a copy of a 1948 Broadway musical, right down to the kooky girl-friend. I kept waiting for the chorus to break into *I'm Just a Girl Who Can't Say No!*" There were loud guffaws, although Feehan's director Ted Fortosky and his blonde wife Danielle were not amused. Kramer shook his head sadly when the commotion died down. "What I was hoping for," he said, "was a different vision of Saskatchewan."

"I think the students got a lot of Saskatchewan into it on their own," said Danielle worriedly. "One scene, you remember, where the girl is upset because the gopher wouldn't help her find a man? The students put in that scene by themselves."

Kramer grinned crookedly. "I wonder how the feminists in the audience felt about that scene." Shouts of laughter. "I thought that scene was offensive," added the animateur, not laughing back. "It was," agreed LaRoche. "It *was* offensive and it is frightening to see things like that still on the stage." It looked as though the meeting was going to get rough, anyway, so LaRoche took a breath and waded in.

"I wish I could have heard the words of your song," he told Shelly Schwieder, one of the high school actresses. "I could hear what you said, but I couldn't understand a word when you started to sing." Shelly looked confused. "I had trouble breathing," she confessed. "And the microphone always seemed to be in the wrong place."

"Just technical. Mm?" nodded LaRoche helpfully, but without much conviction.

"One question is," continued Kramer, "how many communities within a hundred-mile radius of Saskatoon still use a wall telephone? There was one in the play."

"The time of the action kept jumping back and forth," said Ted Fortosky defensively. "I don't think we can attack the wall telephone. I mean, this happens all the way through, the dipping back and forward."

A blond young man propped against the wall leaned forward. "I would submit that the total reality of Saskatchewan is that we're not as far ahead as we think we are." There were shocked cries of "oh, oh!" and someone shouted from the crowd:

"As a Saskatchewanian I resent that." The young man shrugged. "I don't think the remark was in bad taste. Why don't you take a survey?"

Another young man who introduced himself as Ray Pierce of the Dalhousie Musical and Dramatic Society of Halifax said he was sorry but he found it hard to get interested in *Saskatchewan I'm Coming Home*. "I think it was created for a specific occasion which is now past. And I couldn't help thinking last night whether the cast was still back there in time with the centennial celebration. I'm wondering now what is going to happen with all that enthusiasm. Are you going to do the damned thing all over again? Or are you going on to something new? To me that's a helluva lot more important than whether you edit a scene out of last night's bloody production." There was a spattering of applause.

"I think Ray has a good point," agreed LaRoche, looking more savagely like Rasputin than ever. "Forget that show and try something else. Think about today and see if you really have anything important to say in this production. If you don't, don't say it."

Everyone was beginning to fidget. Then a bearded man dressed in jeans and a tattered sweatshirt got slowly to his feet. "I come from Saskatchewan," he announced very clearly. "I'm working in the East now and I'm going to work professionally. All I can say is that I was ashamed at what I saw here last night. I was amazed that things as awful as that were still being produced in my home province." He turned in the silence and walked away.

Dr. Harry Hay, dressed in a sporty checked jacket and razor-creased pants, was asking visitors in the auditorium corridor how they had liked *Saskatchewan I'm Coming Home*. "Lively show, wasn't it?" he beamed. "And it made us some money. That's the main thing!"

The children of Saskatoon were already beginning to invade the Centennial Centre. Twenty seven shows! In the Confederation Room, groups of tots were sitting on the floor while members of the No Name Theatre of Winnipeg (which had been backed by a Local Initiatives Program grant) played games lumped under the ambiguous title of *On the Way to Carberry*.

"What's your name?" asked No Name cast member Isabelle Van Humbeck of a wide-eyed six-year-old. "No, let me

23

guess. Does it start with D?" The child shook his head. "Does it start with Z?" No, it didn't. "Tell me then," coaxed Isabelle. "B," whispered the child. "Um," Isabelle rolled her eyes. "Boris?" No. "Bangaway?" No. Giggles. Whoever heard of a kid called Bangaway? "Bobby?" Yes. "Oh, goody!"

After some minutes of this, the children were invited to guess the names of the entire No Name cast while a member played a flute. Parents trying to sit unobstrusively around the walls of the Confederation Room shifted uneasily in their chairs and there was the beginning of a move toward the door.

Theatre Canada's program for Monday offered a veritable cornucopia of events for children and festival participants throughout the day: theatre workshops for young thespians interested in mime, marionettes or theatre games. More children's theatre. On stage in the main auditorium La Troupe de l'Université de Moncton were rehearsing their controversial entry, *La Nuit des Assassins*. In the lobby, volunteers still sat stony-faced behind the wickets waiting for the rush of demanding Saskatoon theatre-goers.

In the first-floor Saskatchewan room, the executive committee of Theatre Canada bypassed the theatrical fare and assembled for a meeting. A general conclave which would include less exalted Theatre Canada supporters – a gathering grandly known as Governors' Court in former DDF days – was planned for the following Saturday. Now, approximately twenty members of the top organization brass out of a possible fifty, were spotted around the room. Because the organization had always been steadfastly bilingual, arrangements had been made for simultaneous translation.

On Sunday, a crew from Montreal had erected a green soundproof tent in the corner of the Saskatchewan Room and two translators, one to handle French, the other English, sat at microphones behind a plastic window. A technician bustled around the room placing floor microphones so the incarcerated translators could hear what was going on. Then, everyone in the room was handed a transistor receiver with an attached ear-plug.

Everyone, that is, except Yvon Dufour, a Theatre Canada member-at-large as well as chief animateur, and Jeanne Sabourin, a national office staff member. Mme. Sabourin replied to questions in both English and French. Dufour, even though he spoke both languages fluently, preferred to use French exclusively. When he spoke – which was often – everyone in the room except Mme. Sabourin hurriedly plugged in their transistors. On the other hand, when English speakers took the floor, no one bothered to tune in. The English-to-French translator worked as per contract at these times, but it was clear from his attitude that he knew he was talking into the air.

A sheet detailing the budget for Theatre Canada's fiscal year ending March 31, 1973 showed the translation service at Saskatoon would cost $4,400 (the service would also be used at three theatre conferences during the week), $3,500 of which was donated by the Secretary of State's department. Theatre Canada was expected to meet the balance of the bill.

Helen Smith, looking crisp and presidential and with the dog-show incident clearly forgotten, sat dead centre at the head table facing the representatives of her executive. John MacPherson sat correctly on her right and further below the salt Don Nixon, a Theatre Canada volunteer from Ottawa, scribbled away at the minutes. There was an air of mixed anticipation and apprehension in the room. During the morning, in fact, Eve Gilstorf, a Theatre Canada employee who worked under the title of Director of Public Relations and Administration, predicted the get-together could spark some fireworks. This seemed appropriate enough, however, because it happened to be Victoria Day.

Nothing much happened for a long time. There was a series of speeches by Yvon Dufour about an omission in the minutes of the previous executive meeting that "disturbed" him. His reactions, he complained bitterly in French, had been very strong at the time and there was nothing recorded to show the reason why. "In my opinion," he said, "it was a very irritable situation, prejudicial to the French element of the festival." Everyone sat glassy-eyed with earplug cords dangling across their chins.

Jeanne Sabourin briskly joined the mysterious French discussion, the instantaneous translator fell hopelessly behind, and the English-speaking members of the executive looked confused. After more rapid talk, it turned out that Dufour had protested at a meeting in April about the Saskatoon festival committee's campaign to omit some of the French plays. This, apparently, had not been spelled out in the minutes of the previous get-together.

After some forty-five minutes of baffling banter, Helen Smith asked Dufour if he would be happy if a new statement concerning the Saskatoon affair were included in that day's minutes. Dufour shook his head energetically and said *"non."* Well, how about if a statement was attached to an amended version of the previous minutes? Dufour smiled, said *"oui,"* then everyone unplugged their ears and wondered if that could be construed as the fireworks. There were grateful glances at the door as Jean Walters, regional representative for Saskatchewan, arrived with an urn of tea.

While the cups were still clattering, Helen Smith said something about presenting a 1971 policy paper newly-revised by Philip Spensley of Montreal that would review the current structure and objectives of Theatre Canada. She asked Dr. Spensley to sit at a microphone on her left and everyone finished nibbling at their cookies and prepared to listen.

Dr. Spensley was one of the animateurs commissioned by Theatre Canada for the Saskatoon festival. As everyone in the room knew, he had been survey co-ordinator for the policy paper which led to the reorganization of the DDF and the emergence of Theatre Canada. There was a respectful silence as the bearded, English-born Montrealer took his seat at the head table.

"First of all," he said quietly, "I feel there are three major jobs that the organization has before it now in terms of our viability. One is finance. We all know that. We need a campaign in there, including fund-raising. I think public relations is a second matter. And I think the third is a membership campaign."

There was no comment from the floor, so Dr. Spensley forged ahead. Eve Gilstorf passed around copies of his policy paper. The paper, explained its author, would be subject to change as the organization evolved and the current revisions actually reflected some of the things that had influenced the organization one way or another during the previous year.

There was a mild skirmish in English and French concerning the official name of the organization but everyone eventually agreed they liked Theatre Canada-DDF. The primary goal of Theatre Canada, it was also agreed without too much argument, was "to be a catalyst on behalf of all Canadian theatre." Dr. Spensley had originally written "amateur" Canadian theatre "thus contributing to Canada's cultural identity" in the paper. But Dufour argued in

French that the organization should be a catalyst for *all* kinds of theatre and that the cultural phrase had political connotations. The offending words were instantly deleted.

The executive officers looked with interest at the eleven clauses clustered under the heading of Functions and agreed to most without comment. Papers fluttered as Dr. Spensley read them aloud:

* To co-ordinate on a co-operative basis amateur theatre activity on a national level.

* To be a national theatre resource centre which would, through its contacts with the total Canadian theatre scene, make information available to anyone wanting it.

* To keep a finger on the pulse of amateur theatre and to recommend, and where necessary, initiate appropriate action.

* To be the national and international spokesman for amateur theatre in Canada, wherever appropriate.

* To co-operate with all allied disciplines; dance, music, art, radio, television, film and so forth.

* To encourage, arrange and/or sponsor national theatre conferences.

* To encourage, organize, sponsor and/or produce national festivals.

* To administer funds for the training of animateurs for the encouragement of amateur theatre.

* To stimulate the training of animateurs.

* To stimulate the writing and production of Canadian plays.

* To improve amateur theatre management.

A few words were switched around during the discussion and Yvon Dufour wondered whether the organization could actually reach the objective of being the national and international spokesman for amateur theatre in Canada. Would that include amateur theatre in Quebec? There were a lot of polite noddings about this at the head table but there were no changes to the fourth clause. Dr. Spensley was beginning to look pleased at the committee's reception to his paper. He went on to a section dealing with the restructuring of the board of governors and the election of a new group of vice-presidents.

Ears pricked up at this. New group? Now the policy

paper was becoming personal. The author cleared his throat. "Actually, what I've done here," he said delicately, "is to put the jobs of committees and the top officers together so we can co-ordinate the work of the organization. For example, I'd like to see the immediate past president serve as public relations chief and head of the regional committee. After all, Helen has been doing this work anyway and I think she should be given this official job next year. I'd like to see the secretary of the organization act as director of the membership committee. . . ."

The assembled Theatre Canada executive shifted uncomfortably in their chairs. "But I've never seen it done like that before!" protested Bea Ramsay, member-at-large for Regina.

"Maybe I'm not explaining myself very well," said Dr. Spensley, leaning on his forearms. "Look, we operated last year without a secretary and for the most part without a treasurer. I've talked to Jean-Pierre Beaulne, our vice-president legal about this and we both feel we should choose a secretary who could also be in charge of membership. In other words, not just a corporation person but an individual who is also a bloody good campaigner."

The mood on the floor began to deteriorate. "Dr. Spensley," said Pat Bcharriell, member-at-large for Kingston and Press Liaison for the Saskatoon festival. "Never in all my experience have I ever seen a past president put down as chairman of the p.r. committee or chairman of any other committee for that matter. I just can't see any logic in doing that. I think it's wrong! I think it's change for the sake of change. Why, good heavens, the secretary becomes the membership chairman!"

Philip Spensley drew his hand wearily across his brow. "This is not supposed to be a constitution, you know. These are merely suggestions for policy. All we're saying is that it might be a good idea to have a secretary who could do this kind of thing."

Arguments began to buzz across the floor. Okay, so there would have to be better structured committees that would definitely do their job. Okay, so it might be a good thing to take a hard look at members in the organization and what they were doing for Theatre Canada. But didn't the presidents and past-presidents do PR work anyway without being officially tied into the job? Was the policy paper actually trying to change the structure of Theatre Canada or switch people around?

"Look," said Pat Beharriell, "I know how important this all is, Madame Chairman. But a lot of people here want to go to the five o'clock play. Couldn't we refer this problem to a committee?"

More arguments. Why not use the old policy paper now and think about changes next year? But wouldn't that paralyze the organization in vital areas? Some of the officers began to drift out of the room. Dr. MacPherson said very deliberately that there were surely ways of finding a solution to the whole question of work responsibility without restructuring the organization all over again. Dr. Spensley protested back that please, he begged the executive to see his paper was not an attempt to restructure the organization at all. The changes really were minor.

Dr. MacPherson again spoke deliberately and suggested that all that was needed without making drastic changes in the structure was to fill some jobs already vacant and to elect two new vice presidents, not a whole group. There seemed to be some relieved agreement about this, although Dr. Spensley was now running his fingers agitatedly through his hair. A motion was put forward that Theatre Canada continue with the original policy paper with the few minor changes already adopted and that Dr. MacPherson's suggestions be okayed for the coming year.

Dr. Spensley laughed dryly. "I hope you realize I don't have a burning association with this thing. I was *asked* to do the job. But I have the feeling that at this minute the organization is failing to come to grips with its problems. It is wrangling a bull and not grasping it by the horns. You've got it by the tail! There's been a hue and cry about survival and here you have the opportunity to come to grips with it and you're passing it by."

Madame President said something about a kettle of fish, and the meeting – now with half of the executive absent – went on to discuss its financial report. It was confirmed that the organization carried a deficit of $21,035 versus $15,255 the previous year. The Secretary of State had been vigorously lobbied to provide Theatre Canada with $302,000 a year which, according to Dr. MacPherson would certainly help solve the funding headache. Right now, though, the whole thing was in limbo and no one knew when the answer from Gérard Pelletier would come through. "Election year!" sighed Bea Ramsay.

Commented Mary Jane Scott: "We're not going to allow

29

Theatre Canada to die! If it does," she continued, looking around the small representation in the room, "it will be over our four dead bodies."

An air of gloom settled over the group. Helen Smith peered over her reading glasses and said with a tight little laugh: "Why, we haven't even got a quorum!" She began to stash away her papers.

In the corridor outside the Saskatchewan Room, Eugène Gallant, director of Les Feux-Chalins of Moncton, New Brunswick, was rapping with Glynis Leyshon, a member of Company One of Vancouver. Company One was one of the three fully-professional groups invited to the 1972 Theatre Canada Showcase. "There's one aspect of theatre festivals I don't like," said Gallant. "People talk too much, not knowing what they're even talking about. And they go around and around! I went this afternoon to two plays. *Babel* from the St. Francis Xavier Performing Group, Antigonish and *Chamber Music* from the Sir Robert Borden High School in Ottawa."

Gallant is a thin man with shining eyes and lank hair and a teacher at the Université de Moncton. He threw up his hands in a Gallic gesture. "Afterwards, I just wanted to leave, quite satisfied with the performance. But we had to *know*. Theatre people are the worst people to have around when you see a play. They're going to destroy everything. They're not going to accept it, even if it's good. I love working with kids, you know. Your group must have had lots of fun doing *Tale Theatre* for the kids today."

Glynis nodded. "After *Tale* we talk to the kids. But they don't want to analyze the play at all. I suppose they're still so involved in the magic."

La Nuit des Assasins from the Université de Moncton was a triangle play about three teen-agers in an attic who were acting out the murder of their parents. Seats in the Centennial Auditorium were one-third full. After the play, Yvon Dufour asked cheerfully whether the English-speaking members of the audience minded that the play was entirely in French. The consensus was that it hadn't mattered.

There was a lot of talk about body language meaning more than the spoken word at times, and Dufour, looking very pleased, stepped down from his objective role as animateur and pronounced: "I think we can agree that tonight we have seen some *superb* theatre." There was a rattle of applause. Then, someone from the front row asked loudly: "Why is French-Canadian theatre better than English-Canadian theatre?" Dufour laughed and shrugged.

Canadian playwright George Ryga was supposed to arrive in Saskatoon for a Theatre Conference on Canadian writing but sent a telegram explaining that he was ill. Instead, animateurs Ken Dyba, dramaturge of Theatre Calgary, Roland LaRoche, Ken Kramer and Andrew Allen of the Canadian Broadcasting Corporation (who had been sent to Saskatoon to hand out six CBC bursaries to promising participants) sat at the head table in the Saskatchewan Room and led the discussion among a group of approximately twenty-five interested individuals. Even though there were no exclusively French-speaking members in the audience, the elaborate arrangements for simultaneous translation were still provided.

 The conference pivoted almost entirely around the subject of subsidization of Canadian playwrights by government agencies. "I simply don't know what the problem is when this is argued against," said Kramer. "Shakespeare was subsidized. Michelangelo was subsidized."

 "Molière was subsidized," added LaRoche in French.

 "The trouble is," Alan Aylward, a member of the professional Canadian Puppet Festivals of Toronto commented from the floor, "anybody could jump on the subsidy bandwagon if we had policies like that."

 "But if an artistic director reads the script and he likes it and he wants to invest the time in doing it, surely he can be trusted to recommend subsidy for the author," argued Dyba. "He should be able to get financial help for the writer to come to his theatre and develop the play or for future work."

 At the back of the room, animateur Sean Mulcahy, Irish-born artistic director of Edmonton's Citadel Theatre, got to his feet. Mulcahy, as usual, was impeccably dressed, very much Centre Stage and ready to enunciate so that no one could miss a syllable.

 He began his small speech by saying he would like to throw one or two questions in the air and let them hang there for a moment. "I've got about 120 Canadian plays lying on my office floor at the moment and most of them are garbage. About three are bearable. We seem to have reached a situation where the Canadian playwright has become a Different Kind of Person." Mulcahy wondered whether Canadian poets were thinking of insisting that bookshops sell at least fifty per cent Canadian poetry. Or that Canadian artists would insist on the same national quota in the galleries. Why was so much ink being spilled and so much air-time being devoted to the Canadian *playwright?* "It seems," Mulcahy thumped on, "that the playwright wants the government to molly-coddle him. To ask a theatre like the Citadel with a subscription list to put on fifty per cent Canadian plays, good or bad, is taking a dreadful liberty. Why not novelists? Why not sculptors? That's all."

George Ryga's *The Ecstasy of Rita Joe,* performed by the Medicine Hat College, was staged on Tuesday night and Harry Hay was smiling broadly in the foyer as a two-thirds capacity audience filed into the Centennial Auditorium. After all, Indians were familiar in Saskatoon and word had got around town that the Medicine Hat group was going to present a pretty smooth production.

After the final curtain, the cast – all of them white but suitably tinted – squatted on the floor of the stage and animateurs Sean Mulcahy and Ken Dyba coaxed the audience to crowd closer to the front. "Will you *close the door please!*" Mulcahy shouted to the ushers. "Otherwise I will lose my temper because of the noise." Outside in the foyer, a Ukrainian group from Saskatoon Folk Arts Council was beginning to tune up for the evening's Green Room party. "I find it very difficult to talk during a czardas," quipped Mulcahy.

As everyone probably knew, continued the Citadel's director, these after-play chats were *entirely* informal. There would be no judgements by adjudicators, a word which he assured the rapt audience had *vanished* from the language. In other words, he hoped to exchange ideas and if there weren't any ideas there would be no exchange. Giggles. "To kick this off," said Mulcahy, "I'd like to say that if there are any people here who took part in this afternoon's theatre conference on the future of the Canadian playwright, may I respectfully draw their attention to Mr. George Ryga and his play."

The audience construed this to mean Mulcahy liked *Ecstasy*, so there was a burst of applause. After telling everyone he now intended to be totally impartial, Mulcahy said he would hand the discussion over to Kenneth.

Dyba decided that impartiality was out. "I think we've seen some very nice work here this evening and I've just learned the cast did a flat-out rehearsal this afternoon. So this was the second performance within a few hours. I'm very impressed by that." Dyba said he had also discovered that Theatre Canada had subsidized Ryga to work with the Medicine Hat group during rehearsals and *that* was interesting. The audience applauded again.

Someone in the audience asked whether there were any real Indians in the cast of the play and director Dorothy Jones said no, everyone was white. There were only about two Indians living in Medicine Hat, so it had been tough getting her cast into the skin of the play. George Ryga had been a great help, of course. Another member of the audience said he thought the members of the cast were great Indians and there was more applause.

A girl in the third row then stood up and said she liked the play but it made her feel ashamed of living in a society which had such rotten racial prejudices. Mulcahy came quickly to the front of the stage, pointed an accusing finger and said loudly: "I resent that. *You* might be prejudiced, young lady. The person sitting next to you might be prejudiced. But *I'm* not prejudiced. I would ask you not to generalize about the society we live in." Groans, laughter and applause.

The backstage, unionized crew began to strike and the set and the clatter was appalling. Mulcahy whipped behind the curtain and the audience listened in fascinated silence as his muffled voice was heard arguing with the workers. When he emerged, his face was flushed but the clatter went on. After a while, the questions from the audience and the answers from the stage became almost inaudible. "Louder!" shouted some onlookers from the side of the auditorium.

One question, repeated twice, hit its mark. What did the director think was the worst problem she had in putting on the play in Saskatoon. Dorothy Jones giggled a little then replied: "The lighting."

Mulcahy leaped forward. "I quite agree," he barked.

33

"Butchers! Butchers! I think it's a crime that a director brings a fine play like this to a theatre and has it butchered by the lighting." Laughter and applause. Dorothy Jones smiled wanly at Mulcahy's outburst. She started to speak, but the backstage noise was now deafening and the czardas was invading the auditorium. People began to drift toward the doors.

Sean Mulcahy's remarks about the lighting of *Rita Joe* made headlines in Saskatoon's *Star-Phoenix* the next day and the director found himself having to apologize. The lighting, it seemed, had been handled by the Medicine Hat College's own man, not a Centennial Auditorium staff member. As Dorothy Jones was forced to explain to a reporter: "He simply didn't have the time to get used to the equipment and get the cues right."

Even though it was only halfway through the festival, the mood at the Centennial Auditorium was changing from Early Frantic to a weary but warm Spirit of Family. Faces began to become familiar. People were beginning to call each other by their first names. There was Helen and Harry and Marian and Sean and Jeannie. The participants billeted at the University of Saskatchewan admitted they were having a ball. The day after *Rita Joe* made such a hit, three members of the cast housed at the Bessborough were arrested after throwing beer bottles out of a hotel window.

"The pressure was off," another member of the Medicine Hat crew explained. "The kids were just celebrating. Everyone is having a wonderful time."

At the Green Room get-togethers, participants from groups across the country were beginning to discuss the Saskatoon Big Bash. "I like it for a lot of reasons," said Bob Curtis from the Tec-Voc Travellers of Winnipeg who were presenting an original rock musical called *The Fool's Jewel*. "One is that it's non-competitive and so it's friendlier than the old DDF used to be. We're still really competing with each other, of course, because we all want to show we can do well. Theatre Canada? Well, anything that brings people together has to be okay."

"I think the non-competitive showcase idea is more constructive than the competitive festivals of the past," commented Bob Ring of the Dalhousie Musical and Dramatic Society which was scheduled to perform Irwin Shaw's *Bury the Dead*. "I'm all for it continuing this way. There's no way a single adjudicator can look at a play and understand all of its aspects – lighting, directing, acting, everything."

Bob sipped at his beer. "It's a challenge for some groups to get to the festival, of course. There's no travel allowance any more. The Nova Scotia government was going to help our kids but it backed out at the last moment. But we'd made the commitment to come to Saskatoon and the cast chipped in to pay their own expenses. We cancelled our train reservation and travelled for three days by bus. Why did we come? Well, this is one festival where you can meet people from right across the country who are interested in theatre. That's really something."

On Wednesday night, Harry Hay pulled a slip of paper out of his pocket and beamingly announced the Saskatoon festival had already grossed $9,000, a figure that surpassed Ottawa's entire box-office take in 1971. However, he admitted he was still miffed about the French-Canadians and their attitude at the festival, especially that man Dufour. "He scarcely speaks to me any more," complained Dr. Hay. "And I'm not anti-French, you know. Remind me not to get involved in a thing like this again."

On Thursday afternoon, Charlie Blake, a Hospitality Committee Assistant, was fussing about arrangements for the Lieutenant-Governor's visit to the festival that night. There would be two flags draped over the vice-regal box, Charlie explained importantly. The Canadian flag would be on the Lieutenant-Governor's right hand and the Saskatchewan flag on his left. No, he wasn't planning to drape flags over the other official boxes but he admitted it had been discussed.

Actually, pondered Charlie, there would be three official boxes in use. Senator Buckwold was coming, you know. Then there was the Big Brass of Theatre Canada and a representative from Rothmans Pall Mall of Canada, who were one of the organization's financial angels, and officials of the CBC. Perhaps more flags would be in order. It had been tough getting information about how to drape the flags on the Lieutenant-Governor's box, though. The local library didn't seem to know, so finally he had telephoned the Air Force. They had the whole thing down pat.

He bustled out of the room and encountered a man

from the Centre's maintenance department. "Charlie!" said the man. "We've got a problem. Someone has stolen those damned Canadian flags!" Charlie's face whitened and he staggered a little. "Oh my God," he gasped.

On Friday, the talk of the festival was about how odd Thursday night's play *The Disintegration of James Cherry* had been and how rotten it must have been for the Lieutenant-Governor. And did everyone know the story about how the Hospitality Committee had to find some flags at the last moment?

James Cherry, performed by the group from the University of New Brunswick had received the worst pasting so far of any play invited to the festival. Criticisms flew at the young director and his cast from animateurs, annoyed members of the audience and other participants. The Lieutenant-Governor himself did not attend the after-play row. Instead, Harry Hay spirited him off to the VIP cocktail lounge, presumably to be revived.

Theatre Canada president Helen Smith smiled tightly when asked what she had thought of the James Cherry play. Well, she said diplomatically, there had perhaps been *better* plays presented at festival. But next year, it had already been decided, there would have to be stricter selection techniques. The national office had received forty-nine applications from groups, both professional and amateur. Seventeen had come to Saskatoon and she admitted that in many instances, mainly because of shaky Theatre Canada finances, the selection committee had relied on advice from the regions when issuing invitations. That would all have to be changed.

She sank into a chair in her presidential suite and admitted the week was beginning to wear her down. The socializing in the new organization was *nothing* like it used to be in old DDF days, but still. . . . Well, there were the mandatory cocktail parties. The midnight meetings of the executive. Interviews. The plays. Decisions, decisions. . . .

Oh, it wasn't that she didn't *enjoy* festival. As a matter of fact, she had learned a great deal from the Saskatoon experience. It had helped consolidate a lot of ideas about Theatre Canada in her own mind. "For example," she said, resting her head against the back of her armchair, "it has convinced me more than ever that we were right to turn the annual festival into a non-competitive showcase." She remembered she once had a singing teacher who had been an adjudicator at music festivals in England. He had been dead against competition. "He told me," grinned Mrs. Smith, "that after listening to thirty-five girls sing *Cherry Ripe*, he began to give marks for legs."

The joke seemed to cheer her up and she obligingly checked through a mimeographed Helen Smith biography which had been issued by the Theatre Canada publicity committee. "I haven't even seen this," she said, and read it aloud with added comments.

"Born in Avonlea, Saskatchewan, Helen Smith was raised in Dauphin, Manitoba. She has resided in Ottawa and presently makes her home in Victoria, B.C. *Right*. Mrs. Smith has been both actress and producer-director. *That's for sure*. She has been involved with theatre since high school days – *I can scarcely remember that* – and was once best actress award winner of a DDF Regional Festival. *Oh yeah!* Her background training includes music and theatre. She taught speech arts."

Mrs. Smith lit a cigarette and read on: "An active community worker, her interests have included the Victorian Order of Nurses and family children's service work as well as University of Victoria volunteer work. *That makes me sound so busy*. Helen has been a DDF/Theatre Canada board member for seven years, a former festival chairman and president of the organization since 1971. She is married to Hershell Smith, lumberman, has four children – *three boys and a girl* – two grandaughters, horses, cows, chickens and geese. *God, quite a menagerie*."

The door of the presidential suite opened and John MacPherson walked into the room. He looked agitated. "Problems?" asked Mrs. Smith. Dr. MacPherson spoke a little less deliberately than usual. "I'm just mad," said the Theatre Canada vice-president. "It's Ray Pierce of the Dalhousie Musical and Dramatic Society. They did *Bury the Dead*, remember? Well, he had a television interview with the CBC objecting to our scheduling of rehearsal times and technical facilities. And if that's the best Theatre Canada could do, he said he'd keep his company in Halifax."

"Wow!" said Mrs. Smith.

"He's been rehearsing that thing since last October!" said Dr. MacPherson. "And he had as much time in the auditorium as everyone else here. As a matter of fact, we opened up the place for him at six o'clock in the morning."

Mrs. Smith puffed silently at her cigarette and Dr. MacPherson went on: "Anyone who takes a show on the road with 170 lighting cues and can't tell anyone what they are at the last minute . . . well, that's amateurism of the worst kind. He's the great showman who got his invitation to Saskatoon, then withdrew his play from our regional festival in Nova Scotia. The festival, incidentally, was booked into the Dalhousie auditorium. But Pierce would not allow his technical crew to work backstage. Then he sent us a bill for the auditorium rental. We lost $2,000 on the regional because of that man."

"That's what makes it so frustrating for us," said Helen. "We fought like hell to get that group here, but they've been more trouble than anyone else. I mean, how are you to know? These are the variables." She threw up her hands. "Well, that's showbiz."

Governors' Court – or Theatre Canada's general meeting as it is now more modestly dubbed – was held in the Saskatchewan Room on Saturday afternoon and Helen Smith smiled happily over her glasses as the chairs filled up. Harry Hay was there, looking exceptionally cheerful. There was a small silence when he approached Yvon Dufour, said something to him, then actually shook his hand.

The Theatre Canada executive and the inevitable crew of simultaneous translators were present and there were also some representatives of the regions and a few interested participants. Eve Gilstorf handed around the agenda: Minutes of the last General Meeting. President's report. Reports from the regions. Report of the 1972 Festival. Report of the 1973 Festival. Financial Report of the Corporation. Report of the nominating committee and election of members of the board.

Mrs. Smith read from her notes, thanking individuals for their support, reading the regrets of officers who could not make it to Saskatoon and dispensing the information that the top brass of Theatre Canada had been meeting endlessly and tirelessly throughout the year and at the current festival. "It has become evident," she said, throwing a quick glance at the group over her glasses, "that major funding must be found in order to expand." The group gave a collective sigh.

Everything was going swimmingly, it seemed. There was a mild commotion at the back of the room when Philip Spensley decided to stretch out on the floor, but he was allowed to rest in peace. Mrs. Smith sailed into the last paragraph of her report with what sounded like a small prayer: "It is to be hoped that when finances permit, the staff and members of the board will be able to get around this country, to communicate personally and to realize to a greater extent what the needs are. We want to build closer liaison with all people working in Canadian theatre."

The meeting heard the mandatory collection of reports from standing committees ("we've had to figure out what *is* a Canadian play, where *are* the Canadian plays"), regional representatives (Yvon Dufour, representing Montreal, spoke again in French but during English speeches, the translator simply leaned on his hand) and John MacPherson retold his melancholy tale about the long wait for an answer from the Secretary of State's office. "To date," he said, again deliberate, "we have still to hear about our request for $302,000 a year. Our first brief was in March, after which there were three supplementary submissions." Again there were sighs.

But now, everyone sat up straight. It was time for Harry Hay to talk about the Saskatoon Festival. There was an anticipatory shifting of chairs as the white-haired chairman settled himself in front of a microphone (the English-to-French translator still leaned silently on his hand) and began to talk. *Tiens!* Was he about to complain about those French plays again?

"Madame Chairman," commenced Dr. Hay, "we had quite a year getting this thing organized, you know. Our mayor became a senator. The government of the province changed. And the manager of the Centennial Auditorium had a heart attack. The only thing that didn't happen was that the Festival Chairman didn't get pregnant. Now, I hear there's some talk in the national office as to whether these festivals should be organized by professional or local people. I think it would be a shame to take the voluntary thing away because it involves so many people in the community. If you get the thing too well done, it's not going to be any fun at all." Laughs. Harry was going over big. Everyone relaxed.

"Ah!" exclaimed Bea Ramsay of Regina. *"Touché."*

"Now I know there's been some criticism," Harry went on, conscious of his impact, "of some of the programs, particularly

39

the children, being oversold." Oh, oh. Harry *was* going to talk about the plays. "Well, you know, with this change of government and so on, the Saskatchewan Arts Board was going to give us $10,000 and they decided to give us $5,000. But right now, the Arts Board has exactly $700 in the bank because the provincial government hasn't given them any cash. Our hair has been turning greyer because we must have that money. So you see, all along the line we've had this matter of the ugly dollar. That's been the basis for some of these things happening."

Another thing, he went on, few other festival chairmen had done something like putting on a high school show on kick-off night. But he'd done it because he knew it would help the budget, even though he realized the show wasn't of the highest calibre. "That's about all I have to say at this time, Madame Chairman," Dr. Hay wound up. "It's nice of you to invite us to hold the festival next year, but I'm afraid we'll have to decline."

"I saw four shows today," said seven-year-old Barbara Crouse in the foyer of the Centennial Auditorium that afternoon. Saturday was Children's Day at the festival and the building was awash with marionettes, gophers (borrowed from *Saskatchewan I'm Coming Home*) and large black cats with floppy ears and yards of whiskers. "I liked the puppets best," added Barbara.

"And there was this guy dressed up like a lady and she, I mean he, chased another guy all over the place," chimed in Cindy Hill. "I didn't have lunch, but I got to the bathroom all right."

Laughed eight-year-old Randy Crouse: "The boy sitting next to me didn't get to the bathroom. He laughed so hard, he peed his pants."

The final performance at the 1972 Saskatoon Big Bash was a production of *Hadrian the Seventh* with costumes rented from Stratford, Ontario. It was performed by Saskatoon's Gateway Players, a group which Harry Hay argued would sell tickets like crazy. After the show, director Robert Hinitt told the sizeable audience that the budget for the production was $600, which was all the Gateway group had in the bank after completing their last season. However, the Festival Committee supplied $1,089 to offset extra expenses.

There was an attempt by the animateurs (all of them

40

except a hospitalized Philip Spensley were on stage for the final night) to get the audience drawn into a discussion but it was clear that Festival was just about over and few really wanted to dissect the play. Instead, those who tarried in the auditorium began chatting about that week in Saskatoon.

Okay, commented someone in the orchestra seats, so perhaps the best plays from Canada didn't come to Saskatoon. But maybe that was a good thing. The groups that did not come up to standard would obviously go home after learning a good deal from the best stuff they had seen. Someone else disagreed with this. Maybe people working in theatre got something out of the week, but how about the ordinary people of Saskatoon? Perhaps there should have been stiff elimination competitions to bring the best work from the regions.

Sean Mulcahy again took centre stage. One thing he had learned from the festival, he said, was that everyone in the theatre – professional or amateur – were colleagues. People working with community groups should learn from those who had more experience. But the learning process, he agreed, should not be at the expense of the person who forked out his cash to see a play. There had to be compromise. "Perhaps the festival should be at two levels. Workshops and experimental theatre during the day. Then, really fine productions from across Canada during the evening performances. It would seem unfair to spread the word, you might say, by bypassing those without whom theatre people could not exist. *The members of the audience.*"

Outside in the Green Room there were sounds of music, but when those from the audience discussion got there, the band was already packing up and the bar was closed because of Saskatoon's Saturday night liquor laws. Groups of kids hung together like clusters of bees, singing "Auld Lang Syne," and some were weeping. A boy and a girl sat on the floor, their arms twined around each other. Two earnest, long-haired men were swapping addresses.

Madame President swept by, saying that Harry Hay, bless his darling heart, had already gone off to regional representative Jeannie Walters' farewell party and there would be taxis for any Theatre Canada people who wanted to come. "Why don't we get some dancing started here?" a kid asked shrilly. Nobody responded. After a while, everyone wandered dreamily toward the glass doors of the almost-empty Centre.

41

PART TWO

Beginnings

CHAPTER TWO

The Way It Was

1. From Neptune to the Road

The link between Theatre Canada's 1972 Showcase
in Saskatoon and the first recorded theatrical performance on
territory that would become the Dominion of Canada might
seem to be pretty frail. But the thread does stretch across four
centuries, even though it later tangled, and once almost dis-
integrated. Whatever its critics might think of its usefulness or
quality, the Saskatoon festival could be called an example of
Canadian theatre rather than theatre *in* Canada. Some of the
plays were imported – though many were not – but basically,
the showcase was in direct contrast to the touring theatre
from the United States and abroad which dominated the
Canadian stage for so long.

Like Saskatoon, in fact, the big show in 1606 was
– by necessity not design – a locally-produced effort. Called
somewhat ponderously *The Theatre of Neptune in New France*,
the play was a marine masque written by a young Parisian
lawyer named Marc Lescarbot to celebrate the return of the
Governor, the Sieur de Poutrincourt, to the French fort at Port
Royal. The Governor, accompanied among others by geographer
Samuel de Champlain, had been on a voyage of exploration
to the south, and as Lescarbot later wrote: "we were expecting
the Governor's return; whereof we had great desire, the more so
that if evil had come upon him we had been in great danger of
mutiny. I thought to go out and greet him with some novel
spectacle, and so we did."

43

One day, some romantic Canadian movie director might make a film out of that autumn scene on the waves off Port Royal. The ingredients of spectacle are all there. The decorated entrance to the wooden fort that was the explorers' Habitation. Roast venison turning on the outdoor spit. Hogsheads of wine "which did not come amiss and caused certain of the company to make gay dogs of themselves." An astonished audience of Indians, the people of chief Membertou. Voyageurs and "gentlemen of the company." Lescarbot himself directing from the shore. The fleet of canoes skimming toward the governor's two-masted barque, bearing gifts and a royally-robed Neptune surrounded by his six noble Tritons. "They were French verses made in haste," Lescarbot wrote concerning his play, though apparently he thought enough of the work to have it published on his return to France.

"Hail to you Sagamos," Neptune shouted across the waves (Sagamos is an ancient word for captain), "rest and remain awhile/ Come, listen to a god who welcomes with a smile/ And if you know me not, great Saturn was my sire/ Brother am I to Jove and Pluto, god of fire." The first Triton recites: "By right great Sagamos, you name your luck as rare/ Because a fostering god has promised you his aid/ In this important work, wherein with dauntless care/ And hardy venturing your conquest bold is made." And finally, Neptune concludes the masque: "Come then, chefs, cooks and boys, all of you make good cheer/ Scullions and pastry cooks, let soup and roast appear/ Ransack the kitchen shelves, fill every pot and pan/ And draw his own good portion for every eager man."

Apparently Marc Lescarbot's extravaganza at Port Royal was a smash hit with de Poutrincourt and his crew. But it is difficult to find any further references to theatrical entertainments in New France until 1640, when a group of amateurs – probably regimental officers – staged a performance of Pierre Corneille's *Le Cid* in honor of the Dauphin's birthday. It is significant that some historian felt the occasion was worthy of record. Theatrical performances were rare events at that time, mainly because of the towering disapproval of the clergy. Corneille was occasionally tolerated because his work "exalted the will and subordinated passion to duty." Jean Racine's plays were also staged from time to time, particularly those based on biblical themes.

But the real row about theatre in this country during the seventeenth century boiled up in 1694, when Governor Louis de Buade, Compte de Frontenac, decided he would like to encourage an amateur group to stage a production of Jean Baptiste Molière's *Tartuffe* (the religious hypocrite), possibly as a wry dig at the cautious gentlemen of the cloth. When word got out about Frontenac's wicked plans, Bishop Saint-Vallier flatly forbade the performance on pain of excommunication for all concerned. The scandal caused such shocked reverberations around New France that theatre in the area languished for some time.

As a matter of fact, there is a scarcity of information about theatrical activity on Canadian soil – except in universities and some garrisons – until September 1768. An advertisement in Halifax's *Nova-Scotia Gazette* reads:

> BY PERMISSION
> At the THEATRE in Halifax
> By the *American* Company of Comedians, On Friday, the 2nd. Inst. will be presented, a Tragedy, call'd JANE SHORE.
> To which will be added a FARCE call'd,
> THE VIRGIN UNMASK'D;
> Or, an Old Man taught Wisdom.

C. Bruce Fergusson, now provincial archivist for Nova Scotia, has admitted in his article *The Rise of the Theatre at Halifax* that details of this early visitation by an American touring company is shrouded in mystery. It is not known, for example, precisely where the performances were given, though Fergusson guesses they were probably staged at a local coffee house. He is also not sure whether the members of the American Company of Comedians were the first travelling players to give performances in the town. It seems probable, though, that Halifax became an early target for groups of strolling actors because of puritan attitudes towards the theatre that were sweeping the American colonies. Not only was the population

45

of Halifax booming in the eighteenth century; it also included officers and men of several regiments and ships of the Royal Navy, all of them seeking entertainment and diversion.

Theatre, in fact, became somewhat of a vogue in Halifax in the 1770's. Not long after the American Company of Comedians staged *Jane Shore*, a rash of correspondence concerning the drama appeared in the *Nova-Scotia Gazette*, some of it suggesting that the theatre was a perfect medium for political propaganda. Other letter-writers, however, argued that "this diversion could bring in foreign vice," and that "theatrical performances are the blemishes of human nature, the plague of reason and the ruin of virtue." Even so, a local entrepeneur named Robert Fletcher announced he would print and sell a comedy of five acts called *The Jealous Wife* written by George Colman, and "Don Joseph Azevedo at the Pontac Coffee House" declared he would publish a tragi-comic farce called *The Present Times* which was "to be acted by a set of Comedians shortly expected; at a new Theatre in the *enchanted castle*, at the Palace of the Sons of Liberty." Newspaper records show that two plays, *The Suspicious Husband* (written perhaps by the author of *The Jealous Wife?*) and *The Citizen* were staged by "the Gentlemen of the Army and Navy" in April 1773 "for the benefit of the poor in Halifax." Early in 1774, another notice appeared in the *Nova-Scotia Gazette* about "a new Comedy of Three Acts; proposed to be acted in the Theatre in this Town, entitled *Acadius, or Love in a Calm*, "for the benefit of poor Housekeepers or the late sufferers of Fire."

The prologue to *Acadius* (which was published in the *Gazette*) sounds as though Halifax playgoers were already convinced their town had become the theatre capital of North America:

> In less than half Man's Post Deluv'an Age;
> In this Septentrion Clime, there was no Stage:
> No Sock'd or Buskin'd Thespis, in a Cart;
> In Drols or Plays, e'er played, any Part,
> But Interludes, in savage Nupt'al strain;
> Were often heard, throughout the whole Domain;
> As were the warhoop, and knell, Death song;

In voices, hoarse or shrill, Stentor'an strong!
The Muses, then, knew not, of these frozen Climes:
So sent no Cargo, here, of Prose or Rhymes.
But Arts and Trade, at length being wafed o'er,
From British Isles to this Acad'an Shore;
Disciples, then, of the Parnass'an Train;
Adventur'd, over, the Atlantic Main;
Some came from all the Muses, saving one,
Her name, I think, is Thalia, she sent none;
(Tho' Patroness of smiling Comedy,
Of laughing Farce and pleasing Melody)
'Till lately one of ancient British Birth,
Came here; with fine Song, second handed Mirth;
Which growing stale, to keep the Frolick up,
Resolv'd one Night, on Comic food to sup;
Food Al'ment'ry on which poor Poets feed,
And live upon; thro' Life, a life, of need;
A hearty Meal's digestion did begat;
A Theatric, Comic (but ill shaped) Brat.
                                        CALLED,
Acadius or Love in a Calm.

Despite the self-congratulation in Halifax that home-grown theatre had really arrived, there was still opposition to "profane entertainments." Ranted one outraged citizen: "Indeed vanity is not the worst article against the Plays and their makers, their actors and promoters which (after all the late expense of sweat and struggle to defend them) are generally such wretched instructors of the age as to teach and credit nothing more than its profaneness and debauchery and help set the sparks of lust and passion all in a flame."

Few bothered to listen. In 1781 there was talk of building a theatre in the backyard of the Old Pontac Coffee House "for the acting of plays during the winter" but a local worrier pointed out that there could be "fatal consequences" if the building caught fire, and the idea was temporarily dropped. It was not until February 1789 that Halifax's New Grand Theatre opened with performances of *The Merchant of Venice* and *The Citizen* presented by the "Gentlemen of the Army,

Navy and Town." According to historian Fergusson, more than a hundred different plays, operas and farces were presented at the New Grand until it was taken over by professional managers Charles Stuart Powell and a Mr. Baker in 1797. Until that time, all of the shows were staged by local amateurs. Prices of admission varied from five shillings for a box seat to two shillings in the pit, and it was requested that persons would not stand on the seats or wear their hats at the time of performance. Everybody, it seemed, had a relaxed time at the New Grand. "It is wished," reads one theatre notice, "that whistling or any other unbecoming noise might in future be omitted."

While Nova Scotia was discovering the pleasures of the stage, Quebec was slowly relaxing some of its rigid views toward theatrical performances. In 1774, English officers in Montreal finally vindicated Frontenac and staged Molière for the first time in this country. A few years later, a professional company from Albany junketed into Montreal with productions of *The Taming of the Shrew* and Hall Harton's *The Countess of Salisbury*. But garrison play-acting was one thing and professional theatre was another. The Albany company tried to counteract public criticism by advertising their plays as "lectures" but it soon became clear that the tour was a flop. In 1798, Rickett's Equestrian and Comedy Co. of Philadelphia made a reasonably profitable trip to Montreal and Quebec, but it was not until 1804 that a Mr. Ormsby "from the Theatre Royal, Edinburgh" advertised that he "respectfully informs the ladies and gentlemen of Montreal that he intends (with their approbation) to establish a company of comedians in Canada to perform in Montreal and Quebec alternately. The theatre of this city is fitted up in that large and commodious house next door to the Post Office where will be presented this evening a comedy in five acts called *The Busy Body* to which will be added the much-admired farce called *The Sultan*." Ormsby produced a number of creaking comedies during his short stay in Montreal, then left Canada bitterly convinced that the northern colonials were not at all responsive to culture.

An English traveller and historian called Lambert wrote to a friend in England after sampling Montreal's theatrical fare at the time: "There is a theatre in Montreal but the performers are as bad as the worst of our strolling actors . . . yet they have the conscience to charge the same price nearly, as London theatres. Sometimes officers of the army lend assistant to a company but I have seen none except Col. Pye and Capt. Clarke of the 49th who did not murder the best scenes of our dead poets. It may be seen how despicably low Canadian theatricals must be when boys are obliged to perform the female characters, the only actress being an old superannuated demi-rep whose drunken Belvideras, Desdemonas and Isabellas have often enraptured a Canadian audience."

Undaunted by Mr. Ormsby's misadventures in Montreal, however, a Mr. Seth Prigmore sailed optimistically into town in 1807, rebuilt "the commodious house next door to the Post Office," and called it the Montreal Theatre. He tried valiantly to make his enterprise work by imposing no-drinking rules in the gallery and making sure that there was adequate heating in all parts of the house. He also tried to capture the imagination of Montrealers by staging a production of *The Tempest* and handing the part of Miranda to "a young lady of the city in her first appearance on stage." Nobody seemed to be overly enthusiastic about Seth Prigmore's Montreal Theatre. After a year, he moved away and left the shaky field to a Mr. Allport who was apparently a poor actor but a superb scene-painter. He was also, according to historian Franklin Graham in his book *Histrionic Montreal*, somewhat of a boor. Well-known English actor John Bernard visited the city in July 1809 with the intention of making some stage appearances. But he wrote to a friend: "I found a company playing in Montreal as deficient in talent as in numbers. I tried to perform but quarrelled with that low fellow Allport."

Predictably, Allport went the way of his disillusioned predecessors. But yet another theatrical hopeful, John Mills, took over the theatre in 1810 and even ventured to Quebec City to clean up some extra cash. Mills' offering to playgoers in Quebec was a mish-mash of scenes from *Macbeth* in which he used a kilt borrowed from a military officer and as daggers, two white-handled dinner knives filched from a downstairs tavern. As Franklin Graham has recorded: "The Governor General and his pretty young wife were there. All the married officers and their wives were present, besides the fashion of Quebec." The theatre, though, was in a fearful state of dilapidation. Mills had built boxes, but the ticket-holders could shake hands with each other across the floor. "It was a brilliant audience," wrote Graham, "but many left after suffering through a highland fling." The performance ended "merrily enough" with the band of the 8th Regiment playing *Rule Britannia*.

The War of 1812 had a dampening effect on theatrical activity in Canada, though there was a successful visit from Ceyatano's Spanish Circus. In 1818 things were livelier in Montreal when the Mansion House Theatre opened on College St. Yet another playhouse opened its doors on Notre Dame St. in 1821 and in 1822 the New Market Theatre on Jacques Cartier Square appeared on the theatrical scene. In 1825, though, Montreal got its first real theatre of class and distinction when the Hon. John Molson backed a $30,000 subscription campaign to build a two-storey building on St. Paul Street which he called the Theatre Royal. Molson picked actor Frederick Brown to manage the place and it opened on November 21, 1825 with Reynolds' comedy *The Dramatist*. Brown then announced a season that had something for everyone: *Speed the Plough. The Wonder, or a Woman Keeps a Secret. Richard III. Hamlet. The Way to Get Married.* Clearly unsuperstitious, he closed out the Theatre Royal's first season – during which he used both American professionals and Canadian amateurs – with a play called *The Road to Ruin.*

The following year, Brown chalked up the greatest coup of any theatrical manager to try his luck in Montreal by persuading the celebrated English actor Edmund Kean to tread the boards of the Theatre Royal. Kean made his Canadian début on July 31, 1826 as Gloucester in *Richard III*. Later in the season he played in *The Merchant of Venice* (as Shylock), *Othello* and *King Lear*. According to critics of the time, his performances were "electrifying."

Kean – a vain and sensitive man who was also a slave to the bottle – was in his element amongst the awe-struck Canadians. He was lionized at public dinners and entertained lavishly everywhere. Criticism of any kind, however, infuriated him. During one performance he stood on his head in a chair, to the delight of the audience. Someone shouted from the balcony: "Another tumble, Mr. Kean!" The actor, aware of the fact that his drinking habits were no secret, thought the man had yelled "another tumbler," and rushed out of the theatre, into the street and straight to his bed at the Masonic Hall Hotel. A theatre employee was sent to explain what the playgoer had really said and Kean was persuaded back on stage. In Quebec City, at a Command Performance before the Governor-General, the actor met some Huron Indians who cheerfully agreed to create him a member of their tribe. Excited with the novel idea, Kean accompanied the Indians to their camp and was ceremoniously dubbed Chief Alanieouidet. Back home, he commissioned a full-length painting of himself in Indian costume and was occasionally glimpsed wearing his Canadian war-bonnet around the streets of Dublin and London.

Montreal continued to attract well-known names from abroad. Edmund Kean's son Charles visited the Theatre Royal with a production of Massinger's *A New Way to Pay Old Debts* (one of his father's successes) in 1831. Charles Kemble and his daughter Fanny came with four plays, *Venice Preserved, Much Ado About Nothing, School for Scandal* and *The Lady of the Lake*. A letter from Fanny to actor Charles Matthews in London, describes what it must have been like to tour around Canada in the first half of the nineteenth century:

> You would not have to complain of want of hospitality . . . but the unspeakable dirt and discomfort of inns in Montreal and Quebec, the scarcity of eatables and the abundance of fleas and bugs, together with the wicked road from Saint John to Laprairie would make up a sum of suffering for which it would be difficult to find adequate compensation. People intolerable . . . the jargon they speak is intolerable.

While theatres were succeeding or folding in centres such as Montreal, Quebec City and Halifax, the drama had slowly been gaining support in other parts of the country. There was a performance "for public charity" in Saint John, New Brunswick, on February 28, 1789, which the *Royal Gazette* hailed as the town's first theatrical event. The play was a comedy called *The Busy Body* "to which will be added *Who's The Dupe*" and it was staged at Mallard's Long Room on King St. The performance was apparently so newsworthy, *The Gazette* sent a reporter to review the show: "Saturday evening last was presented in this town *The Busy Body* and *Who's The Dupe* by a company of gentlemen. . . . Some of the company displayed comic talents which would have done honour to the British theatre and it is justice to say that all exceeded the expectations of the most favourable of friends."

The gentlemen actors of Saint John were kept busy with their amateur play-acting until the final years of the eighteenth century and into the nineteenth. In 1810, however, Saint John attracted its first professional thespian, a Mr. Powell who gave a performance in an attic which some local had grandly christened the Drury Lane Theatre. Six years later, an American professional company unpacked its trunks in Saint John and began staging regular productions (even though letters to the local *Courier* complained of their "ribald nature") and other professionals from below the border followed. Later, more theatres were built to accommodate the touring groups and amateur dramatic activity was forgotten as interest in the city's commercial life began to grow.

Across the country in York, Upper Canada, dramatic performances by amateurs were enjoyed by the English settlers as far back as 1809. In 1810, a group which called itself The Company from Montreal rented a ballroom to present a Scottish melodrama called *Douglas or The Noble Shepherd.* In the 1820's, though, the name of Frank's Hotel began to crop up in reports of local theatrical performances. Frank's stood on the north-west corner of West Market Street and Market Lane and apparently boasted an upstairs room that could more or less accommodate an audience of one hundred. Theatrical accommodation in York improved during the 1830's and forties but the names of few of the playhouses – or converted lofts – survive. Meighan's Ballroom is one name that appears in early letters and in 1824 some professional companies which began venturing into York from below the border used the place on their circuits through Rochester, Buffalo, Kingston and Niagara Falls.

The Upper Canada Gazette and Weekly Register of October 7, 1824 announced that a Mr. Archbold and his Western Theatre were coming to Meighan's "to enliven and remove tedium of long winter evenings." The article continued that there were many hypocritical religionists "who rail against the stage. But the stage may be converted into one of the best schools for practical morality where virtue and vice are placed in the strongest possible point of view."

Spots like Frank's Hotel and Meighan's Ballroom began to look pretty drab to playgoers as York began to grow up. The first real theatre in York — now renamed Toronto — was the Royal Lyceum, built in the mid-1840's on King St. In the beginning, times were shaky for the new playhouse. It was first managed by a group of amateur showmen who had moved in from a converted Methodist chapel across town and rumours were always flying about the rows between disgruntled touring companies and the theatre's front office. One travelling player who visited the Royal Lyceum in its early days, and obviously saw possibilities in the foundering playhouse, was a man named John Nickinson. Nickinson was British-born but had become a well-known actor-manager on the North American theatrical circuit. In 1852, he and his actress daughter Charlotte settled briefly in Utica but the following year, they packed their bags for Toronto and acquired the lease of the Royal Lyceum.

The new Nickinson management was launched in March, 1853 with performances of *The Rough Diamond* and *Faint Heart Never Won Fair Lady*. It was the beginning of a six-year stay for Nickinson in Toronto and during that time the city's theatre-lovers saw many of the celebrated actors of the day. The Royal Lyceum booked Charles Matthews. The Toronto-born Queen of Melodrama, Clara Morris, was said to have made her début there. Charles Couldock, the English Shakespearean star, emoted on the Royal Lyceum's stage. But times were bad in Canada during the late 1850's. Torontonians began to patronize the Royal Lyceum less and less, and in 1858 Nickinson checked his dwindling funds, then decided to travel south again. The theatre drifted from management to management during the next decade of depression, then was destroyed by fire in the early 1870's. In 1874, with the Canadian economy taking an upturn, the playhouse was rebuilt and reopened under the name of the Royal Opera House.

Actually, 1874 was a momentous year for the theatre in Toronto. While the Royal was going up, a group of citizens called the Toronto Opera House Company clubbed together to give the city yet another theatre. The playhouse was called the Grand Opera House and was built in all its wedding-cake glory on Adelaide St. West. The *Canadian Illustrated News* commented at the time: "Montreal theatre-goers will have reason to be envious. . . ." But the Grand needed a manager and the Opera House offered the job to someone they knew: Charlotte Nickinson (now Widow Morrison) who was, coincidentally, treading the Toronto boards at the time. She accepted with pleasure. After assembling a company, she opened with a gala performance of *A School for Scandal* (guess who played Lady Teazle?) on September 21, 1874.

For the next few years, business at Mrs. Morrison's Grand Opera House boomed. Admission was twenty-five cents to all parts of the house and the playbills also promised such extra delights as "the elegant prismatic reflecting sunlight chandelier which will be lighted by electricity every evening at a quarter to eight o'clock." The plushy Grand was burned in 1879, but although it was rebuilt a year later (it was eventually demolished in 1929), Mrs. Morrison's heyday was already over. Disenchanted with a system which relied on a Big Star supported by hack players, the owners waved her goodbye in 1878.

In the meantime, other well-known names were capturing the imagination of theatre audiences across Canada. In Montreal, Charles Dickens appeared at the Theatre Royal with a cast of amateurs in May, 1842. Writing to a friend in England, an excited Dickens wrote of his acting experience:

> I really do believe that I was very funny. At least I know I laughed heartily myself and made the part a character such as you and I know very well – a mixture of F. Harley, Yates, Keeley and Jerry Sneak. When Lord Mulgrave and I went out the door to receive the Governor General, the regular prompter

followed us in agony with four tall candlesticks with wax candles in them and besought us with a bleeding heart to carry two apiece in accordance with all the precedents.

Reporting on Dickens' play-acting début in Montreal (the three one-act plays concerned were *A Roland for an Oliver*, *Two O'clock in the Morning* and *High Life Below Stairs*) Franklin Graham acidly commented: "With all my great respect for the memory of Mr. Dickens, his account would lead us to believe he had been the whole show. In fact, the dickens and all and the others buffoons."

Graham was kinder to Barry Sullivan, the great Irish tragedian who played Montreal in 1859. Sullivan apparently brought an extensive repertoire which was a strain on his supporting company and the prompter. At one point, in fact, the actor decided to act as prompter as well as star in a play, but lost his temper when a member of the cast suddenly asked for help in the middle of a dramatic death scene. "Am I to prompt you when I am *dying!*" he shouted, then rushed off the stage. After a short interval, he was induced to return to finish dying in discreet silence.

Actors such as Sullivan, Tyrone Power, Sr., John Wilkes Booth and Thomas C. King played Montreal, Quebec, Toronto and sometimes Kingston during their visits to Canada in the early and mid-nineteenth century, but it took years before the celebrated names of the theatre travelled further west. In British Columbia, British soldiers and sailors brought an interest in amateur theatricals to the Pacific seaboard and old files of the *Colonist* and other British Columbian newspapers show there were musicals, minstrel shows and straight dramatic presentations staged on ships or in converted halls from 1850. By 1860 there was a log theatre in Victoria called the Colonial and in 1865 there were four theatres catering to a population of 5,000. Most playhouses specialized in Shakespeare. According to Michael Booth in an article on theatrical taste in the early Canadian west published in *Canadian Literature*, the *Daily British Colonist's* attitude to Shakespeare was one of "awful respect and reverence." The newspaper once described *Hamlet* "as the

sublimest production of the pen of the immortal Bard of Avon."
However, it criticized a performance of *As You Like It* for the
retention of "several objectionable passages which have long
since been discarded as ill suited to the present age of refinement."

Victoria apparently depended on San Francisco for
dramatic talent in the 1860's and seventies. The usual professional circuit was San Francisco-Victoria with stops in Washington and Oregon and an occasional side trip to New Westminster.
Booth says that because of the tedious trip by sail or steam
from San Francisco, Victoria's theatres were often dark or audiences had to suffer through mediocre productions. He describes
a performance by one company which staged *Macbeth* in the
Victoria Theatre – a playhouse which the *Colonist* extravagantly
described as a "commodious and elegant temple of Thespis."

The curtain rose on a cotton plantation set, which
had done service for *Octoroon*, backed by a door
and parlour windows draped with claret curtain, a
preposterously free rendering of the blasted heath.
The company laboured under a poverty of actors and
acting talent. The murdered Duncan kept reappear-
ing, first as a supplementary witch then as the
queen's physician. One of the witches, a bearded
six-footer with a glass screwed into one eye, sang
his part from the score in his hand as he leaned
against a tropical tree. (This was still Davenant's
semi-operatic *Macbeth* with Locke's music). The cotton plantation gave way to much tattered and very
extraordinary mountains and water, but the parlour
and curtains remained, now changed into wings.
The banquet tables were totally bare and the four
actors at each table remained motionless during the
banquet scene, except for one who peeled an apple
while Macbeth was distracted by Banquo's ghost.
Macbeth and his queen were enthroned
on shabby horsehair chairs placed on a large packing-
case which bore in large letters the name of the ship
that brought it. The climax came in the conjuration

scene, where there were only three actors to represent the line of eight kings. Each could be perceived, after one appearance, crawling hastily under the back scene to join the procession from behind, each king enveloped from head to foot in a sheet. Unfortunately, one of the sheets caught on a nail and the actor's struggles to free himself could easily be seen through the dilapidated back-cloth. No kings came forth. The performance stopped. At last the breathless actor appeared in tatters, the lower half of his sheet torn away to reveal tweed coat and trousers. The audience broke into a perfect shout of uncontrollable laughter.

By the 1880's, however, the number of touring companies — dominated by "name" actor-managers — was increasing everywhere, even in Victoria. Canadians, the foreign professionals had discovered, were eager to see their shows. New theatres were being built throughout the country and big money was to be made in a land which had little indigenous theatre of its own. The word spread fast in the American states, in France and in Britain, and as the nineteenth century waned, the great theatrical safari into Canada had begun.

2.   "Let's hit the road and clean up in Canada"

The blossoming of The Road, or the golden age of touring as some call it, has plenty of detractors today among both professional and non-professional theatre groups. The argument is that The Road, which was almost completely controlled by foreigners, did not represent Canadian drama and that it probably stifled any local attempt to establish a truly national theatre. There might be some truth in this, although those who have defended The Road on the grounds that it at least allowed Canadians to glimpse some of the greatest international stars of the day, point out that there seemed to be little interest in developing plays and players in this country, anyway.
       Some Canadian names did appear along the highly-

competitive Road. There were the seven Marks Brothers from Christie Lake, Ont. (Bob, the eldest met a travelling magician called "King Kennedy, the Mysterious Hindu from the Bay of Bengal" in the 1870's and resolved to launch the family into showbiz) who achieved recognition in the nineties. The Marks Brothers played small towns throughout Canada and into the United States and they catered to the average taste. Their plays — many especially commissioned for the company — featured identifiable heroes and villains and had such ringing titles as *Children of the Slums, Harvest of Sin* and *A Mother's Heart*. Bob Marks was once quoted as saying: "The great appetite of the masses of show-goers is for melodrama. Despite what the experts say, melodrama is one of the great perennials in the theatrical business." That, according to the head of the Marks family, was the secret of the company's success.

Then there was the Summers Stock Company which was based in Hamilton, Ont. at the turn of the century and occasionally packed its bags and ventured out on The Road. Programs which have survived show the company (headed by comic actor George Summers) presented such popular melodramas and farces as *A Wife's Honor, True Irish Hearts* and *Resurrection*. The McDowell Company of Canadian actors, led by American-born E. A. McDowell, toured western Canada and parts of the United States in the 1870's and eighties. Apparently McDowell based his reputation on the better commercial hits of the day such as T. W. Robertson's *Caste* and *Ours*, Dion Boucicault's *Arrah-na-Pogue* and *Colleen Bawn*, though he was not above trotting out *East Lynne* and *Uncle Tom's Cabin*. Franklin Graham wrote of the McDowell Company in his book *Histrionic Montreal*, though the story concerned the company's experience in Emerson, a small town south of Winnipeg:

> The "theatre" was an old warehouse full of farming implements and boxes. The place had but two exits one of which was from the platform to the prairie, where tents had been rigged up for the company. There was not a house nearer than a mile, and, as everybody came on horseback, the outside was like a horse fair. Soap and candle boxes formed the back

seats, champagne and brandy cases being in front. The Inhabitants were anxious for the company to remain a second night, which they could not do on account of being booked elsewhere, so another performance was given that same night at 11:15. A Canadian political burlesque, *H. M. S. Parliament* written to *Pinafore* music was given. The orchestra consisted of a church organ.

Another Canadian company which upgraded its repertoire to include better-written stage successes was the Tavernier Company headed by Albert Tavernier and his wife, Ida Van Cortland. Like the McDowell group, the company staged *Arrah-na-Pogue, Colleen Bawn* and another current smash, *Camille*. But then, according to reports, the Taverniers considered themselves to be serious thespians rather than mere *entertainers* such as the Marks Brothers. Tavernier himself trained with the McDowell company and Ida spoke her first lines under the stern eye of Mrs. Morrison at the Grand Opera House in Toronto. As a critic for the Toronto *Mail* commented after viewing Miss Van Cortland's performance in *The Two Orphans* in March, 1878:

> Miss Van Cortland has long since given the public proof of her unquestionable powers as an actress but few would have imagined she could have acquitted herself so well in the onerous part of Louise. . . . The character of the poor blind girl, with its transitions from despair to hope, the unobtrusive resignation with which she bears her troubles and the quite unmistakable joy manifested at their happy close – all these marked the true artist, and indicate for this young lady a still more successful future.

Albert and Ida met when they were both playing parts with the touring Nannery Company in Newfoundland in 1879 and were married the following summer in New York. They worked for several foreign touring companies but in 1881 they decided to form their own group, originally called the New York Comedy Company, with Ida Van Cortland as the star. In the years to come, the Canadians – well aware of the tough competition from abroad – toured in the Maritimes, Ontario, as far west as Winnipeg and south into the bordering communities of the United States. Some of Ida Van Cortland's reminiscences as an actress during the days of The Road have been preserved in family documents: "The annual appearance of the company in each town was an event looked forward to by old and young. The children met me at the stage door and clung to my skirts. I had the following of the 'home' or 'family' public, which is the best public upon which any manager can depend." And she wrote of her stage work:

> Camille was one of my strongest parts. I had knelt at the feet of Modjeska, and had won my inspiration from her, for while playing Nanine with her in this piece at Mrs. Morrison's, I had sobbed my heart out with my head in her lap. . . . Nor was this girlish hysteria, for even after years of experience, emotion aroused by such parts, in me at least, was real. If I had to move the people, I had first to move my own heart, and many a night, I have been so overcome I have been carried off the stage when the curtain fell.

The Tavernier Dramatic Company as the group was finally called, travelled The Road until 1896 when Ida Van Cortland suddenly decided to quit the stage and the company disbanded.

After so many years, it is almost impossible to measure the impact the few Canadian touring groups made on audiences in this country. Clearly, though, it was minor compared with that made by the flood of star-studded foreign companies that eagerly invaded the land. Sir Henry Irving, accompanied by the equally-illustrious Ellen Terry, first toured Canada in 1883 and was so impressed with his reception he returned for five more tours. One earned his company $200,000, a fortune in the late nineteenth century. Sir Henry was obviously intrigued by his visits to Canada, though. Once, he asked Toronto *Mail and Empire* critic Hector Charlesworth if he could wangle a meeting with famous oarsman Ed Hanlan. Charlesworth arranged for the two men to get together and was astonished to learn that Sir Henry was an authority on the subject of sculling. But the actor must have missed the activity and bright lights of London's West End. "Why do Toronto merchants close so early?" he once asked Charlesworth wistfully. "And where do they go at night?"

Building interests in centres such as Montreal, Toronto and Winnipeg responded to the demands of The Road by quickly providing accommodation for the stream of touring groups. A roller-skating rink across the street from the Grand Opera House in Toronto was converted and called the Toronto Opera House. The Princess Theatre rose phoenix-like from the ruins of the old Academy of Music in 1895. The Royal Alexandra was built in 1907. Shea's on Victoria Street in Toronto appeared in the early part of the twentieth century. In Montreal, there was the Crystal Palace Opera House, the Théâtre Française and the Grand Central Dime Museum, which featured English vaudeville then French comic opera. There was Le Monument Nationale on St. Lawrence Street and "the most beautiful theatre in America," Her Majesty's on Guy Street which opened in 1898 with a performance of E. E. Rice's *The Ballet Girl*. In Winnipeg, there was C. P. Walker's theatre which not only accommodated the touring companies but managed its own circuit through Regina, Saskatoon, Lethbridge, Calgary, Edmonton, Vancouver and Victoria.

The box-office boomed, the foreign syndicates moved in to supply local managers (among the most powerful: The Theatrical Syndicate, the Shubert Theatre Corporation, Klaw and Erlanger – the major stockholders of The Theatrical Syndicate – Northwestern Affiliated Theatrical Circuits and, later, the Anglo-Canadian Booking Office) and the theatrical tourists kept coming. Minnie Maddern Fiske toured with Ibsen's *Rosmersholm* and a play called *Salvation Nell* in 1909. Sir Johnston Forbes-Robertson brought a production of H. V. Esmond's *Love and the Man* which Charlesworth insisted was a "ghastly affair" about a rotter whose vices had paralyzed him but still plotted from the depths of his wheelchair. "Everyone tried to be kind," Charlesworth has written in his memoirs, "but it was quite obvious before the evening was half over that the play was doomed and irreclaimable. It dragged out its existence in other cities for a few weeks while Forbes-Robertson made up his mind what to do about it. Finally, he decided on *Hamlet* (his greatest role) as a stop-gap but there were problems. The cast travelling with him had been selected for *Love and the Man* and they were untrained in Shakespeare. Finally, Canadian friends came to the rescue and actors who knew the play were rounded up.''

The Road brought Maude Adams to the Canadian circuit in Sir James Barrie's *What Every Woman Knows*. Marie Dressler came back to her home country to show what Broadway polish could do for an actress. Lily Langtry had the local schoolboys chanting: ''Go tell the Jersey Lily . . . that the sights will knock her silly . . . climbing the Golden Stairs.'' When Mrs. Patrick Campbell played Toronto in Bjornson's *Beyond Human Power* she selected her own entr'acte music from the works of Grieg, her favourite composer. After the performance she sent for her manager and furiously asked why the Canadian orchestra leader had not played the music as ordered. The terrified conductor was summoned, put to the question, then nervously admitted his orchestra *had* played Grieg. He was sorry that Mrs. Campbell had not recognized it. The great star shrugged. She loved Canadian audiences and Canadian box-office receipts. But orchestras in the colonies were, well, positively *colonial*.

Yet it was the receptive Canadian box-office that lured such stars as Maurice Barrymore. Julia Marlowe. Lola Montez. Sir John Martin-Harvey, who came with his celebrated play *The Only Way*. Sir Frank Benson. Matheson Lang. George Arliss. Sir Barry Jackson. Alla Nazimova. Sarah Bernhardt, who once tangled with the church in Montreal because of the play *Adrienne Lecouvreur* which deals with the fatal rivalry between the actress Adrienne – an admitted courtesan – and the Duchesse de Bouillon, a woman of questionable morals. Bernhardt was threatened with instant excommunication if she dared appear in *Adrienne Lecouvreur*. She laughingly ignored the threat, to the cheers of an SRO French-Canadian audience.

The powerful foreign syndicates crowed with satisfaction. So maybe stars like Martin-Harvey, Matheson Lang,

Beerbohm Tree and Lewis Waller were in their professional decline when they came to Canada. Maybe the dramatic material being exported down The Road was becoming pretty threadbare. But the Canadians were still plunking down their cash, weren't they? And after all, that's what really mattered.

CHAPTER THREE

The Two Vice-regal Schemes

1.   "With a view to encouraging the sister arts"

Locally-produced theatre, either amateur or professional, was scattered thinly across Canada in the first decade and a half of the twentieth century. The country was still in the iron grip of the syndicates and, although there was bitter criticism of the standard of entertainment being shovelled into their theatres, Canadians – as they later did as far as imported movies, records and publications were concerned – accepted what was being fed to them from the United States and abroad with docile passivity.

"Canada is the only nation in the world whose stage is entirely controlled by aliens," mourned influential critic Bernard K. Sandwell in 1911. Theories varied as to why. Canadians who went to the theatre tended not to consider drama as a serious art-form, possibly because of the long-standing belief in the country that anything connected with the *professional* stage – even superior fare – was in questionable taste. Few Canadians were genuinely active in theatrical circles. Those who were truly stage-struck invariably fled to New York or London.

The church's constant pulpit-thumping about the poisonous evils of professional theatre still influenced a large segment of the community. Significantly, there was never any important move among Canadian business interests to compete with the foreign invaders. Governments and universities showed supreme disinterest in providing theatrical accommodation as a boost for native talent. Canadian cash invested in the building of opera houses was not intended as an incentive for local stage hopefuls. The theatres were constructed to accommodate the touring companies and in many instances they were built by American interests, anyway.

The picture was somewhat different as far as amateur theatricals were concerned. Performances of suitable plays by ladies and gentlemen who were not hell-bent on commercial gain were tolerated and even encouraged – provided the group had background. Background meant that the amateurs belonged to some respectable institution or that the group had beginnings anchored in military, academic or socially-acceptable history. The long-established Garrick Club of Hamilton, Ont. was staging amateur productions in the first years of the century and so was Toronto's venerable Dickens Fellowship Players and the Margaret Eaton School of Literature and Expression. Ontario's London Dramatic Club was a mere shadow of its prominent amateur predecessors but still, it had Roots. So did such groups as the University Dramatic Club of Montreal, the Ottawa Players Club and the Toronto Garrison Dramatic Company.

Plays produced in Canada by Canadians, in fact, were generally equated with recreational activity. The grubby work of professional theatre was being handled – very much like garbage disposal – by paid outsiders. Despite the anguished writings of newspaper and magazine critics, it was not until 1906 that an unimpeachable voice suggested that locally-produced music and drama might actually be worth encouraging on a national scale. And that a serious interest in theatricals need not necessarily lead to hell or social suicide at all.

The voice came from Government House in Ottawa and belonged to Canada's ninth Governor General, Lord Albert Henry George Grey. It might be a splendid idea, decided His Excellency in the Fall of 1906, to hold an annual competition "with a view of encouraging the sister Arts, Music and the Drama, throughout the Dominion of Canada." For amateurs only, of course. He was prepared to offer two trophies for the winners of the twin contests and a special committee of gentlemen was rounded up to flush out qualified judges. Lieutenant-

Governors in the provinces were asked to co-operate so the competitions would be organized at the highest level.

The announcement – which received little prominence in the press – came as somewhat of a surprise to Canadian society. Earl Grey, a sensitive-looking man with correct, military manners, had been in Ottawa since 1904 and this was the first hint of the fact that he was interested in culture. An intriguing rumour had once got around that he had been a financial angel for a prominent English actress (Toronto journalist Hector Charlesworth later revealed that the lady was Mrs. Patrick Campbell), but most Canadians who knew anything about the Governor General thought he was incurably preoccupied with cricket, football (he donated the Grey Cup to Senior Rugby), conservation and penal reform.

Certainly His Excellency's official speeches provided few clues to explain his sudden urge to become a patron of the arts, though they made it clear he was a rampant Imperialist: "Canada . . . whose lovely sparkling winters make her one of the brightest jewels in the British Crown. It is the proud mission of the Anglo-Saxon race to maintain and advance the cause of civilization throughout the world."

And did these flowery phrases sound as though they were uttered by a representative of the Crown who apparently harboured a bohemian interest in the stage?

> It is because I regard the British Empire as the most potent instrument that has ever been fashioned for spreading the blessings of equal rights, of Imperial Justice, of Christian Service and true chivalry that I regard it as the greatest privilege allowed to any man to proclaim himself a British citizen and to have the power of placing his services at the disposal of the King, who is the invisible incarnation of the race.

There have been several attempts to guess why Earl Grey suddenly decided to launch his Musical and Dramatic Competition. One idea, suggested by Charlesworth, is that His Excellency grew nostalgic about his past associations with the London theatre, cast a pitying eye over Canada's floundering native theatrical and music scene and was moved to inject a little adrenalin into it. Another is that when Lord Grey officiated at the opening of the parliament buildings in Alberta, he was impressed with a local choir which performed during the ceremonies and decided that vice-regal patronage of such groups would be useful. Public Service, after all, was a tradition in his family. Both stories probably hold water. Not long after his return to Ottawa from the west, the Governor General talked to some prominent individuals in the capital, put together an executive committee and announced that his first contest would be held some time in the spring of 1907.

Because "racy" press coverage was not encouraged during the Earl Grey Musical and Dramatic Competitions (there were five of them between 1907 and 1911), little objective information about them survives. The contests were not preceded by playoffs and were supposed to be open to "all amateur companies in Canada and Newfoundland." But the executive committee reserved the right to reduce the number of entries "in case the total exceeds the number which can be conveniently accommodated during the week of the competition." By scanning the names of theatre groups invited to the music and drama fests – "accommodation" was limited to nine at the most – it seems that either blue-blood entries alone bothered to apply or the committee wielded a sharp hatchet. One participant at the 1911 competition in Winnipeg, Dora Mavor Moore of Toronto, insists that hatcheting of socially-unacceptable groups was fierce. Players were always royally entertained by the host city's elite and social acceptance was apparently considered quite as important as good diction and dead-on top notes.

Earl Grey, though, left most of the details of contest arrangements to his committee and clutch of lieutenant-governors. In 1906 he did take time from his frequent blitzes on jails in Ottawa, Toronto and Montreal to approve a list of rules. These have been preserved for posterity, along with adjudicators' remarks at the competitions.

The Governor General also fussed over his competition trophies, idealistic sculptures designed from his own scribbled sketches by Louis Philippe Hébert. He talked Canadian actress Margaret Anglin (who had achieved stardom and respectability abroad) into presenting a bracelet to the best actress in the drama section and English actor J. E. Dodson was persuaded to bestow a ring on "the gentleman considered the best actor." Later, committees in Winnipeg and Toronto also offered gold, silver and bronze medals for individual winners in instrumental and vocal music and the Governor General himself added yet another drama prize for "purity and beauty of diction."

The executive committee in Ottawa (chaired in the beginning by Sir John Hanbury-Williams who knew more about military strategy than stagecraft) sweated over the Rules and came up with an exotic set of regulations. Plays, the committee decided, should not be less than one hour and not more than an hour and a half including scene changes – a rule which must have had groups agonizing over what scripts, or parts of scripts, to choose. With a wave of the hand as lavish as Cecil B. DeMille's, the committee decreed that dramatic casts must include at least six persons "and no more than fifty." No professionals were eligible to enter but amateur groups – which could well have benefited from expert direction – were allowed to employ a stage manager.

The "principal qualities by which the dramatic competition will be judged" were indicative of the social and cultural mores of Canada at the time. The executive committee ruled that marks would be given for (a) excellence of the company in acting together as a unit (b) grace and ease of carriage and manner (c) diction (d) the promptness of entrance, exits and the picking up of cues (e) dress and (f) make-up. There was nothing in the marking system which concerned play selection or sets and lighting.

Six amateur dramatic teams showed up in Ottawa for the first Earl Grey competition of 1907. The names of the groups sounded like a Who's Who of recognized Canadian non-professional theatre. St. Mary's Dramatic Class of Halifax managed to beat their way to the capital with a production of *Captain Swift*. The select Toronto Garrison Dramatic Company came with what seemed like a diplomatically-chosen entry, *His Excellency the Governor*. The Garrick Club of Hamilton brought two plays, *The Deacon* and *Kitty Clive*. The Ottawa Dramatic Club presented *Gringoire*. Montreal's University Dramatic Club staged *Arms and the Man* — in less than ninety minutes. The Winnipeg Dramatic Club brought a home-made Canadian play, *The Release of Allan Danvers*.

Allan Danvers was presented on the final night of the contest and, to the astonishment of the Winnipeg group, carried off the Drama Trophy. Years later, Leyden Shiller, a member of the cast, remembered how the original Canadian play was conceived. The local Winnipeg committee had apparently asked a Major Devine, D.S.O., to form a company to represent the city at the Ottawa competition. "Major Devine decided," Shiller told a *Winnipeg Free Press* reporter in 1938, "that we would have to write a brand new script to fit into the one hour and 30-minute time limit. The plot of *Allan Danvers* was blocked out by Major Devine over a plate of devilled kidneys in the old Marriagi Hotel. It was finished with the help of two collaborators, Ernest Beaufort and Wilson Blue, at that time on the staffs of the *Free Press* and the *Telegram*." Despite its celebrity at the time, there is no record as to whether the play written over a dinner-plate was ever presented on a stage again.

Interestingly — even though groups which participated in the five Earl Grey competitions were made up of the very best people — vice-regal opinion was that the adjudicators should pull no punches with their criticisms. After all, one of the reasons for the contests was to stimulate interest in the arts and the Governor General believed that expertise would develop only if the groups were told about their faults. The judges took Earl Grey at his word.

Adjudicators for the first drama contest in Ottawa were Langdon Mitchell from New York theatrical circles and Mrs. Kate Douglas Wiggin Riggs, whose main claim to fame was that she had authored *Rebecca of Sunnybrook Farm*. According to recorded comments, the critics leaned over backwards to make sure the privileged amateurs were not mollycoddled. To begin with, the 1907 report read, the standard of work among the companies would have to be drastically raised if the Governor General's competition was to be a success.

"There are two weaknesses in amateur companies which are almost insuperable," the report went on. "The first of these is the slow picking up of cues. In this latter the professional is often at fault as well. But nothing makes so bad an impression. No matter how good the individual actors are, the performance becomes listless. Unconsciously, the audience becomes bored." Later, it continued: "In another point the amateur frequently errs; this is in not directing his glance at the person to whom he speaks, or who is speaking to him. Too often the eyes are fixed upon the feet of the person spoken to."

The Garrick Club of Hamilton earned honourable mention in the 1907 competition. St. Mary's Dramatic Class, which had trekked all the way from Halifax, came in last and also had to endure a lambasting from the two judges:

> The general impression which the performance made was one of extreme slackness, slowness in picking up cues, inexactness in movements and general spiritlessness. The setting of Act I was excellent but there should not have been a spittoon under the table, to the actor's left. A large ash-tray on the table with a little water in it would have obviated the necessity of what was to the eyes of the audience, a spittoon. . . . The diction of the company was decidedly inferior. Vulgarity of enunciation should be visited with a severe penalty.

Acutely aware that their efforts could be mercilessly dismembered by the Earl Grey judges, however, other groups eagerly applied for the honour of appearing at the second music and drama competition in Ottawa, 1908. The Governor General and his executive committee again decided to look around New York for a judge, and chose theatre critic F. F. Mackay. Mackay was clearly briefed so precisely as to his duties that his remarks on the final night of the festival sound suspiciously like a lecture to a group of unruly schoolboys:

> That it is not necessary for the actor to actually experience the various sensations described by the author may be shown thus: In seed-time the farmer plants his corn and when it appears above the ground the

crow comes from the adjacent forest and plucks the sprout to get the sweet swollen kernel.

To prevent the ravage of his crop, the farmer takes an old suit of clothes, stuffs the trousers and coat with straw, fastens a pair of boots on the figure, puts a hat on the top, making the form resemble, as nearly as may be, the shape of a man. This figure the farmer calls a scarecrow. It is placed in a prominent place in the field. The crow, seeing this sign of a man, flies away. May we not assume that the crow flies away because it feels fear? What does the man of straw feel, who produces fear in the crow? The actor, if he be a true artist, is the sign that begets sensations in the auditor.

It took more than an hour for Mackay to deliver his homily but eventually it was learned the Earl Grey prize for drama had been won by the Ottawa Thespians. The Margaret Eaton School of Toronto had brought along a one-act play called *The Society for the Protection of Suffering Servants* and – unimpressed by background – Mackay waded in: "The stage setting was bad, furniture poor and inappropriate, the acting a grotesque burlesque of even the possibilities of life."

Commenting on an actress in the company who assumed the role of protean actress playing bits of seven distinct characters, Mackay said:

> There were seven different characters set down for impersonation and not in one single character of the seven did the lady, either in make-up or speech present the art of interpretation. She was unnecessarily loud in voice and grotesque in action. The art of comedy is to present the probabilities of life; and the art of force is to present the possibilities of life. But in this performance there was not even the possibility of life, just dramatic slaughter.

Earl Grey, recognizing that his competition had to be diplomatically moved to other Canadian centres, decided to stage it in Montreal the following year and to import New York producer John Corbin to handle the drama contest postmortems. There was one French play, *Les Précieuses Ridicules*, entered in the 1909 competition but the drama trophy went to the John Beverley Robinson Amateur Players of Toronto. In 1910, the contest was held in Toronto itself and another well-known group, the Dickens Fellowship Players, clinched the drama trophy.

That year, however, was a significant turning point in the character of the Earl Grey competition. It was even predictive of ideas and issues that would haunt the organizers of the Dominion Drama Festival decades later. For one thing, the Governor General made the unprecedented decision to use Canadian adjudicators – and members of the press at that. The journalists he picked, of course, were scarcely muckrakers: Toronto critic Hector Charlesworth, whose authoritative voice still echoes posthumously in Canadian theatrical circles; B. K. Sandwell who then still lived in Montreal (this caused comment in social circles because of a story that Sandwell had once been refused entry to Toronto's exclusive York Club); and, lastly, Ernest Beaufort of the Winnipeg *Free Press*, who had helped write *Allan Danvers* in 1907. The competition was staged at the Royal Alexandra Theatre but no one bothered to tally the number of Torontonians who turned out to see the plays.

The point on record, though, is that Hector Charlesworth and his colleagues predicted that the question of play selection would have to be tackled by future contest committees. "We believe that amateurs materially increase the value of their performances when they produce plays of definite literary merit and it is our regret that other considerations did not permit us to give the award to one or the other of these productions," the adjudicator's report read that year. "We would suggest that in future contests the artistic value of the play itself, apart from the acting and ensemble be a factor for consideration by the judges."

As in other years, the adjudicators were firm with the competing groups. Candians, Earl Grey noted with interest, were apparently not squeamish about rapping the knuckles of other Canadians. His decision was vindicated.

72

It is an axiom with all dramatic judges that one important role badly played is sufficient to ruin a production. We have in mind the production of *Jack Straw* by the London Dramatic Club, the most ambitious and handsomely staged production of the series which was put out of the running for the trophy by the fact that its leading part was incompetently played while others who gave evidence that they could play the role were seen in minor parts. . . .

The Toronto Associate Players, which staged *A Country Mouse*, were scolded: "Had the company spoken tolerable English it would have received sufficient marks in depth of individual excellence – apart from acting – to rank it with the first or second company." If that failed to deflate the group the next remark was obviously designed as a crusher:

Without posing as purists, we think there are certain plays which pass current in the theatre of today which should not under any circumstances be staged by amateur companies containing young and inexperienced girls.

An example of this class of play was seen in Arthur Law's farce *A Country Mouse* which reeks with veiled suggestion and we considered it fortunate that the objectionable last act of this play, which was condemned on its original production in London, was omitted. Harmless though the piece may be in its general effect on the average audience, it can easily be seen that any father might reasonably object to his daughter taking part in so cynical a production, the very humour of which turns on a lack of modesty and of respect for the established conventions of morality.

By the end of the 1910 competition, Earl Grey had come to rely on Hector Charlesworth both as a friend and an advisor on matters theatrical. The critic's leadership in handling the adjudication team at the Toronto music and drama contest

73

pleased the Governor General and strengthened his belief that the Dominion in which he was serving as the King's representative could one day stand on its own feet culturally – with the continued encouragement of Britain, of course.

In an all-out gesture of confidence, he invited Charlesworth to be the sole adjudicator of the 1911 competition to be held at the Walker Theatre in Winnipeg. It would be the last contest before Earl Grey surrendered the governor generalship to Queen Victoria's son, The Duke of Connaught. Charlesworth, highly flattered by such a blue-ribbon accolade, immediately accepted. Although, as usual, there was scant publicity concerning the 1911 music and drama competition, there is no doubt Earl Grey's invitation boosted the Toronto critic's already enviable reputation among less distinguished writers. In later years, Charlesworth's seemingly endless series of books of journalistic reminiscences were among Canada's first home-grown best sellers.

In Winnipeg, nine contesting groups were listed for the drama competition. Five were from the city itself – a fact which Charlesworth publicly deplored. Rules and regulations for the music as well as the drama contest varied little from other years. Choral societies had to sing Von Herzogenberg's *Christmas Song* and the group could bring along up to 150 vocalists. the mixed voice choruses of not less than twenty-four and not more than sixty were committed to sing Elgar's *How Calmly the Evening*. Orchestras of not less than thirty and not more than sixty were stuck with Von Weber's Overture to *Der Freischütz*.

Over at the Walker Theatre, Charlesworth sat bravely through plays presented by the Ottawa Players Club, the Edmonton Amateur Dramatic Club (which clinched the trophy), the London Dramatic Club, the Margaret Eaton Associate Players of Toronto, plus those staged by the five local companies. There was the Philanderers Amateur Dramatic Club (Major Devine, D.S.O., again turned up to steer the dramatic tiller), The Strollers Club, the Bohemian Company of Players, the Winnipeg Thespians and the St. Alban's Dramatic Club.

Hector Charlesworth's post-competition lecture in 1911 seemed less abrasive than in other years. It is possible he realized that his words would be the last to be uttered at a national gathering of Canadian theatre groups for the next twenty-two years. "The showing made in Winnipeg was greatly superior, both as to extent and excellence, to that which was seen at Toronto a year ago," he began carefully. There were gasps of relief. Then Charlesworth continued: "Despite the high standard of excellence shown by the majority of companies taking part in the competition, however, there were one or two offerings that were beneath criticism and which tended to throw the whole competition into ridicule."

He plowed on: "If the drama is to remain a preservative force it must be by the cultivation of a refined and elegant diction which shall be a corrective of the ordinary colloquial speech of the street. Elegant diction does not mean a stifled or affected utterance. It means a combination of elegance, vivacity and refinement which produces a sense of satisfaction in the ear and the intelligence."

Charlesworth also noted that amateur groups were beginning to get the hang of picking good plays for production. "Pieces like *She Stoops to Conquer, The Tyranny of Tears* and *A Pair of Spectacles* represent the best that has been achieved in clean English comedy. *David Garrick* is theatrically effective and interesting. *Lady Huntworth's Experiment* and *Liberty Hall*, while not so important, are nevertheless clean and pleasant entertainment."

Perhaps, mused Charlesworth, 1911 was the beginning of significant stirrings on the native theatrical scene. Perhaps the five Earl Grey competitions would "stimulate an intelligent interest in an art, too much neglected, which has fallen largely into the hands of men without ideals." He was wrong. After the Governor General's departure, the drama contest was dropped and no one was ever to discover whether the annual theatrical get-togethers might have developed into something more than cultural happenings staged by the country's amateur elite. The Duke of Connaught half-heartedly patronized a music festival sponsored by the Imperial Order of the Daughters of the Empire; then even this leftover from Earl Grey's poetic experiment vanished into the gunsmoke of 1914–18.

2.　　　　　The amateurs are coming, the amateurs are coming .

Even after the five Earl Grey Musical and Dramatic Competitions faded into a mothballed memory of smiling trophy winners, silk hats and gaudily-uniformed equerries, local theatre-lovers continued to hope that the contests had helped establish some kind of united front for native theatre in Canada. The situation, however, looked downright bleak for a time. After 1911, scores of groups either disbanded or limped along in regional isolation until they were killed off by the First World War. But then, the war also clipped the wings of the foreign syndicates. Some of the larger cities still attracted companies from below the border but The Road was clearly coming to a dead-end and there was virtually no professional Canadian theatre to bulldoze its way to national recognition.

The theatrical groups that did survive after 1911 and through the war, justified their existence by patriotically producing entertainments for the troops and cheering up the folks at home. The Ottawa Drama League – which actually got going after Earl Grey sailed for home – was even recognized as a useful institution by the federal government and granted the use of the Victoria Memorial Museum's auditorium in 1915. The group was just beginning to swing into action when the Parliament Buildings were gutted by fire and the Little Theatre was taken over by a homeless House of Commons. Scenery was removed, props were packed and the League resigned itself to staging occasional productions at the Russell Theatre in Ottawa until the House on the Hill was restored.

The Canadian drama scene looked more lively in Toronto, Montreal and Vancouver during the First World War. The Players Club of the University of British Clumbia suddenly came to life and began staging wartime productions in 1915. The Dickens Fellowship and the Arts and Letters Clubs of both Montreal and Toronto doggedly ignored shortages of both personnel and supplies to provide theatre on the home front. The Players Club of Toronto (which grew out of the Victoria College Players Club) was organized in 1916 by a group of University of Toronto dons led by Lieutenant-Colonel Vincent Massey. Players Club productions were limited during the war years but at least the club was breathing. Toronto even produced a few theatrical luminaries: Dora Mavor with the Ben Greet Company (the young actress had received an honourable mention at the 1911 Earl Grey Festival but had been so disillusioned with the "pointless socializing" among the amateur groups she vowed to work toward professional status). Then there was Nella Jefferis at the Toronto Conservatory, who would tread the Broadway boards in 1917 with Lionel and John Barrymore. And at the Dickens Fellowship, Torontonians crowded in to watch the polished performances of Basil Morgan.

It was a time of waiting, uncertainty and frustration for those who cared for the theatre in Canada. Although there was a deep national urge for self-expression, other matters took precedence. The community needed to be distracted from the war news, of course, and the Boys needed to be entertained, but somehow, bandage-rolling and other volunteer chores seemed to loom more importantly than play rehearsals and set designing.

After the Armistice, though, the floodgates opened for the community theatre in Canada and by 1930 – when the touring companies had been well and truly squashed by the depression – amateurism had entered its Golden Age. Nonprofessional theatre became so powerful in the country, in fact, that many observers of its rise believe it blocked the evolution of the professional system. "Canada has gone amateur!" a prominent English actor is reported to have exclaimed somewhat derisively in the late 1920's. The amateurs themselves, remembering the humiliating days of the Syndicate and the country's failure to boost local professionalism, were proud of their new muscle. Money, recognition and patronage were showered on the emerging local groups. Amateurism meant "love," didn't it? Enthusiastically, the lovers rode the crest of the post-war wave of nationalism. Those yearning for professional status were forced to seek work in New York or London or among the few foreign stock companies which bravely bucked the new threat of cinema to take up temporary residence in Canada.

The first real sign of the coming amateur boom was in 1919 when, after eight years of work, Hart House was completed at the University of Toronto. The building, intended as a place where "members may discover the true education that is to be found in good fellowship" was a gift from the Massey estate. Amateur actor Vincent Massey himself – by then out of the army and an active director in the family firm of Massey-Harris – took a fascinated interest in equipping the basement with a sophisticated Little Theatre and allowing the university's Players Club to become its chief tenants. Director Roy Mitchell, formerly of the Arts and Letters Club, was coaxed back from New York to take on the job as the new theatre's managing director.

There were other early amateur stirrings. The Dramatic Club of the University College Alumnae Association – a women's organization – made its first public appearance in Toronto with Molière's *Les Femmes Savantes* in 1918. In Montreal, two separate attempts were launched in the Fall of 1918 to organize little theatre groups "free of religious bias." One was headed by Rupert Caplan, a former director with the YMHA Players. Another was under the chairmanship of war artist Charles W. Simpson who was once connected with the Trinity Players, an influential group which had performed in a musty basement furnished with kitchen chairs in the early years of the century. Simpson joined another former Trinity player, Basil Donn, and the pair decided to call their new group the Studio Players. Both the Caplan and the Simpson-Donn plans fell through. Influenza swept Montreal that year and suitable theatres could not be found.

In 1919, though, the Court Players suddenly popped up and staged a production of H. A. Vachell's *Case of Lady Camber* at the Stanley Hall, followed by C. Haddon Chamber's *Sir Antony* at the prestigious His Majesty's Theatre. The following year, a group called the Community Players came on the scene and, simultaneously, the Court Players disappeared.

Across the country, the movement was beginning to roll. In Winnipeg, the Community Players began to plan productions in a small house on the corner or Main Street and Selkirk Avenue. The Vancouver Little Theatre was organized in 1921 and miraculously found its own playhouse. By that year, too, Hart House Theatre was already making an impact on Toronto's theatrical circles and observers from Queen's

University in Kingston and McGill in Montreal were poking around the auditorium with plans of their own to build theatres along similar lines.

In Ottawa, the Drama League got the Victoria Memorial Museum auditorium back in 1923 but somehow, observed the League's policymakers, Col. Henry Osborne, Duncan Campbell Scott and Mrs. Dorothy White, the place now seemed strangely inadequate. After all, community drama was catching on all over the place and it might be a good idea for the League to think about building a Little Theatre of its own. Twenty years before, a suggestion like that would have sparked hoots of laughter, but the League people were serious. By 1926 they were churning out leaflets urging theatre-lovers in Ottawa to support their campaign for a $60,000 building fund. "We've had all kinds of strange homes," Col. Osborne told one fund-raising meeting. "Parish halls, obscure rooms, the Museum theatre. Now we want a theatre as good as Hart House in Toronto." The League got one in 1928, at the corner of King Edward Avenue and Besserer Street and amateur theatricals had become such Big Time, the auditorium was opened by the Governor General, Viscount Willingdon.

The following year, community theatre was grabbing space in the press clear across Canada. In November, 1929 Sir Barry Jackson, founder and director of the Birmingham Repertory Theatre, talked to an audience in Edmonton and thumped away at the need for a national theatre in Canada. "One day," he commented, "I hope to see Canadian cities take as much pride in their theatres as they do in their grain elevators."

Sir Barry obviously hit a nerve. A few months later, a new group called the Edmonton Little Theatre Association was not only formed to stage a full season of plays but other amateur companies from Calgary, Medicine Hat and Lethbridge joined with Edmonton – under the leadership of Lethbridge director E. G. Sterndale Bennett – to organize an Alberta Drama Festival in 1930. So who needed professional theatre when everyone was having such a good time? As feature-writer Zee Pauline Trotter reported breathlessly in the Edmonton *Journal* that year:

Rehearsals of the Little Theatre Association are fascinating! "Come here, Louis and tell me if I've got this stomach in the right place!" This cry of distress from Mr. Rogers Robinson whose cleverly convincing acting carries the association's last play of the season, *The Farmer's Wife*. Mr. Hyndman, star of *The Goal* which was the Little Theatre's first production, in sweater and shirtsleeves, was busy moving stage scenery but stopped to assist with the Applegarth farmer's refractory waistline.

"A skin you love to touch," murmured Mrs. MacDonald gently as she rubbed grease paint onto the countenance of a young man in the garb of a country yokel. "Why didn't you shave old dear?"

"I thought the stuff would stick better if I didn't," explained the rueful actor.

In a later issue of the *Journal*, there was a story about the Edmonton Little Theatre's need to find a home and how Frank Holroy, the group's scenic artist, was creating stage settings "with sacking and ordinary paint. Seen from the audience and under proper lighting, the canvas curtains indeed appear to be exquisite oriental hangings."

Even the editorial writers – who had ignored such fripperies two decades before – were catching the theatrical fever. Glancing up from its gloomy pontifications concerning the Great Depression, the *Journal* decided cheerfully in 1930:

The Little Theatre has given a new hope to those who are anxious to have the spoken drama flourish and to have it adhere to high standards. The movement has expanded at a rapid rate during recent years in all parts of this country. Professor Baker of Yale has listed 1,800 names of producing organizations. It is estimated that 100 of these present from four to twenty-five plays a year! Alberta's participation to the fullest possible extent in this most encouraging development is exceedingly desirable and a promising beginning has been made.

Toronto's Hart House Theatre was still the major showcase of amateur theatricals in the early 1930's and many of its original players had stepped up the ladder into the English professional companies which were presenting repertory seasons in the city. Vaughan Glaser's Company managed to present six successive series of plays in Toronto from 1921 to 1927. The Cameron Matthews English Players stayed for two years. Charles Hampden's British Players dug in between 1925 and 1926. Then there was the English Repertory Company, backed by an optimistic Theatre Guild of Canada, which tried to make the professional grade in 1927–28.

Even so, it was Hart House and other amateur companies such as the T. Eaton Co.'s Masquers and the Imperial Oil Players Guild which seemed to be making the most enduring impact on the town. Hart House itself had gone through several organizational changes since 1919. Instead of reporting directly to the University of Toronto, for example, the theatre had now become the responsibility of a Board of Syndics headed by Vincent Massey. Massey– who continued to dabble in acting during the 1920's, together with his stage-struck younger brother, Raymond – had also switched Hart House directors four times since the departure of Roy Mitchell in 1921. Although the theatre had presented a staggering total of a hundred plays between 1921 and 1925 it was no secret that it was in constant conflict with the philosophies of the university's Players Club and that income of the expensive little theatre could be better.

Bertram Forsyth, a director with solid local and overseas experience, became chief of production after Mitchell resigned in 1925, but the years with Hart House were tough for him. The Vaughan Glaser Players proved to be formidable competition and Forsyth desperately began to choose plays for their popularity instead of quality. The ploy failed to work. In university circles, the story was that Forsyth left Hart House with a deficit and Massey testily brought in yet another experienced director, Walter Sinclair. Frustrated with constant budget-cutting, however, Sinclair resigned in 1927 and moved to New Orleans. Hart House's fourth director in eight years was Carroll Aikens, an energetic westerner who had brought drama to the fruit-growers of British Columbia's Okanagan Valley as far back as 1920. Aikens was a success for a time. He healed the rift with the Players Club and presented a series of successful productions: A. A. Milne's *Make Believe*, Bernard Shaw's *Major Barbara*, Shakespeare's *Comedy of Errors*. There was talk of Hart House expanding by forming an independent experimental group, an idea probably goaded into the open air by Herman Voaden, a Toronto playwright and director who was constantly railing against amateur organizations which failed to be adventurous in their choice of plays.

Aikens quit Hart House in 1929 and Vincent Massey decided to be cautious about settling on a new director. Edgar Stone, a young man with theatrical background who was then employed by Ontario's Motion Picture Branch, was asked to take over temporarily. Eventually, Massey asked him to stay. It was 1930 and news from around the Dominion made it obvious that the Theatre of the People was hitting the big time. The old Trinity Players, with Basil Donn as director, had been enthusiastically revived in Montreal. Yet another local venture, The Theatre Guild, headed by dynamic young socialite Martha Allan and Rupert Caplan (who had tried unsuccessfully to launch a group in 1918) staged A. A. Milne's three-act mystery *A Perfect Alibi* at Montreal's Moyse Hall. News was that the Guild (which quickly switched its name to the Montreal Repertory Company because a Theatre Guild existed in New York) would also have a French section. French-Canadian groups in Quebec were always popping up, anyway, though they were constantly merging, dissolving or changing their names.

In Nova Scotia, the Theatre Arts Guild of Halifax began staging productions in a "playhouse" that seated less than 200 spectators yet managed to cram in dozens more. The rain leaked through the backstage roof and actors had to stand on duckboards in the basement dressing rooms. When members of the audience were finally forced to sit through performances in their raincoats, director Leslie Pigott and Guild leader James L. Robertson talked their way into accommodations provided by the Navy League Building.

On the western shores of the Dominion, community theatre had grown from the Vancouver Little Theatre of 1921 and the Victoria Little Theatre to the British Columbia Drama

Festival of 1932 under the presidency of bristly theatre militant Major L. Bullock-Webster. In Saskatchewan, the Little Theatre was booming, with members eagerly crowding in from towns and villages across the province. The Manitoba Drama League, boasting such formidable and influential backers as John Craig of the Winnipeg Little Theatre, Lady Margaret Tupper (whose lawyer husband, Sir Charles Tupper, was a grandson and namesake of Sir John A. MacDonald's celebrated cabinet minister) and George V. Ferguson of the Winnipeg *Free Press*, could count sixteen member groups in Winnipeg and 106 on the provincial register. Even in unemployment-plagued New Brunswick, the Saint John Theatre Guild optimistically began to make plans for increased theatrical activity in 1931.

Over in London that year, Vere Brabazon Ponsonby, the Ninth Earl of Bessborough (an Irish, not a British title) was being entertained by friends at the Savoy Hotel before sailing for Canada to become the Dominion's new Governor General. "I hope," said the tall, pale Earl to a friend who had just returned to England from a visit with Canadian relatives, "that there is plenty of theatre going on over there."

The friend sipped thoughtfully at his sherry. "Abandon any such hope, milord. Theatre in Canada is dead."

3.   The Great Idea

The information that theatre was non-existent in Canada shocked and depressed Lord Bessborough. Although he was well-known in England as a gentleman politician (he sat as a Conservative MP in the House of Commons in 1910 and from 1913 to 1920), a soldier with the British Expeditionary Forces and a millionaire margarine manufacturer, friends knew his real obsession was with the theatre.

Rowland's Castle, Bessborough's luxurious home at Stansted Park in Hampshire, boasted the best-equipped private playhouse in the kingdom. Even the toughest critics from the London newspapers were glad to accept invitations to Stansted to review the Society of Stansted Players' expensive productions of Shaw or Shakespeare. The plays themselves were always staged for some worthy charity such as repairs for the nearby Chichester Cathedral or the Radium Fund of the Royal West Sussex Hospital, but Bessborough employed professional directors and liked to think the productions were taken seriously. Rehearsals went on for several weeks and the entire cast stayed in the rambling castle, pampered and fed by Bessborough's domestic staff.

The audience which attended the plays was invariably aristocratic (Lord Louis Mountbatten and his wife were constant guests) and names appearing on Stansted programs included Lady George Cholmondeley, the Hon. Denys Buckley, Major Arthur Clarke-Jervoise and – always a source of good copy for visiting journalists – Bessborough's dashing young son and heir, Viscount Eric Duncannon. Bessborough himself liked to appear on stage in the flowing robes of a king or a duke and he fancied himself as a set designer.

So the theatre in Canada was dead? The somewhat introverted Earl whom one British writer described as "a man who dances as if in a dream," (the truth is that he was a little deaf) admitted later in a 1936 *London Morning Post* article that the prospect sounded rather dreary. "When I arrived in 1931, I found road company activity dead," he wrote. "Theatres had been taken over by film companies. Depression had practically killed touring by professional companies from abroad." However, duty to King and Country came before human yearnings for theatrical entertainment and Bessborough arrived smilingly in Halifax to assume his duties as George V's representative in this uncultured outpost of Empire. His swearing-in ceremony, in April 1931, made the front pages because it was the first event of its kind to be broadcast clear across Canada.

Another snippet of news about the Bessboroughs grabbed the romantic attention of Canadian readers. Lady Bessborough, the statuesque daughter of Baron de Neuflize, Governor of the Bank of France, was known to be pregnant. Staggered by their responsibility, Government House officials ordered the vice-regal train from Halifax to crawl to Ottawa at a cautious thirty miles per hour. It is not known whether either the new Governor General or his wife protested that the interminable trip would be as likely to induce a miscarriage as a bumpy

84

ride. In any case the Bessborough infant – the couple's third child, suitably christened George St. Lawrence Ponsonby – was safely delivered in a Montreal hospital a few months later.

In the meantime, Bessborough was discovering to his delighted surprise that life in the Dominion was not quite as theatrically sterile as he had been told it would be. For one thing, there was the Ottawa Drama League and its cosy Little Theatre practically at the front door of Rideau Hall. Hart House in Toronto was operating more smoothly than it had for years under the direction of its new manager, Edgar Stone. There was Martha Allan's Repertory Theatre in Montreal. Talks with the executive of the ODL (which was summoned to Government House within weeks of Bessborough's arrival) cheered the Governor General still further when he learned that the Little Theatre movement, in fact, was flourishing healthily throughout Canada. He had scarcely unpacked his Saville Row wardrobe when he received a letter from Lillian D. Myers of the bustling Saskatoon Little Theatre suggesting that a Governor General with such a strong interest in drama might care to do something about unifying Canada's proliferating groups. Perhaps a Canadian Drama League might be the answer? The notion – a nostalgic reminder of his tie-in with the British Drama League – clearly stuck in Bessborough's head. As he was to remember with perhaps unintentional Imperialistic overtones on his return to England five years later: "Drama leagues had sprung into being all over Canada. Instinctively and without any prompting or previous consultation, Canadians laid the foundations of a peoples' theatre. They did what their ancestors in England did in the Middle Ages."

Bessborough lost no time in sampling the fare at the best little theatres in Ottawa, Toronto and Montreal, and Government House aides quickly realized that vice-regal visits should include an evening of drama if possible. Unlike his predecessor Earl Grey, sports events interested the new Governor General only slightly. He enjoyed bridge almost as fanatically as he did the stage (he became so absorbed in games, his guests were often kept nodding over their cards until dawn) but he seldom read a book and he displayed a stony disinterest in music and painting. Vincent Massey was not in Toronto when

Bessborough dropped into Hart House to see a play in the summer of 1931, but Edgar Stone wrote to his home, Batterwood House in Port Hope, Ontario, about the vice-regal visit and mentioned that the Governor General had dropped a hint about "doing something for amateur dramatics." Thoroughly intrigued with Stone's report, Massey sped a note to Bessborough's private secretary, Allan Lascelles.

What was all this about a Bessborough plan "within the sphere of amateur dramatics?" What did His Excellency have in mind? He was very much involved in theatre himself, he reminded Lascelles, so he asked him to pass on the word that he would be glad to co-operate in any way. The letter was the beginning of Massey's association with a national movement that would be the source of personal satisfaction, irritation, doubt and sometimes embarrassment until the day he died.

In 1931, however, Vincent Massey was in the mood to think seriously about an enterprise that might have seemed an unimportant distraction a few years earlier. The slightly-built, grave-faced head of the wealthy Massey family had already strayed from his board room at Massey-Harris in Toronto to become Canada's first ambassador to Washington from 1925 to 1930 and the life of a diplomat obviously suited him. At the end of the term his personal friend, Prime Minister William Lyon Mackenzie King, asked Massey to accept the post as High Commissioner in London. Massey – anxious to get back into diplomatic harness again – immediately accepted. His luggage was already packed when Mackenzie King's Liberal government was defeated in the July 1930 general election and Conservative R. B. Bennett took over as Prime Minister.

Massey, who was a staunch Liberal, could have automatically resigned the London job. Instead, smarting with disappointment over the turn of events, he decided to ask Bennett for instructions. It was a stormy meeting in Ottawa. The Prime Minister made no bones about the fact that the appointment was unacceptable, and Massey – always the gentleman – backed down. As he later remembered: "To bring the disagreeable episode to a close, I said that in view of his statements on the subject of the High Commissionership and his intentions with regard to the appointment, my only course was to offer my resignation. He agreed and gave me to understand that it was accepted." Massey's diplomatic career swung restlessly in limbo for the next five years.

At the time of his enquiry to Allan Lascelles about Bessborough's "amateur dramatics plan," though, Massey and his wife Alice were preparing for a trip to the Far East. Massey was checking through his itinerary one morning when a large envelope arrived from Government House enclosing several pages of typewritten foolscap marked "private and confidential" and a covering letter from the Governor General's secretary. He flipped through the pages. They contained details of a plan for "an annual Dominion of Canada Drama Festival," that were staggering in scope. Conscious of his powerful influence as the king's representative in Ottawa, Bessborough clearly intended to pull out all the stops so his grand design would catch on. He intended to write to "lieutenant governors of the provinces, principals of universities, directors of little theatres and representatives of the boy scouts and girl guides" announcing his interest in organizing a festival "that would create national interest and be of educational value."

A suggested constitution and list of regulations followed. Bessborough would be patron of the festival. The lieutenant-governors of the provinces would all be presidents. The Prime Minister, the Leader of the Opposition and the premiers of provinces plus the chancellors of Laval and the University of Montreal would be named vice-presidents. There would be a huge committee made up of the vice-chancellors of universities, provincial ministers of education, representatives of literary societies, little theatres groups, the National Council of Education – and the boy scouts and girl guides. Bessborough had blueprinted the machinery of the festival as carefully as he designed stage settings. He suggested that an office should be opened in Ottawa and that the festival should be held in the capital every year during the third or fourth week of June.

He had definite ideas, both about the type of competitions to be included in the festival and the competitors themselves. He felt there should be adult and junior teams and that adjudicators at preliminary playoffs (an idea that had evaded Earl Grey) should be local residents "so as to avoid travel."

A committee – yet another committee – would then pick ten adult and ten junior teams from the adjudication reports and a *second* provincial round of playoffs would then be held before paid audiences. The cash from box-office sales at this set of eliminations would then be collected and shuttled to the festival's central committee and used to underwrite expenses for the big Ottawa Final. Each province, decided the Governor General, would select two adult and two junior teams to go to the Final and he urged there should be only "the simplest scenic effects" so everyone would compete on an equal level.

The plays? Well, productions should be no longer than forty minutes in playing time and Bessborough suggested that a list of scenes or speeches from Shakespeare, Corneille, Racine and Molière might be prepared so teams could pick out what they wanted to stage. Finally, he felt there should be an exhibition of set designs at the Final and he also added that it might be a good thing if "a school of producers" be established in Canada. Massey was astonished at Bessborough's massive and ambitious plan. He read Lascelles' covering letter and was relieved to learn that "His Excellency does not intend to do anything about the idea at the moment," mainly because of the depression. Tucking the documents back into their Government House envelope, Massey filed them carefully in a desk drawer and a few days later took off for his scheduled trip to the Orient.

Bessborough, though, was itching to do something about his drama festival plan. In November of 1931, he was out making speeches in Ottawa and Toronto that negated his previous intention of keeping the idea under temporary wraps. "I should like to see as a normal part of our life in this country, dramatic performances taking place of plays by Canadian authors with music by Canadian composers, with scenic decoration and costumes by Canadian artists, performed by Canadian players," he thumped at the Empire Club in Toronto. "The drama can be made not only an artistic but a great educational influence. I visualize a movement that might develop into a great Drama League, Dominion wide. The keen and growing interest in the little theatre and repertory movement extending as it does right across the Dominion from Ottawa, through

Winnipeg and Vancouver, is proof in my mind that a movement for national drama might be born."

After these virtual announcements, things then began to move fast. Lascelles was ordered to circulate a newly-designed draft in December 1931 which included a covering letter from Bessborough declaring his interest in sponsoring a festival. The fresh draft was somewhat different from the one sent to Massey a few months before. For one thing, the word "Dominion" was omitted and the idea was that the festival should begin in the provinces of Quebec and Ontario with other provinces joining only if and when they wished. Bessborough also had second thoughts about the kind of festival he wanted. This time he divided it into two sections, drama and declamation.

"In the drama branch," the new plan read, "teams from any recognized university, college, school, convent, seminary, drama league, little theatre, amateur dramatic society, literary society, boy scout or girl guide organizations in any of the provinces included in the scheme are eligible to compete. Any team not included in the above categories may compete, subject to the approval of the general committee." The draft went on to say that ministers of education would be consulted by the festival's management committee to help find adjudicators for the first-round elimination competitions. The adjudicators' reports would then be submitted to a referee who would pick "six teams in the Drama Branch and six from the senior and junior classes respectively in the Declamation Branch." These would compete in the second round of the competition to be held in Quebec and Montreal (for Quebec) and Toronto and Ottawa (for Ontario) in October. The new draft was fuzzy about how competitors would be chosen for the big Final in Ottawa. It merely stated that a prize would be given by the Governor General to the best team in the drama and the twin declamation branches and that prizes would also be handed out to the second and third teams.

Steaming along with his idea, Bessborough had also got around to naming individuals he would clearly command to work for the festival. As in the first draft, he named himself as patron. But now the enormous list of presidents had been whittled to two: the lieutenant-governors of Ontario and Quebec. There would be eleven vice-presidents, including Prime Minister R. B. Bennett, Mackenzie King, the chancellors of Laval and the University of Montreal – and Vincent Massey. As before, the general committee was enormous and listed such names as Martha Allan, Hector Charlesworth, Duncan Campbell Scott of the Ottawa Drama League, Edgar Stone and, inevitably, representatives of the boy scouts and the girl guides. A brand-new section of the draft stated that both French and English would have equal standing in the competition.

Vincent Massey, now back from his jaunt to the Far East, reacted swiftly to this weighty new communiqué from Ottawa. On January 4, after enjoying a traditional Christmas and New Year's celebration at Batterwood, he wrote worriedly to Lascelles complaining that the plan outlined by Bessborough was "too comprehensive and complicated" to be tackled in the first year. Diplomatically, he suggested there should be a certain amount of spadework done before a final plan could be safely launched. "It must not run the risk of failure," he warned. He agreed Departments of Education should be involved in the scheme and – surprisingly for a man who was the moving force behind Hart House – he gave the nod to the idea of splitting the festival into drama and declamation contests:

> I feel the declamation of dramatic verse would meet with general approval on the part of educational authorities and the general public whereas the drama has not yet been accepted officially as a factor in education. Apart from this, one is still conscious of the lingering Puritan traditions which regard the theatre with certain misgivings. I would suggest dramatic competition during the first year on a conservative and limited basis, while declamation might be carried considerably further.

Massey also argued against the festival not being given national importance from the beginning and suggested that provincial departments of education be asked to run the preliminary playoffs on their own. High schools, he felt, should not be included in the festival at all. He referred to a covering letter from Lascelles which had come with the new draft, hinting there might be a large meeting in Ottawa early in 1932 to discuss the plan. Massey clucked over this and said he believed the idea was not yet mature and that it might be wiser to get a few interested individuals together to thrash things out before going all the way. The whole question of the festival must have gnawed at Massey, however. Two days after writing his letter, and possibly before it even arrived at Rideau Hall, he was in Ottawa with Bessborough, talking about the festival blueprint. He tried to see the Governor General again on January 20, but His Excellency had other engagements. The two men did not meet again personally to discuss the idea until the following May.

But Massey's impassioned arguments clearly made sense to the Governor General. On January 14, 1932, Lascelles was mailing yet another note to those who had received the December communication:

> His Excellency has received many expressions of opinion from educational and other authorities in various parts of the Dominion with regard to the suggested Drama League and Festival. There appears to be general agreement that such a movement would be of national as well as educational value. Much preliminary work, however, would have to be done privately before a detailed scheme of so elaborate a nature could be launched publicly and effectively. The present period of economic depression, during the continuance of which the public announcement and initiation of such a movement would no doubt be inopportune, provides, at the same time, an opportunity for further consultation among those interested and the thorough preparation of a detailed scheme of organization. It is not, therefore, proposed to hold any meeting of a formal character for the present.

By now it was apparent that Bessborough was beginning to rely a good deal on Vincent Massey's expertise as a patron of little theatre and on his intimate knowledge of the Dominion. The Governor General (whom Massey once described as "a very nice fellow, very conscientious and a bit self-conscious and shy") decided to keep his helpful collaborator informed as to what was going on. Memos and suggestions concerning the proposed festival were regularly mailed to Batterwood House, even though Bessborough must have known Massey was busily addressing Canadian Clubs across the Dominion and raising funds for a new convalescent hospital to be built by the Sisters of St. John the Divine. At one point, in July 1932, Bessborough sat down and jotted a personal note to Massey, politely admitting he had read about his visits to different parts of the country "so I hesitate to remind you of your most kind promise to draw up a definite Drama League Festival scheme from the voluminous dossier I inflicted on you."

Massey, in turn, realized he had better do something concrete about pulling Bessborough's obsessive plan into shape and scribbled some proposals which were sent to Lascelles later that month. To begin with, Massey agreed the competition should be in three stages, much as Bessborough had already envisioned: regional, provincial and national. He scrubbed the idea for a declamatory contest and ignored the Governor General's original plan to have senior and junior divisions. "As regards plays," wrote Massey, "I agree with His Excellency that these should be limited to Shakespeare or the French classics on one hand and Canadian plays on the other. Adjudication should be left to local people to find in the personnel of experienced dramatic groups." He suggested that nothing more needed to be done about the idea until the Bessboroughs returned from a tour of the Western provinces they planned after the Imperial Economic Conference in August. "I feel they will see quite a lot of what is being done in drama festivals around the country. After their return to Ottawa I think it might be advisable to call together the committee which His Excellency thought of summoning last spring, then place before them a definite plan for their approval."

The next problem to be faced, Massey added, was finance. Bessborough had mentioned $10,000 as the sum he felt would get the festival moving and Massey optimistically agreed it should be possible to raise this amount "for such an excellent cause." He then suggested that the Governor General approach Col. Henry Osborne, a mild-mannered friend of Massey's who had attended college in Port Hope, to act as director of the proposed festival. At that time, Osborne (whom Bessborough already knew as a founder of the Ottawa Drama League) was working as Secretary General of the Canadian Agency of the Imperial War Graves Commission. Bessborough was only too delighted to recruit such a gentlemanly volunteer and Osborne was willingly roped into the job. The directorship conveniently settled, Massey decided the next step would be to set up provincial bodies of general and working committees, "the former being largely decorative and the latter consisting of practical people." It was a policy that would throw successive wrenches into the machinery of the DDF for the next four decades.

The Bessboroughs, accompanied by their glamorous son Eric Duncannon, made a triumphal progress through the west in the Fall of 1932. Depression-plagued cities such as Winnipeg, Saskatoon, Regina and Vancouver loyally turned out with infantry regiments, brass bands and mandatory troops of girl guides and boy scouts. Farmers waved as the vice-regal railway car clattered by their fields. Ex-servicemen, festooned with military decorations were assigned as chauffeurs of the polished Rolls Royces trundled out to carry the trio to official banquets and receptions. "The kindly manner of the Governor General and the radiant charm of his wife created a deep impression on everyone present," gushed a Saskatoon reporter. "Her Excellency stepped from the balcony of the hotel carrying with her a beautiful bouquet presented by Miss Edith Underwood, daughter of the mayor, charmingly gowned in a dress of blue embroidery, with hat to match. On more than one occasion Her Excellency was addressed in French and gave a smiling reply on hearing the language of the country of her birth."

According to press accounts of the 1932 western tour, Bessborough talked more about Canadian resources than Canadian culture, but he did manage to fit in some plays and meetings with individuals who were later destined to become household

93

names in the Dominion Drama Festival. At John Craig's Winnipeg Little Theatre he saw a performance of *Othello* with Beck Dennistoun as Desdemona. Winnipeg writers have since suggested that the Governor General was so impressed with the play that he thought of founding the DDF on the spot. During the western trip he also met Lady Margaret Tupper and immediately wrote to Massey: "Pleased indeed with the performance of *Othello* in Winnipeg. Lady Tupper will send names for the general committee in Winnipeg. She says she can always get to meetings in Ottawa herself and appears very keen and all for Shakespeare."

Before leaving on his tour, Bessborough had asked Massey to act as chairman of the general and executive committees of the proposed festival and Massey – up to his ears in the project by this time – could scarcely refuse. Gratefully, the Governor General acknowledged from the west: "Thank you for accepting my offer to become chairman. Nothing could be a better omen for the success of the venture."

By now, it had been decided between Bessborough, Massey and Osborne that the meeting with individuals interested in community theatre and a drama festival should be held at Government House on Saturday, October 29, 1932, a few weeks after the opening of Parliament. A list of sixty suitable names was prepared which included representatives of little theatre groups and leagues from across the nation and, for influential ballast, names such as Sir Charles Gordon, president of the Bank of Montreal, Mr. Justice Surveyer of Montreal, Sir Andrew Macphail and Sir Robert Borden. No one refused an invitation.

4.   "A red-letter day in the annals of Canadian drama"

From its very beginning, the Dominion Drama Festival stressed the importance of order, the right thing and protocol. Before the October 29 meeting, a memo was sent to all invited guests that must have sent them scurrying for their tailor's telephone number or copies of Harper's Bazaar. "The meeting will be held in the ballroom of Rideau Hall at 2:45 p.m.," read the message from Ottawa.

Guests will arrive at the Front Door and be shown into the Chinese Gallery. At 2:35 p.m., Their Excellencies will receive their guests who will be introduced by Mr. A. F. Lascelles, assisted by Lt. Col. E. Mackenzie. After passing Their Excellencies, guests will go into the ballroom and be shown to their seats by Lt. Col. H. Willis-O'Connor and Capt. Colville who will reserve places in the front row for Her Excellency and House Guests. His Excellency will then seat himself at a table in the Ball Room with his back to the dais. At the conclusion of the meeting a buffet tea will be served in the dining room.

Fortunately for those who had fussed with their finery, that Saturday was cool and clear in the capital. By 2:20 p.m., the leaf-spotted driveway of Government House was jammed with rented limousines, taxis, gentlemen sporting top-hats and ladies white-gloved to the elbows. Few recognized each other. Possibly none realized they were about to be admitted into a unique family circle that would stubbornly endure for years, despite financial crises, outside criticism and insurrection within the ranks. The guests stared curiously at each other across the ballroom as they waited for the meeting to begin. Lady Tupper from Winnipeg was already dispensing salty comments among those closest to her chair. D. Park Jamieson, a lawyer from Sarnia, Ontario, and an influential member of the local little theatre sat quietly, a carnation in the buttonhole of his director's suit. E. G. Sterndale Bennett from Lethbridge stared thoughtfully at the ceiling through his spectacles, a faint smile on his lips. Little theatre enthusiasts Caroline Crerar and Arthur Brain from Hamilton, Ontario, waved across the room as Catharine Brickenden from London, Ontario, sailed regally to her seat. There was a small ripple of laughter as an impressed gentleman hastened to hold "Cizzie's" chair.

Everyone recognized Martha Allan from the Montreal Repertory Theatre. Who could mistake that slicked-back blonde hair, the quick gestures, the expensive clothes of a young woman whose father, Sir Montague Allan, owned the Allan Shipping Lines and a massive Montreal mansion called Ravenscrag? Was it really true that she smoked *cigarettes?* There were murmurs of interest as Vincent Massey took his seat next to that nice man, Col. Henry Osborne. As usual, Massey was dignified but friendly. Personally, he was pleased about the conference. Edgar Stone, the director of Hart House, had been invited to attend but Massey decided to act as representative of the Toronto area as well as chairman of the steering committees and Stone was told to stay at home. Massey turned to shake hands with Rupert Davies of Kingston and Dorothy White of the Ottawa Drama League.

Lord Bessborough himself was in fine form that October afternoon. Hiding his shyness behind sheafs of prepared notes, the Governor General was clearly elated at the excited response to his drama festival idea. He rose to his feet to a storm of applause, smiled, bowed slightly in reponse then told his guests: "Now that the Little Theatre has gained so strong a foothold in this country, there is, without any doubt a great opportunity for its development along national lines, with the ultimate objective of creating a national drama." Community drama, the Governor General continued, "brought people together, especially in the long evenings of the winter." The audience listened to Bessborough's speech with hushed and approving attention. Next on the agenda was the matter of the Dominion Drama Festival itself. Should it be born here and now? There seemed to be no real dissenters, but discussion about a possible festival went on for an hour or so. Vincent Massey finally got to his feet and gravely moved it be adopted that there should indeed be a drama festival. The motion was seconded by Mr. Justice Surveyer of Montreal and carried by the meeting.

It developed that, for the time being, the competition would be confined to "established amateur dramatic societies." These would include little theatre companies already producing, university, literary society groups and so on. The list of "suggested" short plays was again brought up at the meeting but guests felt there should be no rigid rules about this. Everyone had to agree it was "desirable to develop a national drama and consequently original Canadian plays will be encouraged," but how this would be achieved was not made clear.

But by then, a spirit of camaraderie had developed among the guests and there was a hint of festivity in the air. Everyone happily applauded when it was announced there would be an election of festival officers, or as it was termed at the meeting, "an election of a general committee." Bessborough was duly named patron, to more excited applause. The lieutenant-governors of the provinces, the Prime Minister and the federal Leader of the Opposition, provincial premiers, university heads, church leaders, provincial ministers of education and presidents of established theatre groups were all lumped into the committee, to pleased head-nodding from those present. Bessborough, after all, obviously meant business if he could gain the support of such heavy artillery. There was more approval when other officers were named. The Rt. Hon. Sir Robert Borden, president. Vincent Massey, chairman. The Hon. Athanase David, provincial secretary for the province of Quebec, first vice-chairman. Col. Henry Osborne, vice-chairman and honorary director. Sir Charles Gordon and Beaudry Leman, Montreal financiers, were quite suitably named as honorary treasurers.

There would be an inner conclave, it seemed. Sir Robert Borden. Vincent Massey. Athanase David. Col. Osborne. The two treasurers and one representative of each province to be selected by the little theatre groups themselves.

"Saturday October 29, 1932 should be recorded as a red-letter day in the annals of Canadian drama," wrote a *Globe* reporter who was at the meeting:

> The Little Theatre movement has been greatly benefited by the steps taken at this conference in Ottawa and will be still more greatly benefited by the carrying out of the plans made for the Dominion Festival. In the first place, the fact that the whole higher governmental and educational apparatus of the entire country, together with leaders in almost all the other walks of life is giving official sanction and active support to an undertaking solely designed

to foster the development of the Little Theatre, strikingly validates every claim made by enthusiasts as to the profound importance of that institution both socially and culturally. The dignity and prestige of the Little Theatre movement are immensely enhanced by this tremendous endorsation. Finally, all groups will please take notice that a Dominion Drama Festival is now actually in being, that detailed announcements of eligibility, requirements, general plans may profitably be considered for competing in some sort of Regional Preliminary Festival, whether at home or at a district centre, before the end of January.

In the ballroom of Rideau Hall, chairs scraped, chatter boomed louder and the impressed group of little theatre addicts edged toward the dining room and that promised buffet tea. Then there was a startled hush. The Countess of Bessborough came through a door holding her young son, George St. Lawrence Ponsonby. With cluckings and clapping, Canada's community theatre elite showed they recognized drama at its very best. After an entrance like that, how could the Dominion Drama Festival possibly fail?

CHAPTER FOUR

The First Years

1. **"Now, we've got to get organized. . . ."**

Vincent Massey seemed to be swept along as optimistically as everyone else when the Dominion Drama Festival was spawned in October, 1932. One of his first practical acts of confidence was to instruct the Massey Foundation to make a grant of $2,500 to the project. A covering note to a foundation officer read: "I questioned the wisdom of some of the features of the idea in its early stage. But now I think it is a valuable undertaking."

These can be construed as enthusiastic words from Massey. Although he was known to be passionately fond of the theatre, both because of his interest in Hart House and his occasional flings at acting (he once played Pope Pius VIII in a production of Paul Claudel's *L'Otage* and wore the Roman Catholic Archbishop of Toronto's amethyst ring for the run of the play), his stormy impatience with errors in Hart House management and his cautious view of amateurism itself were almost as celebrated. Writing in a 1922 issue of *Queen's Quarterly*, in fact, Massey put himself on record as a cynic as far as the future prospects of Canadian drama were concerned. "It is easy to be as witty about Canadian drama as about the Canadian navy," he commented: "Each at the moment may seem to represent a well-meaning but insignificant effort to complete our national equipment – to suggest a pious aspiration rather than reality." At that time, Massey noted, Canadian drama represented perhaps twelve or fifteen produced plays.

"Amateur theatre suffers from two evils – preciousness in art and instability in finance. If commercial theatre errs in trying to give the public what it wants, amateur theatre makes the frequent mistake of giving its public what it thinks it ought to want – often sublimely confident that food to be wholesome must be unpalatable."

Even so, the top-level support behind Lord Bessborough's Dominion Drama Festival must have convinced Massey that the odds for success were tilted in its favour. Although he had been elected president of the National Liberal Federation and had planned a gruelling schedule of political speeches, he dutifully allied himself to the festival dream and worked with Henry Osborne (who had dug into a corner of an office rented by Ottawa lawyer and theatre buff John Aylen) and Bessborough to get the plan moving towards its scheduled climax in April, 1933.

Regulations were the first problems tackled by the gilt-edged DDF executive and there had to be some serious thinking about the preliminary elimination contests designed to sort the men from the boys. Before the first Final Festival in 1933, the entire question of regional structure and adjudication was confused. There was general agreement that there should be Western and Eastern Quebec competitive regions and also Eastern and Western Ontario regions. After some argument, Urban Toronto was finally declared a region in itself because of the number of powerful groups competing there. Other regions for the 1933 Festival were lumped into natural provincial boundaries.

But then there was the question of language. Should some regions be split again into separate playoffs for English and French groups? And how? "The whole position of the French groups will bear discussion," Osborne wrote worriedly to Massey in late December, 1932. "Should we, for example, have a regional adjudication in Montreal to include French groups from Eastern Ontario as well?"

After further discussions and correspondence, it was decided that both Eastern Ontario and Western Quebec would be divided into French and English sections. Montreal would host both playoffs with separate adjudicators. Ottawa would look after the French round in Eastern Ontario, Kingston would take the English regional.

The work of organizing the festival at the regional level continued frantically through November and December. Osborne was continually jotting notes to Massey – which eventually caught up with him in Port Hope – praising or complaining about areas that were zooming ahead or dragging their heels on the regional scene. Western Ontario earned a gold star from the beginning. D. Park Jamieson (the dapper lawyer with the carnation) was scarcely back home from the Ottawa meeting before he was summoning little theatre groups to London, Ontario, to form a Western Ontario Drama League. "Great activity under Jamieson in Western Ontario," enthused Osborne's progress report to Massey in mid-December, 1932. "B.C. seems to be progressing under Gomery's charge, though there are some difficulties on the Island, apparently. Prince Edward Island, nil. Western Quebec, including Montreal, no definite word as to entries expected. Eastern Quebec, still in the dark."

The choice of available and suitable adjudicators for both the regional and final DDF festivals was to haunt the organization until 1970, and Massey himself got a taste of things to come in 1932. Not that there was a shortage of applicants. Before the first regional playoff in Kingston during February, 1932, Osborne's desk was flooded with letters from excited theatre-lovers who fancied themselves in the exalted role of Dramatic Judge for a festival so highly endorsed by the top personages in the land.

"Possibly Merrill Denison would be satisfactory for Montreal," Osborne mused to Massey after thumbing through the pile of applications. "Toronto is a bit of a nut to crack. What would you think of B. K. Sandwell? If Toronto presents a special difficulty we might, if necessary, get someone to run up from New York though I think we should avoid that if possible. I've not eliminated the possibility of a person being selected within the region itself. This is because British Columbia has already written that Carroll Aikens would be satisfactory to them."

Massey replied with crisp notes that were in contrast to Osborne's somewhat emotional outpourings. "I think that so long as we keep to the rule that adjudicators must come from outside the area involved in the principal contest we will probably find quite a choice of available people," he ruled with matter-of-fact directness. Not long after, he scribbled a short memo to Osborne saying he was thinking of asking Tyrone Guthrie to judge a preliminary competition. He remembered the director had been in Canada in 1930 doing a series of radio plays and that he had been an adjudicator in the National Festival of Great Britain. In the meantime, however, Osborne continued to sift through correspondence, worry over non-activity in some regions, and shuttle off suggestions for regional judges to Massey, who either approved or disapproved of them. S. Morgan-Powell, the Montreal drama critic, was finally asked to judge the English division in Western Ontario. E. G. Sterndale Bennett got the assignment in Kingston. "In writing to them," Osborne wrote to Edgar Stone at Hart House in January, 1933, "I stated that all expenses in connection with the matter would be borne by the Central Committee."

Stone himself – who had been told by Massey to organize the Urban Toronto regional – was apparently being difficult by asking for *three* adjudicators. Osborne complained: "I think it's a tall order to pay three adjudicators for one region. Other regions have been content with one. However, perhaps in the case of Toronto there would be no travelling expenses." He hinted to Stone that it might be a fine thing if the regions helped with the financing of the Ottawa Final Festival. "Six groups from the Ottawa Drama League have worked out a good scheme," he wrote. "They are going to have a preliminary local showing of their plays then pool the money for expenses. The Kingston committee proposes to billet visiting players." Stone did not snap at the bait.

But then there were other Festival birth-pangs. There had been a nasty mix-up in British Columbia about whether Percy Gomery of the Vancouver Little Theatre (who had been invited to the October meeting) or Major L. Bullock-Webster of the British Columbia Drama Association was organizing the regional playoffs for the area. The rumblings from the west even reverberated around Rideau Hall. A Captain W. C. Innes of Port Credit complained because his group had not been invited to the Western Ontario playoff. "Innes, who runs the Port Credit dramatic group is in a state of tragic disappointment that he did not know his group was eligible for the DDF," Osborne reported to Massey. "He thought it was on a purely invitational basis." Later, Osborne wrote in relief that "Innes has been accommodated. He replaces a Windsor entry which has dropped out."

The question of a suitable adjudicator for the Ottawa Final was beginning to become a crucial problem. Thoroughly aware of possible flack from the regions, Osborne sent out diplomatic feelers as to how local organizers felt about someone being imported from Britain. Martha Allan promptly replied from Montreal that anyone who was satisfactory to Osborne was fine as far as her region was concerned. Other letters were as co-operative and Osborne passed on this information to Port Hope. At the same time he was also asking Massey's advice on other questions. Was the DDF for professionals or amateurs? Should adjudicators be billeted in private homes? Were there any kinds of plays that might be unacceptable? Massey, stopping over at Batterwood House between speeches in Quebec and Toronto, patiently sent on his opinions to Ottawa.

"The DDF is for amateurs," Osborne later replied to enquirers. "There is no objection to the employment of a professional director by a group. As to the players, there would be an objection to a professional actor who is temporarily out of employment and who proposes to resume in the future. On the other hand, there is no objection to a person who has abandoned his profession permanently and is now engaged in another occupation." Professor James A. Roy of Queen's University wondered worriedly if a group could use a professional make-up man and was told that if the man was indeed professional he could do the job, provided he was not paid. Percy Gomery of Vancouver wanted to know whether the hiring of costumes would count against a team. "For example, one team here is doing *School for Scandal* and the cost of making costumes, even with inexpensive material, would be prohibitive." Osborne, after some brow-furrowing, ducked the question by replying that perhaps a certain amount of hiring was unavoidable and that groups could use their own judgement.

And how about the billeting problem? "Should regional adjudicators be billeted in private homes?" Osborne asked Massey in February, 1933. "Margaret Tupper has offered to put up Dr. (Lawrence) Mason herself. Mrs. Brickenden of London has offered to hostess Morgan-Powell. Mrs. Brickenden adds in her letter, incidentally, that 'of course I am embroiled in the London Drama League entries for the contest, but I do not suppose anyone would believe a man of the standing of Mr. Morgan-Powell would be influenced unduly. However, it is for the powers that be to decide.'" Osborne added that his present inclination was to write and say that on the whole it would be best for adjudicators to stay at hotels and that in any case they should not stay with people connected with groups. Massey – plainly bored with the subject of billeting – replied tersely that it was all a difficult question. The central committee should say that such hospitality was undesirable but that the final decision should be left to the regional people. They should have to assume full responsibility. Osborne passed on the message.

By this time, however, Massey found he would have to devote more time to Final Festival matters. Bessborough himself wanted to talk about awards and trophies and Massey was consulted directly. The Governor General enthusiastically decided he would donate the main trophy for the best play in either English or French plus two extra awards for the best play in English and the best play in French. This obviously overlapping idea, which Massey approved, would cause considerable embarrassment to the DDF founders after the 1933 festival. It was agreed that the three awards would be held by groups for a year. Diplomas would also be presented and these would be kept permanently.

Then there were decisions to be made concerning the style and wording of the DDF trophies. It was eventually agreed that the awards should be in the shape of plaques. The design assignment was handed to Alex Scott Carter of Toronto, who was paid $300 for the main trophy and $150 each for the two lesser awards. The Bessborough Trophy itself turned out to be a symphony of blue and gold gesso dominated by the Bessborough coat of arms and surrounded by scrolled designs and appropriate theatrical figures. At the top of the plaque Carter placed the words Dominion Drama Festival, Ottawa 1933. In the middle was the information that this was the "Award of His Excellency the Earl of Bessborough, PC, GCMG, Governor-General of Canada." At the bottom of the plaque there was a space for the names of annual winners to be immortalized.

Somewhat uncharacteristically, Massey worried a great deal about the wording of the diplomas. "I don't think they should read 'for plays in French . . . or English,' " he mused to Osborne. "If we're to be exact, they should read 'For Plays *presented* in English or French'. Another possible wording could be 'award for the *competition* for presentation of plays in English . . . or French.'" Osborne, aware that the unflappable Massey was perhaps displaying Opening Night jitters, judiciously remained silent. In February, however, Lord Bessborough himself took one thorny problem out of his colleagues' hands. He suggested a suitable adjudicator for the important Ottawa Final, and Massey and Osborne had no choice but to agree. After all, Bessborough's nominee, Rupert Harvey, came with the highest credentials. He was a well-known British actor and producer. He had toured as an actor in Canada and had played at the Old Vic. He opened the repertory theatre in Bristol. Finally, he had already received vice-regal approval. He had directed the blue-blooded amateurs at Lord Bessborough's Stansted Theatre. What could be more appropriate than that Harvey should be invited to share in Bessborough's triumph of cultural patronage in Ottawa?

2.   **To be or not to be**

Even before the first regional playoff of the Dominion Drama Festival at Kingston in late February, 1933, anyone with even a slight interest in drama must have been aware that something important was going on in Canadian theatrical circles.

First, the October meeting which created the DDF was enough to send editorial writers rushing to their typewriters to assure Canadians that foreign culture was Out and national culture was In. Then, in December 1932 – while Massey and

105

Osborne were struggling with the complex setup of the regionals and the Final Festival – Lord Bessborough decided to sponsor a production of *Hamlet* starring his nineteen-year-old son, Viscount Eric Duncannon. The play would be directed by Martha Allan and be presented first at the Ottawa Little Theatre, then at Miss Allan's Montreal Repertory Theatre. The event sparked a flood of comment, both social and theatrical, from journalists and critics, particularly in Ontario and Quebec. For one thing, Miss Allan had chosen to use the 1603 First Quarto version of the play. It was a decision which sparked bitter attack almost as soon as it was announced.

"The appearance of the First Quarto was totally disregarded by Shakespeare," Thomas Archer complained in *The Canadian Passing Show*. "It has been said that this publication was pirated in the manner of Heywood's plaint 'that some by stenography drew the plot, put it in print, scarce of word trew'." Miss Allan, Archer scolded, should have stuck to the Second Quarto of 1624, which merged with the "First Frolic" to become the accepted text.

Martha Allan herself was distraught by all the fuss – which also spilled over into the British press – and wrote plaintively to Massey during rehearsals which coincided with Duncannon's Christmas break from Cambridge:

> *Hamlet* is taking form and life, but we have had grievous interruption through the Cambridge Authorities who are outraged that we should use any version of text but their own, although they admit it to be but a compilation of the Second Quarto and the First Folio and not a true copy of either. His Excellency is much perturbed and fears the effect of their wrath on Eric if we should insist. I am also much perturbed but I am a producer, not a poet and feel that a literary text, while a solace to scholars, has no place in the theatre, which is for drama and not dialectics.

Although clearly annoyed by the text incident, however, Bessborough took an absorbed interest in the 1932 production. He sat patiently through rehearsals and painstakingly designed an expensive set. (Later Christmas production sets designed by the Governor General were even grander; one for the 1933 staging of *Romeo and Juliet* has since been remembered as "something which looked as though it was built by the Ministry of Works.") A *Montreal Star* reviewer described the *Hamlet* set as "a simple backcloth in blue for the rampart and ghost scenes; a truly Elizabethan bedroom design and for the rest, ascending steps to the throne chairs, alternating with a forestage created by the simple medium of drawn curtains."

The Governor General also had a hand in "suggesting" members of the supporting cast who were picked with meticulous care, both as far as suitability and regional representation were concerned. Beck Dennistoun, daughter of the Hon. Mr. Justice Dennistoun of Winnipeg (who had starred in the *Othello* that Bessborough had seen during his western tour), was chosen as a perfect Ophelia for the highly-lionized young Duncannon. Other thespians were weeded out of groups in Montreal, Ottawa, Toronto and Winnipeg like so many dramatic all-stars.

From a distance of several decades it is now difficult to know whether the critics were delighted with the 1932 production of *Hamlet* or whether they were were too over-awed with the vice-regal sortie into theatre to be thoroughly objective. A sampling of press opinion shows Thomas Archer writing, for example:

> Lord Duncannon's *Hamlet* was not the *Hamlet* Shakespeare had imagined, because of the text. But he possesses a romantic appearance, a beautiful voice and an easy and dashing manner, all of which indicate that in ten years or so he will make a considerable noise in the world of make-believe.

The *Montreal Star's* S. Morgan-Powell (who was to become an adjudicator for the Western Ontario regionals) wrote:

> Lord Duncannon did reveal a keen understanding of the psychology of the character. His voice is melodious and he employs it in general to fine effect,

though he displays at times a tendency to sharp contrasts as between measured cadence and emotional expression. Taken all in all, his Hamlet is one of the most interesting amateur achievements I have witnessed in fifty years of playgoing.

Lord Duncannon Scores Triumph in Exacting Role of Hamlet! gushed the Ottawa *Journal* in a flare headline and followed up with: "From the wings, the ghosts of the great Hamlets might well send kindly salutations to this brilliant neophyte who strives so splendidly to make manifest the magic of the master." The following Christmas, incidentally, after his performance in *Romeo and Juliet* with the Ottawa Little Theatre's Julia MacBrien (whom he swore at during the rehearsals, an indiscretion which caused the young lady's father, Major-General J. H. MacBrien to threaten him with a punch on the nose) Duncannon received and refused an offer to appear in a Hollywood film version of the play.

After all this theatrical excitement in 1932, the DDF regional contests might have turned out to be a series of anticlimaxes, even though a tally by Osborne showed ninety plays in English and twenty in French had been entered across Canada. On the contrary, though, interest began to run high in the press by February 23 when thirteen groups turned up at Kingston's Queen's University to be judged by E. G. Sterndale Bennett of Alberta. The Kingston regional was apparently a drab occasion. Unlike the glittering *Hamlet* of two months before, the one-act plays entered were set against plain-drape backdrops. The choice of plays (or parts of plays) varied – Shakespeare, John Masefield, Eugene O'Neill and so, according to the adjudicator, was the qualify of performance. Kingston itself was plainly chagrined that *Ile* by Eugene O'Neill, presented by Group B of the Ottawa Drama League won the festival and another ODL entry, *Will Shakespeare, Act 4* came second.

"We were not very well satisfied with Mr. Bennett," complained W. Rupert Davies, president and editor of *The Whig Standard* of Kingston in a letter to Vincent Massey, and continued:

He seemed to start out very well but weakened towards the end. I had a very decided feeling, rightly or wrongly, that he was allowing his personal prejudices to influence him too much in his comments and decisions. I think you will agree with me that all things being equal it would have been much better to have given second place to Brockville or Kingston rather than to an Ottawa play which was so largely a one-woman show. Aside from the matter of choosing, in my opinion, Mr. Bennett's greatest weakness was in not giving systematic, constructive criticism on all points. On some plays he would dwell in great detail. Others he gave but brief attention.

Massey, fully aware of Davies' influence replied: ". . . Well, it's the first year of a rather ambitious plan and useful comments such as you have made will help us to avoid this year's mistakes in the future." In the same mail he sent off a letter to Osborne suggesting either the Kingston or Brockville play go to Ottawa as a third entry from the Eastern Ontario region.

In the meantime, the French division of the Eastern Ontario regions was also under way in Ottawa but received only token coverage in the local press. The Western Ontario Drama Festival, held on March 2, 3 and 4 in London, Ontario, fared better with the media. A story that week in the *London Free Press*, in fact, gave a rare insight into how the executive in Ottawa was briefing the adjudicators:

Adjudicating at all festivals is being done on the following system. Acting, 50 marks. Production, 35 marks. Stage presentation, 15 marks. *Acting:* This will cover characterizations, audibility of speech, variation in tone, emphasis, gesture and movement. *Production:* Interpretation of spirit and meaning of the scene; team work, general pace and variation of tempo, grouping and movement, making of points and sense of climax. *Stage presentation:* stage setting, properties and lighting, costumes and make-up.

109

Had standards of judging changed a great deal from those set by Earl Grey in 1907? Continued the *Free Press:*

> The scenes will be entirely in curtains, indicative scenery only being used. It is intended to allow only a 10-minute interval for scene shifting between the plays and in addition to a local staff of six stage managers, each group entering may have their own stage manager.

There was more strafing at the DDF as the regional playoffs moved west. Complaints began to dribble in from the regions that they had heard the executive committee was inviting runners-up as well as winners to the big Ottawa party. Well, their group had come in second. Weren't they eligible to come to the Final too? Osborne began writing a diplomatic series of letters explaining that the DDF executive certainly reserved the right to ask a second team to attend the Final. But the choice, you see, was determined by the adjudicator's report.

When Lawrence Mason, drama critic of the *Globe* in Toronto, finished his adjudication assignment in Winnipeg, Osborne wrote hurriedly to Massey:

> I see from the press there was a dead heat in Winnipeg. If Mason has been unable to select one play I presume we shall be compelled to ask both to attend the Final. In this connection the whole question of issuing invitations in excess of those placed first will want immediate consideration after the regional results are all in. We shall want to look carefully over the whole field from the standpoint of (a) selection and (b) money available.

Mason himself wrote to Osborne about what he described as "a special, rather independent feeling which prevails in Winnipeg." He warned there would be revolt if only one play was invited from Winnipeg while two or more were chosen from Eastern regions.

Osborne, in turn, passed Mason's melancholy intelligence on to a by-now irritated Massey, then added:

> Of course, no difficulty arises if we may consider it as settled that we are to invite a sufficient number of teams to fill six evenings. There are 10 regions presenting English plays and if we issue one additional invitation to Manitoba, Western Ontario, Toronto, Eastern Ontario and Montreal we shall have fifteen plays or just enough to fill five evenings! This will leave the sixth night to be used for three French plays. The two teams in Winnipeg which marked 90 points apiece, incidentally, were *The Man Born to be Hanged* and *Jim Barber's Spite Fence* by Lillian B. Thomas. This last is an original Canadian play.

Later Massey reacted sensitively when he learned that a Hart House production, *Twelfth Night*, had won the Urban Toronto regional. "I hear there is some slight feeling about the award to Hart House," he wrote calmly enough to Osborne in April, 1933. "The selection of a second play from the Toronto area has a bearing on the problem, however. I shall be interested to hear what team it is proposed to invite. It would, of course, be very unfortunate if this was another entry from Hart House." Stone was chillingly aware of Massey's possible embarrassment. After the marks were in, he and Sterndale Bennett sat up one night and thrashed out the question of the Toronto invitations. "The points go like this," Osborne – at Stone's request – informed an anxious Massey:

> *Twelfth Night*, Hart House. *Campden Wonder*, Hart House. *Dear Brutus*, Beaches Library Drama League. *The Thunderbolt*, Hart House tied with Beaches. It is unfortunate, but it does mean two invitations to Hart House. It was felt we could not pass over a group placed second in favor of another tied for third. We've now decided, you know, to ask 18 English plays to Ottawa. So we've asked Sarnia and Victoria. Sarnia is likely to accept but Victoria is doubtful.

111

I'm expecting a wire at any hour. If they cannot come, I'll extend a third Toronto invitation to Beaches.

Massey silently agonized until Osborne hastened to wire that Victoria had declined because of travelling difficulties and that Beaches' *Dear Brutus* would complete the Toronto trio of entries in the Final.

The inclusion of Sarnia was probably a polite gesture from Osborne himself, made easier because of the elastic rulings about invitations. Sarnia, after all, had placed third in the Western Ontario Festival. But Sarnia was the home-town of D. Park Jamieson, already one of the staunchest supporters of the DDF. As Osborne had approvingly noted, Jamieson was the kind of chap who was down-to-earth enough to invite the London Drama League (which won the Western Ontario regional) and the Players Guild of Hamilton (which came second) to bring their plays to Sarnia for a benefit performance. The box-office take, Jamieson informed the pleased Ottawa office, would go towards expenses at the Final.

Then there were other sources of satisfaction for the DDF organizers. The continuing regional playoffs were still attracting plenty of journalistic and social attention across the country. Lawrence Mason, adjudicating in Manitoba and Saskatchewan and reporting diligently for *The Globe*, told of the outrageous lionizing that would alternatively fascinate and bore DDF adjudicators in the future. An obviously impressed Mason wrote of being entertained at Government House in Regina, being escorted around by fawning aides-de-camp and begged to give scholarly talks about the growth of amateur theatre "on radio and at women's clubs in the two provinces." The power of the DDF judge, even then, was apparently so potent that even Lady Tupper turned up at the railway station in Winnipeg to welcome Mason to the city.

On the eve of the first DDF Final in April, 1933, editors around the Dominion were sensing that an exciting national news story was about to come out of Ottawa. But there were some cautious philosophers. "It may be doubted whether a Canadian drama can ever be developed on a purely amateur basis," wrote B. K. Sandwell in *Saturday Night:*

The players are all right; plenty of them are just as good as the average on the professional stage. The playwrights might achieve a considerable height of excellence without becoming exclusively dependent on their royalties for a living. But the direction still remains a problem. Without it, the other two elements will never get anywhere. It must be competent, original, experienced, creative. It must also be continuous over a considerable period of time. Institutions such as Hart House and, in lesser degree, the Ottawa Little Theatre and the MRT can make a large contribution towards this need. Can they do enough? And are they, and is their public, greatly interested in this particular objective? A Canadian drama whose sole impelling motive is a rather self-conscious patriotism is not likely to get very far; and at present that does seem to be the chief preoccupation among both workers and followers in this sphere of our national art.

On April 4, twenty days before the Final Festival was scheduled to begin in Ottawa, Massey and Osborne got together to decide upon whom to ask as French advisor to Rupert Harvey. Harvey's French, it turned out, was not quite as facile as Bessborough had assured the executive. This was surprising to Massey, as he knew the Governor General spoke perfect French. At the meeting, Osborne said he would like to ask Professor St. Elme de Champ of the University of Toronto who had helped out with the DDF director's "helpful list" of French plays in 1932. Massey said he would prefer Marcel Tirol of Queen's University but Osborne politely pointed out that Tirol had been in Canada for just a short time. De Champ, on the other hand, had been around for nigh on thirty years and might feel slighted if left out. But was he *persona grata* in certain French circles?

Osborne decided not to worry about this for the time being. "What we want," he reminded Massey, "is a person to sit with the adjudicator all day Wednesday to advise on questions of language." Massey shrugged and agreed that De Champ was a good choice. After all, Bessborough had handed him another time-consuming chore. The Governor General suggested it might be a nice gesture if all competing players donated a dollar towards purchasing a silver cigarette box for Col. Osborne. Would Vincent look after this? Oh, and incidentally, His Excellency would be pleased to invite both Mr. Massey and his wife Alice to stay at Government House through Festival week.

3. "The spirit of a nation"

One hundred and sixty-eight actors, actresses, directors and stage technicians descended on Ottawa during the weekend of April 23, 1933 to be part of the first Dominion Drama Festival. The regional representation was impressive for those days: Winnipeg. Saskatoon. Quebec City. New Brunswick. Medicine Hat. Halifax. Vancouver. Montreal. Toronto. As DDF chairman Vincent Massey would comment from the stage of the Ottawa Little Theatre on opening night, Monday, April 24: "Eight provinces are represented here at the festival. The number of individuals who will take part have become a rather formidable army. If the festival was held in Europe, teams would have to come together from as far apart as Constantinople, Warsaw and Algiers. That gives you an idea of the geographic dimensions of this Dominion Drama Festival."
The impact of the first DDF Final on Canada's capital was enormous. Theatre was the current vogue because of Bessborough's fascinated involvement, so the Ottawa Little Theatre was packed for all performances. Socially, it even outshone the 1907 Earl Grey competitions. Prominent citizens of the city decided that if the likes of the Governor General, the Prime Minister, Vincent Massey and other notables were backing the DDF, they would outdo themselves to make the week a glittering occasion. Society writers fought to spread the news that the Sackville, New Brunswick, players were first to arrive in town and that they were greeted at the station by Mrs. Dorothy White (by then a member of the local DDF committee and destined to become a president of the association), Mrs. James Parmelee,

Mrs. Antonio Tremblay, Mr. J. H. Stannard and Mr. Jack Meikle.

"Indeed," one report went on, "each party of players was met by Ottawans as they arrived and 90 per cent of the 168 contestants are billeted in the homes of well-known citizens, many of whom previously have taken little or no interest in the development of little theatre. Mrs. A. H. Anderson, a former president of the Sackville Association, in addition to billeting three of the Maritime players within her own home, entertained the entire cast and their friends at a weekend reception." From the station, each drama group was escorted triumphantly to the Ottawa Little Theatre, registered and presented with a silver pin bearing the Bessborough arms and decorated with the blue and red Bessborough colours. Local journalists – happily aware that the Little Theatre was one of the best-equipped in Canada apart from Hart House – hovered, pencils poised, to record the comments of visitors from the boondocks when they glimpsed the place for the first time: "Is this it? Why, it looks like a church!" "Oh no, like a cathedral. It's so calm."

Monday morning, with most of the groups unpacked, registered and wearing the Governor General's silver pin, the calm at the Little Theatre turned into bedlam. At one time, forty-eight actors arrived within five minutes of each other and clamoured for a tour. Where were the dressing rooms? Where was the lighting system? What was being done about arranging rehearsals? "Here we are in the lobby," a local reporter wrote excitedly, "crowds milling around, everyone looking for some-one else. At the far end, a business-like corner with desks, filing cabinets, typewriters, ledgers. Nearby, an easel holding the framed tablet, the governor-general's award, for which all the groups are competing. Here is a table presided over by Miss Mona Coxwell of Samuel French, exhibiting an interesting collection of plays. Col. H. C. Osborne, acting president of the Ottawa Drama League and vice-chairman and honorary director of the festival is in and out during the day, full of charming speeches and helpful suggestions. Mrs. White, one of the most efficient workers, smooths out sundry difficulties. Reporters . . . photographers . . . the telephone rings . . . questions. . . ."

There was a rush to grab a souvenir copy of the 1933 program, a modest publication compared to the glossy productions that would be designed for the festival decades later. The front cover featured a sketch of a drama group on stage and the words "The Dominion Drama Festival, 1933, Final Competition for the Bessborough Trophy. The Little Theatre, Ottawa. April 24th to 29th. Evenings at 8:20 *precisely*. Matinees, Wednesday and Saturday at 2:40 *precisely*." Inside, a special statement that would become a traditional feature of DDF programs read that because of the competitive nature of the performance, each contestant would be given an equal opportunity. "It is impossible, therefore, to permit any disturbance in the auditorium caused by the seating of late arrivals." The program also carried a photograph of Bessborough in his uniform and a reproduction of a hand-written message that was destined to become somewhat of a slogan for the DDF: "The spirit of a nation, if it is to find full expression, must include a National Drama."

The first three plays presented on opening night seemed to have been deliberately chosen for their newsworthiness. There was Eugene O'Neill's *Ile*, presented by the Ottawa Drama League, Group A (one of the plays which caused Kingston to censure E. G. Sterndale Bennett's "biased" adjudicating); J. M. Barrie's *Dear Brutus*, staged by Toronto's Beaches Library Drama League (the group which slipped in under the wire because of Massey's embarrassment over top-heavy Hart House representation); and *Jim Barber's Spite Fence*, written and produced by Lillian B. Thomas and presented by the Winnipeg Little Theatre Members' Night Committee (the play which Lawrence Mason tied with the Winnipeg Masquers' *The Man Born to be Hanged*).

According to reports, the atmosphere that Monday night in Ottawa's Little Theatre was "electric" and the auditorium "had never been more crowded or the audience better dressed." So many locals and out-of-town visitors had demanded tickets, chairs were stacked in the aisles (apparently there were no regulations at the time concerning fire hazards) and some members of the audience perched on window ledges or stood in the exit lobbies. Ottawa's social reporters slavered over the impressive list of official guests: Lord and Lady Bessborough. Sir Robert and Lady Borden. William Lyon Mackenzie

King. Vincent and Alice Massey. Sanford Fleming and his wife. George Black, Speaker of the House of Commons.

"Black evening dresses predominated, many relieved by smart organdie trimmings, sleeves and jackets seeming to be more important than backs," rambled one wide-eyed fashion writer. "Lady Tupper of Winnipeg wore a puce-coloured velvet. She has done much to stimulate the Masquers Club to greater efforts. Sir Montague and Lady Allan of Montreal and their daughter, Miss Allan were there. Lady Allan was gowned in black with red. Miss Allan, the guiding star of the Montreal Repertory Theatre wore a lipstick gown, with beaded jacket. Mrs. Vincent Massey wore a gown of white satin and Miss Ellen Ballon brought a welcome note of colour with her dress of lemon, worn under a high-necked white evening wrap."

Everyone tried, of course, not to stare at the *real* celebrity of the week, Rupert Harvey of London, England. The adjudicator, formally dressed in white tie and tails, sat at a table placed for him at the back of the theatre. He was clearly aware of his awesome responsibilities. He had surrounded himself with reference books, scripts of the plays and mounds of notepaper and pencils. His eyes were riveted on the stage, even while scribbling notes. During intervals between the one-act productions, he disappeared quickly into a private office.

Harvey, whom Bessborough had naturally invited to stay at Government House, tried to be meticulous and helpful during that first festival week. His remarks after performances were objective and not nearly as abrasive as those made years before during the Earl Grey competitions. His comments after the Friday evening's presentation of *How He Lied to Her Husband* by the Montreal Repertory Theatre are typical of the adjudicator's approach to his vice-regal assignment. "This presentation by a group from the Montreal Repertory Theatre Mr. Harvey spoke of as being very efficiently produced technically but too much reliance had been placed on the fact that Bernard Shaw had written a definitely humourous play," read a press report:

> It lacked reality, for although the characters were caricatures, they were definitely alive. The whole ran so smoothly that the players rather over-ran

themselves and did not wait for laughs that they should reasonably have expected to be there. It was also rather too mannered. The play had been brought up to date but Mr. Harvey did not regard this as an improvement, for it is definitely a period piece. Although an ivory holder had been substituted for a fan, the fan sets the period. The husband's attitude in a modern play would be absolutely indefensible.

On Wednesday, the one day on which the festival's six French plays were presented at both matinee and evening performances, Harvey made a remark which was later to cause more sniping at the DDF. According to a newspaper report, "*Les Rantzau* by Erckmann-Chatrian, presented by L'Union Dramatique de Québec came in for special mention by the adjudicator for the extraordinary teamwork displayed by members of the cast which Mr. Harvey described as the best shown in any play, French or English, so far in the competition." As it happened, the winner of the Bessborough Trophy, Richard Hughes' *The Man Born to be Hanged*, staged by the Masquers Club of Winnipeg (a group of T. Eaton Co. employees), had been presented the previous evening. *Les Rantzau* won the award for the Best Play in French.

After the results were published, Vincent Massey received an irate telegram from Col. G. E. Marquis, Parliament Buildings, Quebec City, who complained: "Wednesday evening Rupert Harvey declared L'Union Dramatique de Québec was ahead of all groups so far. Would like to know why the Masquers Club of Winnipeg have been classified as first prize after the turn-about made by the adjudicator. If Quebec is entitled to the Bessborough Trophy we will claim it with energy." Always the diplomat, Massey wired back promptly: "Harvey's remarks on performance of L'Union Dramatique de Québec referred to an individual performance in play and not to production as a whole. This, however, he rated high as final award shows. Greatly regret misunderstanding."

There was another embarrassment for Massey and the DDF's executive after the awards were announced. Naturally (how else could Harvey rationalize the DDF's own terms of reference) the Winnipeg Masquers won the award for the Best Play in English as well as the Bessborough Trophy, a decision which other groups at the festival complained about and which drew criticism from various parts of the country. Massey, recognizing that a former decision had backfired, agonized over the critical comment and wrote to Osborne: "The plan by which the governor-general's trophy *and* the trophy for the Best Play in English or French should go to the same team is not a happy one. Better I think if we had arranged the second-best team get the English trophy if the winner was English or vice-versa." Osborne tried to smooth Massey's feelings by replying that things like that weren't really unusual, it happened in sports all the time. But Massey continued to fret over the controversy. The Vancouver Little Theatre Association had been judged second-best in the English division but this did not rate them a prize. "There's some talk about giving the second trophy to the Vancouver people," Massey wrote Osborne. "But Lady Tupper thought they would not appreciate receiving the trophy now, as it were, by a side door." Nevertheless the Best Play in English award was eventually taken back from the Masquers and handed to Vancouver with as little publicity as possible.

At later executive meetings of the DDF it was Massey who insisted that the program statement concerning awards should read: "Two other plaques will be awarded, for the best presentations in English and French respectively, *excluding* the winner of the Bessborough Trophy."

Reactions to the first Dominion Drama Festival varied across the nation. In Winnipeg, of course, the Masquers were greeted at the railway station with cheers and applause. Editorials in both the city's newspapers bristled with congratulations and reminded proud Winnipeggers that two productions from the city had been invited to Ottawa and also that Winnipeg had won first prize with another play at the Earl Grey contest of 1907. One local columnist wrote cynically: "The winning drama at Ottawa played by Winnipeg performers is entitled *The Man Born to be Hanged.* Quite a lot of persons so born, however, manage to conceal the fact quite successfully."

Predictably, Ottawa newspapers praised the festival. "The final and possibly most important benefit of the festival," editorialized the Ottawa *Journal*, "is the closer cooperation and increased knowledge of different parts of our country made available to those taking part in the plays and those patronizing them. There is nothing a great and widely-separated country needs more than the spirit of union and sympathetic appreciation of the difficulties and problems of this various sections." Other press comments included one from the *Montreal Herald*, which stated that "all but three or four plays were melancholy dramas of suicides and murders." However, the writer continued, "with that brooding intensity and seriousness we shall probably attain a profundity and truth much more essential than the fancy palate-tickling of those bright and scintillating youngsters whose dramas adorn the Parisian boulevards."

In *Saturday Night*, regional adjudicator E. G. Sterndale Bennett shared some serious thoughts about the DDF:

> Where is the movement leading us? Where do we want it to lead us? There is one thing certain. We would not want to see the benefits of the festival confined. If we are to take full advantage of the tremendous energy which has shown itself available we must look upon this year's festival as a stepping stone. Might we even venture to call it a foundation stone, around the above which we might erect a glorious edifice of drama, a National Theatre? Not, perhaps, a centralized plant with its difficulties of maintenance and management but, rather, a brotherhood of effort assisted, guided and encouraged by some parent body.

Sterndale Bennett also urged the DDF to consider both the admission of full-length plays to the festival and the appointment of one regional adjudicator who could travel across the country marking all productions on the same standard. (He mused, though, that this could actually eliminate the need for a final festival.) "It might then be possible to arrange a tour of some of the more meritorious presentations from coast to coast, to give all groups an opportunity to observe the standard they have attained."

The Toronto *Globe's* Lawrence Mason went even further and proposed an entire page of new regulations he thought the DDF should adopt if it planned future festivals. He suggested more uniform interpretation of festival rules, pointing out that some plays in the regions stuck to the official regulation concerning simple drapes and properties while "one company in Winnipeg had as complete a realistic setting as Belasco ever devised, with doors, windows, pictures, lamps, a sewing machine and a vista into a completely-appointed drug store." Mason also worried about time-limit rules which he said "needed clearer statement." Some adjudicators in the regions, he complained, ignored the 20-45 minute play rule and awarded prizes to plays which ran much longer.

"The Central Committee," said Mason, "even invited some of the offenders to participate in the Ottawa Finals." Church and school groups were refused entry into the Western Ontario regionals, the writer went on, yet these entries were formally solicited and duly admitted into the Toronto playoff. "The question of eligibility is too fundamental to be left in quite such a haphazard state. Other dubious points might easily be mentioned such as the question of amateur status, legitimate expenses for stage settings, of participation of one player in more than one production and so on. Most of the existing rules, in fact, are open to grave differences in interpretation."

Mason urged that the DDF give some recognition to groups for originality and imagination:

> In the Toronto regional festival, Herman Voaden's highly original and intensely Canadian play *Rocks* which wholly discards standard realistic methods of production in favour of the most modernistic art-of-the-theatre, was simply ruled out by the adjudicators because, as they frankly stated to the audience, there was absolutely no provision in the marking system for properly evaluating a presentation of this kind. Yet surely our national drama festival does not wish to close the books with the year 1900, refusing any consideration to 20th century stagecraft.

Rupert Harvey made much the same confession about Park Jamieson's expressionistic production of Capek's *The Ant World* from Sarnia, according to Mason. It was apparently beyond the scope of the marking system. In London, too, Morgan Powell declared he had never seen anything like *The Long Christmas Dinner* and did not know how to handle it. "While at Kingston," argued the annoyed Mason, "*Rose Latulippe*, palpably the most brilliant and original production in the festival, failed to win a place because the fixed scale of marks offered no percentage credit for its particular points of excellence." Finally, the *Globe's* critic urged there should be a prize for a Canadian play in the DDF Final "since apparently the major purpose of the festival is to aid in the development of a national drama."

4.   And so, on to the next time.

Lord Bessborough, Vincent Massey and Henry Osborne seemed outwardly unruffled by the flood of criticism and advice that followed the 1933 Dominion Drama Festival. It was decided almost as soon as the capital tidied up after the April Final to do the whole thing all over again in Ottawa the following year. Then, in July of 1933 the executive – apparently taking note of press comment – formally invited a single adjudicator to handle the gigantic task of judging the regional playoffs clear across the land. Only one man seemed suitable for the job: Rupert Harvey.

Yet another July event seemed to coincide with the knuckle-rappings of Canadian journalists. Sir Barry Jackson – no stranger to Canada – wrote to Osborne from Birmingham saying he was aware of talk about a prize for an original Canadian play and that he was offering a trophy for just that purpose. Osborne, who had already been discussing something of the kind with Massey, accepted delightedly. The top brass of the DDF, though, were obviously convinced that more had to be done to convince Canadians that the new organization was committed to encouraging a truly national drama. It was planned to offer a cash prize of one hundred dollars out of slim DDF funds to the author of the best Canadian play in any of the regional festivals. Lady Bessborough also decided she wanted to figure in the awards picture and said she would present "a momento" to the actress whose performance earned the highest marks at the Final.

In the meantime, both Bessborough and Massey were fitting in other commitments as well as advising a harassed Col. Osborne on structural changes in DDF policy. The Governor General made an official visit to mining camps in Northern Ontario not long after the 1933 festival, then travelled to Nova Scotia and back to Manitoba, Saskatchewan and to Regina for the World's Grain Show. The country, he observed sadly in many of his speeches, was still very much in the depths of depression. "But having seen the Dominion during this period," he said at the Boys Farm and Training School at Shawbridge, Quebec, "I think I have learned to appreciate Canadians far more than I would have been able in time of general prosperity. There is nothing more encouraging and cheering than the calm, steady way Canadians have pursued their daily tasks during the difficult period with a supreme faith in the destiny of their country."

Back in Rideau Hall, Bessborough entertained, enjoyed his interminable games of bridge, and pored over the diaries of his grandmother, Lady Charlotte Guest, a woman whom he admired extravagantly. In the late summer of 1933, he was corresponding with his son Eric at Cambridge, suggesting that it might be a capital idea to stage a production of *Romeo and Juliet* that Christmas. Rupert would be coming to judge the DDF regionals so he could direct the play. About the same time, Vincent Massey was organizing a Liberal Summer Conference in Port Hope for the National Liberal Federation and continuing with his speeches across the Dominion. Even so, correspondence concerning the DDF and its future continued to land on his desk at Batterwood and – as chairman – he had to take time to deal with it.

In mid-1933 he agreed with a suggestion from the courtly Henry Osborne that John Aylen – whose Ottawa legal office had been used without charge by the DDF's director – should be named Honorary Secretary General of the Festival.

He also decided, with Bessborough's endorsement, that Osborne should take a trip to England on DDF business, specifically to brief Harvey concerning the forthcoming regionals and also to ask his help in flushing out a suitable judge for the 1934 Final and future festivals as well.

Massey also mulled over the question of whether the festival should admit both short and long plays into competition, perhaps in alternate years. He came to no definite conclusions about this. Bessborough himself was cautious about long-play festivals, reminding Massey that the British Drama League had taken a beating at the box office when it tried out the idea. Massey also chewed over a suggestion from John Aylen that the Final Festival be divided into French and English divisions with a double Bessborough Trophy being awarded to the best entry in both groups. "There has been talk," reasoned Aylen in his new capacity as Honorary Secretary General, "that future festivals might be held in places like Toronto or Winnipeg. I feel the audience for French plays in these cities would be very scarce, so perhaps a split festival would be feasible." After some thought, Massey rejected the suggestion.

The year wore on in a state of suspended animation for Vincent Massey. "Politics in Canada at the moment are – shall I say – stuffy," he complained in a letter to his friend Lord Howard of Penrith in the Fall of 1933. "They need fresh air, the introduction of a new and better technique. . . ." He absorbed himself with family business, work with the National Liberal Federation, Hart House and – of course – the organization of the DDF. Osborne returned to Canada and reported that Rupert Harvey had been co-operative about finding adjudicators and that one man, Netherlands-born J. T. Grein looked promising. Later, Grein (who had a considerable reputation as a critic in England) was formally invited to judge the 1934 Final. To the DDF executive's relief, the elderly Netherlander accepted. Harvey himself arrived in Canada, was installed at Government House as usual, then he and Bessborough flung themselves into the business of staging the Christmas production of *Romeo and Juliet* at the Ottawa Little Theatre and Moyse Hall in Montreal. Christmas was always an important family occasion for the Masseys, but they went to Ottawa to see Eric

Duncannon and Julia MacBrien in the play (which again drew fawning praise from the critics), then waved Rupert Harvey *bon voyage* on his trek as solo regional DDF adjudicator.

It proved to be an exhausting job for the British director – many regional judges in later years would fall, swooning, by the wayside – but Harvey dutifully picked twenty-two groups worthy of an invitation to the spring Final. Three of these were from Hart House and one, a production of Miles Malleson's *Michael* directed by Edgar Stone, would win the Bessborough Trophy. Unlike in 1933, Massey made no comment, either about the large contingent from "his" theatre in Toronto or Grein's adjudication. Perhaps, even at the second Final Festival, those connected with the DDF were getting over Opening Night jitters. The glitter, the Big Names and the frenetic socializing were still important to Festival Week 1934, but this time everyone seemed to know everyone else and the Little Theatre exuded the somewhat cosy atmosphere of an elite club. DDF supporters nodded comfortably over Bessborough's program message for 1934: "A renaissance of the Drama is taking place in Canada. As the success of the Dominion Drama Festival testifies, it is a widely-national movement attended by the most promising developments and by many good auguries for the future; its value as a permanent institution in the cultural life of this country will, I am confident, become more and more apparent in each succeeding year. Bessborough."

Donald W. Buchanan, writing in *Saturday Night*, dubbed the 1934 Final "An Unfestive Festival." Those who had sat through the clutch of gloomy plays were inclined to agree, but were glad someone else had the courage to say so. "My reflection on the finals of the annual Dominion Drama Festival is prompted by the tension produced after six nights and one matinee of mysticism, death and frustration," complained Buchanan. "The winning play, *Michael*, for instance was not only Tolstoyian but the quality of the acting in it, according to the adjudicator, had 'the Russian spirit without affection in the realm of truth.'" However, Buchanan concluded more optimistically, "the performances averaged much higher than last year."

After the 1934 Final, Massey chaired an executive

meeting which decided there would definitely be a 1935 Dominion Drama Festival and that it would again be held in the nation's capital. Executive officer Lady Tupper angrily disapproved of the decision. Surely it was about time, she argued, that the Festival was held at another centre, say Winnipeg? Massey was polite but unmoved by Lady Tupper's outburst. "Lord Bessborough's term as Governor General will expire in September, 1935," he explained coolly from the chair. "Next year will be his last Festival. I do feel it is appropriate that the Final should stay in Ottawa, at least for the time being." Lady Tupper was heard to mutter something like "bosh," or "bash," but Massey sailed on to other matters.

One of these concerned the fact that the Governor General would like to see the DDF incorporated under a Royal Charter and would use his influence to make this a reality. A thoroughly-impressed executive agreed that this was a wonderful idea and Osborne was asked to think about suitable wording and so on. Later in the year, the director reported to Massey that he was tooling around with an idea "something along the lines of the Victorian Order of Nurses." The charter itself made its appearance in May, 1935. It finally put the Crown's highly-respectable seal of approval on theatre in Canada.

Stamped with the Great Seal of Canada, the document was headed: "Bessborough. Canada. George the Fifth, by the Grace of God of Great Britain, Ireland, the British Dominions beyond the Seas King, Defender of the Faith, Emperor of India. To all to whom these presents shall come, GREETING." It explained that the Governors of the Festival "shall be a body corporate and politic under the name of The Governors of the Dominion Drama Festival and may by that name sue and be sued." The objects of the corporation "shall be to encourage dramatic art in Canada by the holding of a Dominion Drama Festival," and the charter went on to say the corporation could grant prizes and awards "for distinctive effort in any of the arts relating to the drama, including, among other arts, the writing of plays, their presentation, mounting, costuming and lighting."

The charter was witnessed by "Our Right Trusty and Right Well-beloved Cousin and Counsellor, Vere Brabazon, Earl of Bessborough, a Member of Our Most Honourable Privy Council, Knight Grand Cross of Our Most Distinguished Order of Saint Michael and Saint George, formerly Captain in Our Territorial Army, Governor-General and Commander-in-Chief of Our Dominion of Canada.

Now that the Dominion Drama Festival boasted a Royal Charter, the next step was to pick its first board of governors. This, according to the charter would be done by the Governor General himself. Writing to Massey, Bessborough said he felt the list should be restricted to the present officers and chairmen of regions. Later, he agreed that a half dozen other individuals should be invited to the first meeting under the charter and should be given governors' status. The extra governors named were Professor E. A. Corbett of Edmonton, Gwillym Edwards of Calgary, Hugh O. Mills of Halifax, Mrs. Catharine Brickenden of London, Nella Jefferis of Toronto, the Hon. Mr. Justice Constantineau of Ottawa and the Rev. Conrad Latour of the University of Ottawa. Bessborough felt there was no one from Saskatchewan, New Brunswick or British Columbia "who might have a claim."

But in 1935, the tides of change were already beginning to erode the original structure of the Dominion Drama Festival. For one thing, Bessborough sailed for home in the autumn and was succeeded in November by Governor General Lord Tweedsmuir. A general election in October catapulted Mackenzie King and the Liberals back into power and Vincent Massey was offered the position of High Commissioner for Canada in London which had been cancelled by R. B. Bennett five years before. He happily accepted the appointment and sent his formal letter of resignation as chairman of the DDF to Osborne in November. One of Massey's last jobs for the Festival at that time was to ask the new Governor General if he would take over from Bessborough as patron of the DDF. Although Tweedsmuir was not really fascinated by theatre (though as John Buchan he was well-known as an author), he accepted.

The Masseys were already unpacking in London when the DDF held its first executive meeting under the Royal Charter on December 7, 1935. Colonel Osborne occupied the chair. The group itself must have been sensitive to the fact

127

that the disappearance of Bessborough and Massey from the DDF could have far-reaching effects on the organization's future. The official minutes of the conclave have an air of The Play Must Go On about them. Significantly, Osborne hastened to cheer the inner circle (which included Lady Tupper, Martha Allan, Park Jamieson, Colin Campbell of Toronto, W. D. Cromarty, John Aylen and Col. Biggar of Ottawa) with the news that Lord Tweedsmuir had agreed to be the DDF's new patron. There was a relieved sigh around the table. Massey had come through again! As for Massey, Osborne went on, he felt the executive should not accept his resignation as chairman. The executive quickly agreed.

The minutes of the rest of the meeting sound like warnings of things to come for the DDF. The question of adjudicators, for example, was emerging as a troubling problem. Thank heavens that Allan Wade of London had accepted the job of regional adjudicator for 1936! But Dame Sybil Thorndike, who had seemed willing to judge the Final, had now turned down the assignment. There was a possibility that the celebrated British director, Harley Granville-Barker might come to Canada but so far he had indicated only qualified acceptance. And this was already December! Then there was the adjudication of French plays. Martha Allan reported that French groups in Montreal wanted Wade to be assisted by Professor Tirol of Kingston and Louvigny de Montigny of Ottawa. As an alternative, the French said they would be willing to select adjudicators at their own expense. There were shocked little cries about this high-handedness from Montreal. After all, the regulations had been circulated and Wade had been officially appointed to judge both French and English entries. The Hon. Director was asked to communicate with the Montreal groups and tell them it was impossible to adopt any special rules for the French.

Outside, a light snow was falling on Ottawa. The executive paused for tea and there was talk about Christmas plans and wasn't Lady Tweedsmuir charming and did everyone know that Vincent's appointment and arrival in London had been so precipitous, his welcome parties clashed with farewell bashes for his predecessor? Everyone hoped that Granville-Barker would come for the 1936 Festival. After all, the DDF should try to make next year's Final really special so the new Governor General would be impressed. Everyone cheered up. Yes, it really looked as though the DDF would survive and grow after all.

It did survive for the next four years (Lady Tupper got it to Winnipeg in 1938 and Jamieson's influence moved it to London, Ontario, in 1939) then it hibernated during the Second World War. It bounced back, though, in 1947 and hung on through controversy, near-bankruptcy and the rise of Canadian professionalism until it emerged as Theatre Canada almost a quarter century later. But in many ways, those last months of 1935 marked the end of the beginning.

PART THREE

The People
and the Problems

CHAPTER FIVE

Politics

1. The Road to the Top

When Vincent Massey sailed for England and his new assignment at Canada House in 1935, he probably believed his close connection with the Dominion Drama Festival had been severed. It must have been a surprise, then (there is no record as to whether he was glad or sad) to receive Col. Henry Osborne's communiqué in December announcing that the executive committee was anxious to keep him as the DDF's chairman. The organization continued to be tenacious about retaining its link with the magic Massey name. Although the High Commissioner now had little opportunity to interest himself in DDF affairs, he was unanimously elected vice-president in 1937 and president in 1938, replacing Sir Robert Borden who died without doing much to oil the wheels of the DDF except by his occasional presence at meetings and festivals. After the Second World War and Massey's return to Canada, his name still stood as president until 1950 (and by then he was thoroughly immersed in other time-consuming projects) when it was decided to place an "honorary" before the title. In 1952, when he was appointed Governor General of Canada, a delighted DDF rushed to Rideau Hall with the request that Massey continue the vice-regal custom of Festival patronage.

"Rather odd, isn't it," Toronto lawyer David Ongley, a comer in DDF executive circles wrote to the organization's staff in Ottawa, "that we should be asking our original chairman to become patron of the whole show?" Massey, of course, agreed to become patron of the DDF and actually was involved more with the organization during his term as Governor General – by attending festivals, writing optimistic messages for the program and so on – than at any time since the early 1930's.

Judging from the miniscule amount of space Massey reserved in his memoir *What's Past is Prologue* for the Dominion Drama Festival, it seems clear that his motives for associating himself with the corporation had nothing to do with a need for extra public recognition. Others who worked for the DDF over the years, however, were obviously convinced that their tie-in with the organization enhanced their lives and careers. Perhaps not too surprisingly, one of the proudest to be connected with the DDF was Lord Bessborough, who wrote to Col. Henry Osborne after his return to England, reporting that a friend had mentioned he had set a modern precedent "equalling that of monarchs of the past" for lending vice-regal patronage to a nation's culture. Osborne himself was clearly flattered by Bessborough's offer of the honorary directorship of the DDF. Through it, he rose from the rather dusty ranks of the civil service to become one of the most awesome figures in Canadian cultural circles. Lawyer John A. Aylen – who had little entrée into the drawing-rooms of the great before he loaned Osborne a corner of his Ottawa office – must have felt amply rewarded for his unpaid work as secretary general of the DDF by his sudden acceptance into high society. Like Osborne, the bespectacled, somewhat nervous man was eventually sought after by writers everywhere for sage comments on the state of the arts in Canada.

The early executive committee and governors of the DDF, of course, were hand-picked by Bessborough, Massey and Osborne either because of their community-theatre connections or their social and financial value to the new organization. Significantly, few individuals approached – however exalted their position – turned down a chance to be connected with the vice-regal cause. Martha Allan of the Montreal Repertory Theatre was naturally a perfect person to be associated with the early DDF. She had money, social position, she could organize and she knew all about the stage. Lady Margaret Tupper of Winnipeg was another ideal choice. Both women

132

were quickly roped into the organization's inner circle.

One executive officer who realized his chance for recognition in 1935 and hung on to it like a bulldog was David Park Jamieson of Sarnia, who had been invited to the 1932 Founders' Meeting, then proceeded to dazzle the DDF's leaders with his flawless performance as a regional organizer. Osborne had his eye on Jamieson as executive material from the beginning. The Western Ontario Drama League – which Jamieson formed – was always first in with entry fees and the region's productions held their own at the Finals. Jamieson himself was a whizzbang at flushing out voluntary help at the regional level. It was discovered that Jamieson was a bachelor who lived with his sister in Sarnia. There seemed to be nothing in his background to account for his fascination with the theatre but for some reason he gravitated early in life to Sarnia's Drama Club as a director. His ambitious and somewhat controversial production of Karel and Joseph Capek's *The Ant World* was the talk of the 1933 Final Festival.

Jamieson's appointment to the original DDF executive under the Royal Charter came as no surprise to those who knew him. Although the young lawyer did not come from such rarified circles as say, Madge Tupper or Vincent Massey, he was "respectable" because of his profession and there was no doubt he was an eager beaver. At Government House parties he was just as nattily dressed as Bessborough himself. He eagerly accepted the DDF tradition of white tie and tails or morning clothes and his speech was unmistakeably prep-school. It was known he was comfortably off as far as cash was concerned and no one, including director Osborne and his loyal aide Aylen, minded that the lawyer from Sarnia was unashamedly ambitious.

Looking back now on the make-up of the DDF's top echelon of the 1930's it seems clear that D. Park Jamieson would eventually grab the organization's tiller. Early honorary treasurers, Sir Charles Gordon and Beaudry Leman were no more than sympathetic figureheads who quietly disappeared from DDF affairs when the Festival was suspended in 1939. Robert Y. Eaton (nephew of Timothy and then president of the T. Eaton Co.), who was elected vice-president in 1937, remained a loyal friend to the DDF into the late nineteen-forties but was not interested in seeking active leadership. H. S. Southam of Southam Press who was elected chairman in 1937 was willing to put up cash but unable to give too much time. The Rev. Conrad Latour of Laval, who also joined the executive in 1937 as mandatory representation from Quebec, invariably found he had more pressing work to do at home. Martha Allan, who might have zoomed to the top as the DDF's first woman leader, died in 1941. Lady Madge Tupper was continually arguing with executive policies and resigned from active DDF duties before the beginning of the Second World War. According to an early DDF memo, Colin Campbell, treasurer of the Central Ontario Regional Committee, was picked for the 1935 executive because he was "safe, comfortable and agreeable and will not have theories or opinions he will try to force through."

Col. Henry Osborne was technically still chairman when the DDF held its first post-war festival in 1947, but his energy was flagging and much of the voluntary organizational work for the revived organization had passed into the hands of his trusted friend, John Aylen. The list of executive officers for 1947 shows those who had hung on, those who had risen from the ranks and those who believed the DDF still had purpose and status after its wartime hibernation. Col. Osborne and John Aylen were still there, of course. But Professor Emrys M. Jones (who was also adjudicator of the 1947 festival) of the University of Saskatchewan had joined the group. Mrs. L. T. White of Ottawa who had worked so diligently as a volunteer in the 1930's was on the list. W. D. Cromarty, an original executive officer, was back and so was D. Park Jamieson. George E. Graham was a DDF newcomer.

Jamieson's influence on the DDF had been evident, though, even before the start of the Second World War. Curiously, later officials of the organization assumed the dapper man from Sarnia must have been created president of the DDF in 1938, and Final Festival programs – even into the 1970's – listed Jamieson as "president" between 1938 and 1952. The fact is, however, that he was never named president of the DDF even though he was in virtual control as chairman. One clue that he exercised a firm hand in shaping policies (while Osborne

134

was still honorary director) is that adjudicator S. R. Littlewood presented Jamieson with a photograph in 1938 enscribed: "to the beloved dictator with gratitude and admiration."

In an interview with *Saturday Night* in 1950, Jamieson mused: "I sometimes doubt the 'beloved' part. I'm afraid I'm inclined to be a dictator in jobs to be done, demanding perfection without regard to human limitations and failings. But I hope I have been mellowing in recent years with my own inability to take care of the jobs at hand."

When Jamieson's name was actually listed on the DDF masthead as "chairman" in 1948, Dr. Alan Skinner of London was picked as his honorary director. Skinner – who had often turned up as an actor in DDF regional playoffs – became a top-echelon partner as unswervingly loyal to the leader as Aylen had been to Col. Osborne. He faded into the background of the DDF when fresh blood entered the corporation in the early 1950's.

DDF legend varies as to why D. Park Jamieson withdrew from the organization in 1952. One story is that he himself was sensing the winds of change and that DDF affairs were becoming too onerous, time-consuming and expensive. (Jamieson poured so much cash into the DDF and signed so many of its notes that colleagues were constantly asking him whether he had an oil-well in his backyard). There was a hint of this during a 1949 meeting in Toronto when the chairman informed his executive that he and Dr. Skinner would no longer be able to give as much time to Festival work as they had in the past and that it would be essential to hire a paid official and secretary. He complained then that the correspondence was voluminous and that as many as twenty-five letters a day had to be answered. His complaint led to the appointment of Richard MacDonald as paid secretary-treasurer then, later, director of the DDF.

Another story is that Jamieson had long been aware of the fact that supporters in the regions were growing restless about his single-handed control of the DDF's destiny and were agitating for a switch at the top. In a memorandum to members of the executive and regional chairmen, Jamieson wrote in November 1951: "There is some suggestion that the organization of the DDF is still not sufficiently democratic and that the Festival is run by a small group in Central Canada. I assure you that neither I nor other officers of the festival are desirous of continuing office indefinitely and would welcome suggestions and nominations of persons to occupy such offices next year." Besides, the glitter of the DDF could have been fading for Jamieson. There was still the glamour of vice-regal parties, white-tie dinners, flower-stuffed presidential suites and suitable protocol, of course. He still believed in the DDF's traditional dream of bringing a national drama to Canada. But money matters were now continually muddying the once crystal-clear DDF waters and he had even given his executive the sad go-ahead to negotiate with a whisky distiller – Calvert's – to provide the festival with a steady source of funds.

In January, 1952 he wrote a quietly desperate letter to Prime Minister Louis St. Laurent outlining the aims of the DDF and referring to Vincent Massey's work on the recent Royal Commission on National Development in the Arts, Letters and Sciences. "I am given to understand your government may shortly give consideration to further implementing the Royal Commission report," he wrote, meaning St. Laurent might implement Massey's recommendation that a Canada Council be created. For some reason, the letter was never mailed.

But by then, the Calvert deal had almost been clinched and the news would be broken to the executive and governors' court at the 1952 Festival in Saint John, New Brunswick. A disillusioned Jamieson wrote to his new secretary-treasurer, Richard MacDonald in Ottawa: "I presume we may have to be doing some entertaining on Saturday night and Sunday and am therefore enclosing cheque for $50 and would appreciate it very much if you could have some flowers in our sitting room and use the rest to buy some Scotch and rye . . . Dewar's Scotch and in view of the impending change, better get me Lord Calvert's instead of the usual poison." Saint John, in fact, would be Jamieson's last big Festival bash as DDF leader. He had already released a statement about his pull-out to Canadian Press which, to his chagrin, used the word "resign" rather than "retire" as he had stated. The story also hinted that the DDF was about to be backed by a distillery. Jamieson complained bitterly about the story – which sparked letters and telegrams of protest from across the country concerning the distillery reference – and MacDonald was asked to rap the knuckles of the reporter concerned.

MacDonald did as he was told, then wrote to Jamieson that the CP editor in charge was indeed apologetic about the misquote, adding:

> I got a call from Vickers and Benson, the advertising agency. They saw the CP story and wanted particulars of the amount which would be involved. They explained they had clients that might be interested. I explained the reference to a distillery as a possible sponsor was made without corroboration by this office and he quickly replied they were not thinking of a distiller. Perhaps we will now get an offer from the United Church.

But who would follow Jamieson as chief of the DDF? At Saint John, the appointment of a new leader (who would now be called "president") was left open to be filled by the executive committee. Eventually, it was decided by Jamieson and lawyer David Ongley that it might be an interesting move to follow the custom of the Canadian Bar Association and pick a president from the region which would next host the annual convention – or in the DDF's case, the Final Festival. In 1953, that would be British Columbia. Enquiries were made by B.C.'s regional representative, Dorothy Somserset of the University of British Columbia, and Donald Cromie, publisher of the Vancouver *Sun* was offered the job. Cromie, who had no connections with the DDF though he had once been president of the Vancouver Little Theatre, reacted with stunned surprise. "No way!" he told Ongley when the lawyer – by then an influential member of the DDF executive – telephoned him from Toronto. Ongley argued with Cromie for some minutes, then finally, with a resigned sigh, the Vancouver publisher replied: "Well okay, I'll do it. But only under two conditions. That all I'm expected to do is look cultured and pour the drinks." Ongley laughed and agreed.

The history of Cromie's one-year presidency of the

DDF (during which Governor General Vincent Massey diplomatically blessed the Calvert sponsorship by presenting the top award at the Final Festival in Victoria, B.C.) was significant only because of the jungle of financial, political and adjudication problems that was growing thicker for the DDF all the time. Most were handled by Richard MacDonald in Ottawa and David Ongley in Toronto. Cromie's term of office as a "name" president ended in Victoria, and Dorothy White of Ottawa was elected as his successor. Unfortunately, the veteran DDF supporter was too ill to attend meetings in Victoria and spent most of her time in bed at her hotel. During much of Mrs. White's term of office, Ongley – now a vice-president – worked as acting president, although the DDF's first woman leader recovered for a brief period in 1955 to take a trip to England.

Then, however, the DDF once again decided to elect a regional "name" president, Mr. Justice D. A. McNiven of Regina. The reasons for the executive choosing McNiven are still shrouded in mystery. The judge had an average interest in theatre, but not even a remote connection with the DDF. However, he was a Name and he lived in Regina, site of the 1955 Final Festival. McNiven was also an elderly widower who celebrated his sudden ascent to the cultural pinnacle of the DDF presidency by taking a bride. He is best remembered for his speech at Governor's Court in Regina, a dissertation about the golden wheatfields of Saskatchewan. The feeling began to grow among those who truly controlled the destinies of the DDF that the presidency plan which had produced Cromie and Judge McNiven was a definite bust.

It must have been a fairly widespread feeling among DDF workers at the time. By 1955, the executive committee of the organization had ballooned from a trim eight in 1947 to a top-heavy twenty-four, augmented by thirteen ex-officio regional chairmen. The overwhelming consensus was that the DDF had now grown important enough to stand an overhaul as far as the choice of top people was concerned and executive committee member Edgar Stone was asked to chair a group to peer into the entire highly-political question. Stone's report, produced in the mid 1950's, was a minor masterpiece of interpretation of the DDF's inbred sense of order.

"We suggest various rules of guidance," the Stone report began. "There should be a first vice-president who, it is expected, will be the next president and is getting experience with that end in view. For the last year or so it has been thought that the president should be elected from the province where the final festival is to be held. We suggest no arbitrary arrangements or policy of this kind should be followed. It should be left open to a nominating committee to make a recommendation regardless of place of residence and with due consideration being given to experience on the executive."

DDF minutes from Regina show the executive and governors approved of Stone's report and recommended that the organization should establish a pattern upon which to plan nominations and "dispassionately assess nominees for their practical, not emotional or sentimental value to the DDF. We propose to be realists." The meeting then agreed it would be realistic to accept Stone's suggestions and establish a "pattern of progression" – much like a royal line of succession to the throne – from secretary up to the presidency. There would be a few roadblocks along the way, however. The first vice-president, for example, would certainly be considered heir-apparent. There would be a second vice-president who would be the immediate candidate for first vice-president. But the third vice-president would be elected as a courtesy to Quebec and was not necessarily in line for the presidency.

The fourth vice-president would be the final festival chairman of the year with a one-year term of office. He or she would not be in line for presidential succession. Fifth vice-president would be chairman of the Theatre Conference (a DDF idea launched in 1949) and not in line for the top job. Treasurer and secretary, though, could be in the running. The DDF's chief treasurer would hold his job for a maximum of three years and would be directly in line for the second vice-presidency and then the presidency. The secretary would be in line for the treasurer's position or he could head straight into the second vice-president's slot if the treasurer decided not to climb.

The first president to be elected under the new rules in 1955 was David Ongley of Toronto, a man who had been working diligently for the DDF since 1949. He would serve a two-year term – as recommended in the Stone report – until 1957. His heir apparent was bustling volunteer Pauline McGibbon of Toronto. F. N. Phelps of London was next in line and – as Quebec representative – Lt. Col. Yves Bourassa was in position as third vice-president. Fourth and fifth vice-presidents were not named, though individuals were found to fill the jobs as final festival and theatre conference chairmen. J. Ewart Mackay was promoted from secretary to treasurer and Roy A. Stewart of Barrie was plucked from the executive committee to become secretary, a strategic position if he had ambitions for the top.

A good DDF president, it was rationalized at the time, should have dedication, expertise and mobility. Ongley, an affable and talkative man, was considered an ideal choice. He was mobile because he was a lawyer who travelled. Although he was no millionaire, he could afford to pay his own way to executive meetings, which were democratically held at various regional centres across the land. He had certainly accumulated expertise during his years with the DDF and besides, he was clearly dedicated, otherwise he would not have carried more than his share of the work-load for so long. There's no doubt, however, that the Toronto lawyer enjoyed his association with the DDF even though he turned out to be the most controversial president the organization ever elected. In 1949, he had quit curling and golf to devote some spare time to the Toronto Final (his legal firm handled Odeon Theatres and Ongley was pressured by Festival chairman Judge Dalton Wells into grabbing the new Odeon on Carlton St., Toronto, for the Final awards luncheon) and later found himself more deeply involved with the corporation. "I felt it was probably a good thing to do something for culture rather than devoting my life to chasing the almighty dollar," he once recalled. "Little did I realize I would be devoting the next years of my life to chasing the almighty buck for the DDF."

After the presidency passed in orderly fashion to first vice-president Pauline McGibbon in 1957, Ongley dropped out of the DDF and returned full-time to his legal practice. He knew he had left the leadership of the DDF in capable hands. Mrs. McGibbon, like Ongley, was a child of the organization. She had worked with it as secretary to D. Park Jamieson (whom she had known in Sarnia), and as social wetnurse to later presidents. She had sat behind exhausted adjudicators, helping them to take notes, reminding them about where the washrooms were located and typing reports with two willing fingers. She was DDF rather than Theatre, but like all of her predecessors she was dedicated to the idea of a truly Canadian drama. Ideally, too, she had learned to conduct meetings in impeccable style through her work with the IODE and she was mobile because she was married to a wealthy Toronto business executive, Donald W. McGibbon, treasurer of Imperial Oil Limited.

There had been changes in philosophy concerning the DDF line of succession, however. Yet another nominating committee report pointed out that if the Stone recommendations continued as DDF policy, secretaries at the bottom of the line would have to wait four years for the presidency if incumbents held office for one year. They would have to wait eight years if the presidency was held for two years. The committee (chaired by Vida Peene, another 1949 Dalton Wells recruit from Toronto) recommended that progression should be "from second vice-president to first vice-president to president." As time went on, however, dropouts from top jobs helped the DDF smooth over the entire thorny question. Problems in the future, in fact, revolved more around persuading the right persons to accept responsible positions than forcing them to hue to the line.

When Pauline McGibbon moved up from her first vice-presidency to the pinnacle, for example, Edgar Stone should have climbed from his spot as second-vice-president. Instead, he dropped out in favour of DDF treasurer, Roy Stewart. In late 1958 when nominating time came around again, there was still another switch when Stewart decided he would like to stay on as second vice-president because of illness, although he was prepared to make way for someone else if necessary. For the next few years, the succession game at top DDF levels looked suspiciously like a game of musical chairs. Lt.-Col. Yves Bourassa, an advertising executive from Montreal and the first French-Canadian to take any real interest in DDF politics, switched places with Roy Stewart and was named president at the Toronto Final Festival of 1959. The Hon. Mr. Justice C. D. Stewart was his first vice-president for his first year in office

141

but Roy Stewart, now recovered, switched places with the judge the following year and was elected president in 1961.

Judge Stewart, in fact, always seemed to be hovering on the brink of the presidency but never quite made it. For some reason, for example, he decided to pull out from the line of progression as first vice-president in 1962 and allow Vida H. Peene of Toronto to slide into the president's chair. Miss Peene was very mobile indeed. She was independently wealthy with an impressive background of cultural good works that had already made her known as the Good Housekeeping Sign of Approval for every organization she deemed worthy of her attention. Miss Peene was also loaded with hard-earned DDF expertise and she was unquestionably dedicated. In may ways, Lord Bessborough would have approved highly of her election to the organization's highest office. The lady was a stickler for protocol and well-bred from the tip of her imported shoes to the crown of her hats. No one had ever heard Miss Peene utter an unseemly word – except once in 1964 while she was waiting in vain for Yves Bourassa to submit his report on a Committee of the Future. Told that the tardy Bourassa had finally decided to hand in his paper, Miss Peene said that the Colonel could "go to hell." The shock-waves rippled around the DDF executive committee for days.

The switching and the juggling for vice-presidencies and the leadership of the DDF went on, unabated, until the organization finally turned itself into Theatre Canada in 1971. Justice C. D. Stewart stayed on as Vida Peene's first vice-president during her first term of office, then suddenly resigned. French-Canadian Jean Pelletier, her second vice-president should then have moved into the important slot but decided to stay put and allow young John Brook of Simcoe to become first vice-president instead. Brook, a DDF supporter who was really Theatre (he was associated with the Simcoe Little Theatre and his wife had won the Bessborough Trophy for her production of *The Boy Friend* in 1959) served for three years, during which the hopping around among vice-presidents became mind-boggling. Only one hung on throughout Brook's term of office: Professor A. J. Shaw, Dean of Romance Languages at the University of New Brunswick.

Interestingly, though, it was the professional treasurer of the DDF, Donald W. McGibbon (Mrs. McGibbon's husband had been pressed into DDF service by Vida Peene because of his financial background) who was in the first vice-president's spot at the 1967 Final Festival in Saint John's, Newfoundland. He was elected president that year and Professor Alvin Shaw, who had stuck steadfastly to the line until he reached the top, followed McGibbon into the presidency in 1969.

How did they all feel about it all? In letters, memoirs or personal interviews, all the presidents of the DDF seem not only to have enjoyed their terms of office but actually to treasure the memory as a highlight of their lives. No doubt the prestige of the position – especially during the earlier days of the DDF – was a dazzling lure. One met the great of the land. One travelled, even though it cost approximately $5,000 of one's own cash a year. One manipulated a cultural organization which had background and tradition. One met people and was treated with respect by regional dignitaries. One played host to lieutenant-governors, high society, important business men and, quite often, vice-royalty.

Even though one's job as DDF president invariably involved the problems of money, regional rows, the constant headaches of biculturalism and the shortage of adjudicators, one also had the opportunity to meet actors, actresses and directors and to rub shoulders with glamorous theatre personalities. One had the satisfaction of knowing that the DDF boasted a mandate to encourage Canadian drama. Who's Who described one as a patron of the arts. And even if one was a judge or a lawyer, a clubwoman or a business executive, one could claim a direct affiliation with Irving, Shaw and Shakespeare.

2.   Then there were the Incidents

Few individuals working within the Dominion Drama Festival have been aware of the full political story behind the various Incidents which haunted the corporation almost from the day it was spawned in 1932. Some of these events, of course, were minor crises which grew out of financial or social problems. Others produced spectacular rows which threatened the order and dignity of the DDF and caused much agonizing in high places. Three Incidents stand out in DDF history as corporation shakers: The Victoria Incident, the Saskatchewan Incident and The Calvert Incident. Those involved in any one of them probably knew little about the others.

The Victoria Incident hit the blue-ribbon DDF executive even before the first Festival in Ottawa in 1933. It began with a blunder, exploded with a bang and ended with a whimper. The incident revolved around Major L. Bullock-Webster of the British Columbia Drama Association, an important figure in Victoria drama circles. In 1910 he formed a little theatre group in Prince Rupert. Then, after serving in the 54th Kootenay Division during the First World War, he returned to the west coast to establish the British Columbia Dramatic School, the British Columbia Drama Association and the British Columbia Drama Festival. Lord Bessborough met the major and talked to him about the proposed DDF during his vice-regal tour of the west during the summer of 1932.

Clearly impressed with Bullock-Webster's qualifications as a regional contact, Bessborough wrote to Vincent Massey in September, 1932 that "Bullock-Webster of Victoria B.C. has promised to send a selected list of B.C. people for our General Committee." Massey received the letter but forgot to pass on the information to Col. Osborne at Ottawa headquarters. Osborne, plowing along manfully with the job of assembling the Group of Sixty that would be invited to Rideau Hall for the October meeting – and unaware of Bessborough's meeting with Bullock-Webster – sent off an invitation to Percy Gomery, president of the Vancouver Little Theatre Association. Hell apparently broke loose on December 9, after the October conclave. A wire was dispatched by Bullock-Webster to Col. Osborne which read:

> Executive committee of B.C. Drama Festival need to know if Mr. Gomery has your authority to organize for our province re the Dominion Festival stop the three members of your committee who are also mem-

bers of our executive were not informed of the organization meeting December 5 in Vancouver.

Astonished to receive this disturbing information at a time when the spirit of enthusiasm and co-operation still hung in the air, Osborne innocently wired back:

> Yes, authority given by following wire dispatched to Gomery November 15 begins it would be appreciated if you as president of Vancouver Little Theatre Association would take initiative in calling meeting British Columbia Little Theatre purpose form a provincial body as indicated draft regulations for Dominion Festival Osborne.

Incensed at this heretical action after his cosy talk with Bessborough, Bullock-Webster immediately called the officers of his association together, told them about the unforgivable slight and promptly tendered his resignation as president. His vice-president, Herbert Pott, loyally resigned as well. Just to keep Ottawa well-informed about the storm, Pott himself wrote to Osborne and broke the news. The resignations, he explained, "were a protest against the ignoring of the British Columbia Drama Festival Association on the executive of which are three members of His Excellency's committee." A copy of the letter was sent to Government House. "Neither His Excellency nor myself have any idea what this is all about," complained Bessborough's secretary, Allan Lascelles to Massey. "I hazard a guess, though, that Mr. B. W. and Mr. G. are not on the best of terms."

In the meantime, a shaken Osborne made yet another error by writing a chiding letter to Bullock-Webster in which he blamed the British Columbia Drama Festival for not letting the DDF know about itself:

> British Columbia was represented at the organization meeting in Ottawa by the personal attendance of Mr. Gomery. It was decided that pending the formation of provincial or regional committees, representa-

tives from each province attending the organization meeting should be taken as representing such local committees to be formed. This was the only practical method by which the movement could be started.

Osborne also wrote to Gomery asking for an explanation of what was happening in the west. Gomery, sticking to his guns as official representative of the prestigious new DDF in British Columbia wrote back that it was true Bessborough had sent for Bullock-Webster in Victoria and had apparently discussed the DDF proposal and its organization at length. This led, not unnaturally, to Major Bullock-Webster's conclusion as expressed angrily to Gomery: "We had imagined that we were being asked to organize the provincial end of the DDF. We were awaiting instructions from Ottawa." Gomery added it was indeed strange that nobody in Victoria thought of Major B. W. as one to be consulted or to participate in the organization meeting. Yet, he complained, "we in Vancouver are being criticized for not doing so."

Not long after receiving this letter, Osborne turned up something that must have shocked him to the backbone: a note from Bullock-Webster dated October 24, five days before the Government House Meeting. It was written on official British Columbia Drama Festival Association letterhead and asked for information about what was happening as far as Lord Bessborough's proposed festival was concerned. The contrite DDF director immediately mailed a letter to Bullock-Webster which read:

I can't tell you how distressed we are here at the unfortunate turn of affairs in British Columbia. The origin of the difficulty is the fact that in the setting up of this office all correspondence which had been addressed in various ways was not completely brought together. I was unaware of the existence of the British Columbia Drama Festival Association and have only now learned you referred to it in a letter written on October 24. Had I been more fully informed there might have been an opportunity to discuss the matter when Mr. Gomery was here having regard to your Festival Association. As matters stand we can only adhere to the arrangements initiated by Mr. Gomery under our authority. We must rely on your goodwill to find the means of practical co-operation.

To Massey, he then wrote that he didn't know whether Bullock-Webster felt he had been ignored by Ottawa or by Gomery. "Gomery may have been a little less than tactful or the Victoria people may be foolishly touchy."

The Victoria people were definitely touchy about the incident. There were several meetings, after which both Bullock-Webster and Pott were coaxed back into the fold, and it was finally decided the matter could be smoothed over if Ottawa agreed the Island could hold its own elimination contest before sending a team to the Regionals in Vancouver. Hearing about this turn of events, Gomery – probably glad to be out of hot water – wrote to Osborne: "It seems to be a reasonable suggestion that Victoria hold an elimination competition, working in conjunction with Vancouver. But so far as I know, the final competition for British Columbia will be held in Vancouver and I am prepared to do my utmost to arrange it all agreeably." Tempers then, were soothed, though letters of protest from Bullock-Webster admirers continued to trickle into the DDF's Ottawa office long after the regionals were over. One, from a J. de B. Aster, blustered: "Major Bullock-Webster is a very prominent man in the Canadian drama unit. We Island people want reasonable acknowledgement of our existence and work." All of the letters were diplomatically fielded by an unhappy Osborne.

Bullock-Webster never forgot "the insult" from Ottawa, though he eventually accepted the job of B.C. regional chairman and worked hard for the success of the DDF until it was suspended in 1939. During the Second World War, he toiled even harder to establish his position as Great Man of the West in the field of Drama and in 1941 he was even planning an International Drama Festival "at the coast" to be held after the war. Then there was his effort to personally create an honour in recognition for work "in the development of the drama in Canada" which he called the Canadian Drama Award. Tenaciously, he set out to make the award as acceptable as the glamourous DDF trophies themselves. The first CDA's were handed out by Bullock-Webster in 1935, and he made sure they were given to the very individuals who had caused him so much embarrassment three years before. The Earl of Bessborough got one. Col. Henry Osborne and Vincent Massey both had to write letters of thanks. Other recipients included Margaret Anglin, the Ottawa actress, E. G. Sterndale Bennett, Lady Tupper and Mrs. Ernest Myers of Saskatoon.

But the CDA's would have to attract the highest recognition if they were to rank with the Bessborough Trophy. During the war, Bullock-Webster was busily seeking patronage from Governor General Lord Willingdon but His Excellency's secretary, Sir Shuldham Redfern, coldly replied that the CDA committee was not a Dominion-wide organization (an opinion which caused hoots of protest at CDA meetings) and therefore not eligible for vice-regal support. The Lieutenant-Governor of British Columbia patronized the awards, however, and while he was waiting to land the big fish in Ottawa, Bullock-Webster worked at gaining support from those in other provinces. In 1945, Saskatchewan, Nova Scotia and Prince Edward Island fell into line. By the following year, the award had been recognized by the lieutenant-governors of all the Canadian provinces and Sir Shuldham Redfern was no longer around because Willingdon had been succeeded by Lord Alexander of Tunis.

"Our chief obstruction, Sir Shuldham Redfern, is no longer at Rideau Hall," Bullock-Webster announced at a CDA get-together. "General Alexander will surely become patron if approached in the right way." The Governor General was duly approached and good-naturedly gave the CDA's his vice-regal approval. By the time the DDF emerged from its wartime mothballs, Bullock-Webster's trinkets had become as sought-after honours for theatre-minded Canadians to receive as the DDF awards. So who had never heard of Bullock-Webster and the British Columbia Drama Association?

The Victoria Incident passed virtually unnoticed by supporters of the DDF but the Saskatchewan Incident of 1949 hit the headlines everywhere and again the foundations of the corporation shook under the weight of controversy and scandal. The seeds of the uproar were probably sown in the nineteen-thirties when the executive committee decided it could invite one play from a region to the Final (invariably the winner) or up to three if they reached what was considered to be first-class standards. Early minutes of DDF executive meetings show recurring altercations between regional chairmen and the top brass about the number of plays invited to the Final from their particular necks of the woods. But with twenty to twenty-four one-act plays being staged at the Finals of the 1930's, the executive had room to manoeuvre politically. Just before the Second World War and immediately after, however, when DDF policy decreed that long as well as one-act plays would be invited (later, only three-act plays were accepted for competition), elbow space became more limited.

There were twelve plays invited to the April 25–30 Festival in Toronto in 1949, seven long and five one-acters. The storm broke in mid-March when S. Morgan Powell, drama critic of the Montreal *Star*, wrote:

> An extraordinary situation has arisen in connection with the selection of plays to be presented at the DDF Festival in Toronto. It has been created by the decision of the Festival Committee that all the winners of the Regional Drama Competition shall not take part in the final competition but only 12 plays be presented. Of these, by some extraordinary decision of the committee, three are productions which did not win any regional competition. No wonder the competitors in Saskatchewan and Manitoba are hopping mad and protest that the Drama Festival is unworthy of being termed a Dominion Competition! Nova Scotia and Prince Edward Island regional festival winners have also been left out of the final competition. Alan MacDonald of Edmonton, who is chairman of the Alberta Drama Board, declares that the DDF selection policy may eventually result in the destruction of the whole festival as a Dominion

affair. Mr. Robert Speaight, the regional adjudicator from England upon whose advice the DDF committee has acted in the matter, insists that the winning regional play should not automatically go into the final competition. This seems an almost incredible decision. One may ask, for what reason, in that case, were any regional competitions held?

The DDF immediately reacted with statements from its biggest guns. Charles Rittenhouse, chairman of the corporation's Extension Committee wrote a letter to the *Star* in answer to Morgan Powell's scathing attack declaring that DDF regulations "to select plays for the finals based on the recommendations of the regional adjudicator and taking into consideration the general standard of production across Canada" were not new for 1949. It had been in operation in 1948, and at meetings that year "authorized representatives from each region were present." Rittenhouse added he did not remember any dissenting voice being raised from the now dissatisfied regions, Saskatchewan and Manitoba. In the second place, wrote the DDF officer, Prince Edward Island and Nova Scotia were both only sub-regions of a single Maritime region and the fact that they were not represented was no argument at all.

D. Park Jamieson, then leader of the DDF (Col. Henry Osborne would die in April just before the Toronto Festival), spoke up early in the row and stated that the committee could not invite any more than twelve groups to the 1949 Final because of the time limit and because a Theatre Conference had been planned in addition to the plays. Explanations, though, proved to be fruitless. On March 29, Vincent Massey – now back from England and still identified with the DDF – received a telegram from Saskatchewan's regional chairman, N. H. Browne:

> Strongly protest committee's decision to eliminate two western provinces in Dominion Drama Festival. DDF established to encourage drama throughout whole Dominion. Is it fulfilling function when 50 per cent from Quebec. This information brought to your attention for whatever action deemed necessary and

advisable so that original purpose of Earl of Bessborough is filled. Copies to H. O. Osborne, H. S.
Southam, J. C. Lalemand, J. A. Aylen.

An exasperated Massey wrote immediately to Park
Jamieson from Port Hope, saying he had received the telegram
from Saskatchewan, and continued coolly:

> I presume that the decision as to the system in force
> this year and last which has led to the elimination
> of the Saskatchewan entry from the Finals was arrived
> at by the Dominion Executive with all the constitu-
> tional proprieties observed. Was the Saskatchewan
> representative a dissentient when this was decided?
> I must of course leave this matter in your hands but
> I should be glad if you will let me know about the
> reply you are sending Saskatchewan so that I may
> be governed accordingly in acknowledging the wire.

Meanwhile, other telegrams and letters were
catapulting towards both Jamieson and the DDF's honorary
director, Dr. H. Alan Skinner in London, Ontario. The Premier
of Saskatchewan, T. C. Douglas, wired:

> Saskatchewan people interested in drama keenly dis-
> appointed that this province not invited to send play
> to the DDF stop difficult to understand how winning
> teams in Manitoba and Saskatchewan can be
> eliminated before Dominion Festival has been held
> stop afraid this will have various effect upon public
> interest in amateur dramatics causing disappoint-
> ment to those who have done much to sponsor same.

There were open rumours that the blue-bloods of the DDF had
turned their backs on Saskatchewan because it now had a Social-
ist government.

"Protest exclusion of Saskatchewan play from DDF
final," wired the Saskatchewan Arts Board. "Adjudication indicated high quality performance stop submit finals should

include best play from each region." Another telegram came from William Reid, president of the Saskatchewan Drama League – who also happened to be director of the disputed winning play, *Private Lives* – which read: "Your decision unbelievable and a serious blow to drama in this province stop reconsideration should be given to this immediately stop Saskatchewan should have equal right to perform in a Dominion Festival." Only one communication helped bolster the quaking foundations of the DDF that week: "No official protest forthcoming from Manitoba Regional Committee we are satisfied with Festival ruling, Donald J. Pope, Chairman Manitoba Region."

But everyone, including the fascinated national media, was waiting for an explanation that made some kind of sense. Both Dr. Skinner and Park Jamieson pored over long letters to dissenters across the country which carefully spelled out the DDF's point of view. Jamieson's statement to the Canadian Press on March 29, 1949, condenses the arguments contained in the flood of mail, though it does eliminate the knuckle-rapping he handed out to Saskatchewan because of the region's insistence on "ignoring the regulations." His press release also left out a piece of information he handed on to many carpers – that both Reid and Browne in Regina had been flagrantly advertising the fact that *Private Lives* would be invited to Toronto and had canvassed for funds on this assumption. Clearly, the Saskatchewan region had embarrassed itself by not digesting the DDF rules and jumping the gun too soon.

The Canadian Press story was carried prominently by newspapers across the land and began with Jamieson's by then weary insistence that Regulations were Regulations. Then it went on:

> Mr. Jamieson pointed out that the division of Canada into regions for the purposes of the DDF is not by provinces but is based on convenience of administration and the number of little theatre groups in any particular area. New regions will be created as may be required from time to time. With practically all groups now entering full length plays, every region cannot be represented in future final festivals. Refer-

ring to Mr. Moray Sinclair's objection that his production of *The Glass Menagerie* was not invited, Mr. Jamieson said that only two plays were presented in the Manitoba region and the regulations require that at least three plays be given to qualify for consideration as a regional festival. To be the better of two plays certainly does not constitute a regional competition under the regulations.

Dealing with the objection that the production of *Private Lives* from Regina had not been invited, Mr. Jamieson said that the decision was strictly on merit and according to the regulations of which this group had knowledge before competing. The executive committee feels that it owes a duty to all competing groups to ensure that the festival is conducted according to the regulations and that the final festival each year is in fact a presentation of the best dramatic work presented in Canada that year.

In his book *The Property Basket*, adjudicator Robert Speaight gives his own version of the Saskatchewan Incident. "I had to choose between a respectable production of *Private Lives* from Regina and an original production of *The Taming of the Shrew* from Peterborough directed by Robertson Davies," he wrote. "All things being equal, I felt the *Shrew* was more suitable to be performed before a governor-general. In other words, an original rendering of Shakespeare was more deserving of inclusion in the Finals than a conventional though correct production of Coward. At the time, I felt I could never show my face in Regina again."

No bombs were thrown at the Toronto Festival, though both Skinner and Jamieson expected the controversy to continue through April and into Festival Week. "No doubt the storm will break out again at the meeting of the governors," Skinner wrote to a friend in Calgary. "We knew this situation was going to occur sooner or later with some region and it happened to be Saskatchewan. But we felt the situation had to be faced some time with so many long plays winning in the various regions and we might as well face it now and get it over."

The DDF meetings in Toronto, however, were relatively calm. Typically, Jamieson met the row head on and read Regulation 13 – the one that sparked the protests in the first place – as though it were the riot act: "Invitations to take part in the final festival will be issued by and in the discretion of the executive committee having regard to the report of the regional adjudicator and the general standard of presentation across Canada . . ." The chairman pressed home his advantage and reviewed the entire matter of invitations, even pointing out that way back in 1947 the regulations were that these were entirely at the discretion of the committee. "In spite of this," he thumped severely, "the press and the various regions ignored the regulations and reports were continually appearing that the winner in the region would go to Toronto." Probably to his own surprise, there was scarcely a whimper from Governors' Court.

The Saskatchewan Incident did have some far-reaching effects on DDF regulations even though, true to tradition, it took time for things to happen. In 1950, when the slice-up of the Dominion grew from eleven to thirteen regions, the committee decided that if a group were placed first in a region and not invited to compete at the Final, the executive would ask the cast and the director of the play to attend the party "provided at least three full-length plays were entered or if an invitation was warranted in the opinion of the adjudicator."

By 1950, though, only full-length plays were being accepted for competition and the DDF – despite its consolation prizes – was being pressured to reduce the number of regions so that winners from all parts of the country could be jammed into the program of eight plays selected for Final competition. Nothing definite was done about the idea until another winning Saskatchewan play, *The Diary of Anne Frank*, was not invited to attend the Toronto Final in 1959 as a competitor. The following year, bruised by yet another blast of western protest, the DDF adopted a fourteen-region, eight-zone adjudication setup. The regulations were also changed so that "the top award winner in every single-region zone and one of the winners in every multiple-region zone shall be invited to the final." The lucky group in the multiple areas would be chosen on the advice of the adjudicator.

If the Victoria and the Saskatchewan Incidents were blows to DDF dignity, though, the Calvert Incident – which directly involved the corporation's revered supporter, Vincent Massey – was a veritable earthquake. The rumbles probably began as far back as the early nineteen-fifties when Calvert Distillers agreed to become major sponsors of a near-bankrupt DDF. The full force of the shock hit at the 1956 Final Festival in Sherbrooke, Quebec.

David Ongley, who was president of the corporation at the time, remembers an executive meeting in late 1955 at the Royal York Hotel in Toronto at which there was a discussion about Calvert Distillers and how the DDF could show its appreciation of the company's financial blood-transfusions during the past years. After all, cities which hosted the Final were always sold out of Calvert whisky during DDF week. But did supporters of the organization buy the liquor at other times? "Dash it all," Ongley told his executive, "I hope they all think about it at Christmas time. Surely one practical way of thanking Calvert is to remind everyone to buy the stuff all year, don't you think?" Officers present seemed to agree with Ongley's suggestion. He filed it away at the back of his mind but brought it up again when M. M. Schneckenburger, a representative of Calvert, was visiting Toronto. "Schneck agreed it was a nice thought," Ongley remembered later. "But at no time did he insist we start any kind of campaign."

The idea, though, continued to nag at Ongley and in April of 1956, not long before the Sherbrooke Festival, he decided to draft a letter to DDF sympathizers concerning Calvert's generous sponsorship. He prepared a list of 3,000 names and Calvert themselves agreed to have the letter duplicated on official Dominion Drama Festival letterhead (which featured Massey's name as vice-regal patron) and envelopes typed. Ongley signed each of the letters personally, sometimes adding an extra message. "One, I think, went to Massey himself," he has recalled. The text of the letter praised the public-minded spirit of Calvert Distillers and outlined what the firm had done to aid the work of the DDF. Fine. It was the final couple of paragraphs which sent dissenters rushing for their pens:

> The executive Committee has established a Liaison Committee to work with Calvert in the mutual interest of both organizations. However, it doesn't require involved plans to do one more important thing. Each and every friend of DDF – and their friends – when the occasion arises can remember and support Calvert. If this is done what does it mean for DDF? First of all, we are saying thank you to a friend – a friend which always leans over backwards to avoid any taint of "commercialism" being levelled against them (and thus to the hurt of DDF) in their valuable contribution. But secondly, and from the selfish viewpoint, and more important to DDF, increased Calvert sales means increased Calvert budgets for DDF to be used in our plans for the development and growth of theatre across Canada. I hope you will agree with me this bears thinking about, and simple action.

One of the first reactions to Ongley's letter was from a Mrs. W. D. Campbell of Maple Creek, Saskatchewan, who was a DDF supporter and an active member of her local United Church's Women's Association. Shocked beyond belief that Ongley – seemingly with the Governor General's approval – was suggesting she stock up on booze, Mrs. Campbell sent the letter with an outraged covering note to the Rev. Ernest Long, secretary of the United Church's General Council in Toronto. Long, in turn, fired off salvoes to Vincent Massey and Prime Minister Louis St. Laurent: "We hold it to be unworthy of Canada that, in connection with a project of which Her Majesty's representative is the patron, the name of the Governor General should be involved in such an appeal as this," Dr. Long's protest to Massey read in part. As well as scolding the Prime Minister, Dr. Long added that it was about time the DDF was supported from the public treasury "so that the Festival may no longer be placed in the unenviable position in which it now finds itself."

St. Laurent slid out from under by replying to Long, suggesting that a letter written to the United Church from Government House (a copy of which had been sent to his office from Rideau Hall) probably dealt fully with the protest. A thoroughly embarrassed Massey clearly believed it did. For one thing, the letter assured Dr. Long, the Governor General had known nothing of the Ongley communication. For another, he felt it should not have been written. However, the letter went on, "the patronage of such a movement implies sympathy with, and support of, its objects. But His Excellency is sure it is understood that the Patron does not, and could not assume responsibility for its administration."

But however much Massey tried to rationalize the Ongley letter, letters and telegrams of outrage kept pouring into Government House. The Rev. F. E. H. James of the Metropolitan Church in Victoria, B.C., wrote that "the United Church of Canada is constantly waging a battle against the inroads of the liquor traffic. We feel that this is one of the greatest problems facing our nation. It is disconcerting to know that such a cultural organization as the DDF is now sponsoring the increased sale of liquor. . . ." Mary Hamilton, president of the School of Narcotic Education in Calgary, wrote about "how very disturbed" she had been about the letter and how her entire life-work had been with the concern of young people. Howard B. Bishop, president of an organization called Human Engineers in New Jersey, sent Massey a pledge card to sign and rapped "It is high time that officials in your country, as well as ours, take a public stand against the use of products representing the Hot Spots of Human Destruction."

And still the messages winged to Ottawa: The Saskatchewan Women's Christian Temperance Union ("In the name of God we will set up our banners"). The Vancouver district Women's Christian Temperance Union ("you can well understand how distressed we were by the letter"). DDF executive members ("we had nothing to do with it"). Alarmed citizens ("drinking has become too prevalent and I dread to think of the future"). The letters were fielded gracefully by Massey's son and confidential secretary, Lionel, but it was clear that Ongley's attempt at Dominion-wide public relations on behalf of the organization's financial angel had badly backfired.

157

The blast hit the DDF president early in May, just as he was about to streak out of Toronto to help organize the Sherbrooke Final. The first rattle came from Dr. Long of the United Church, who asked Ongley "to retract as far as it is in your power." The second was from the Toronto press who wanted to know what the shouting was about. Ongley made a short statement, said he had no intention of retracting his letter and headed for Union Station. At the Hotel Sherbrooke, he wrote swiftly to Lionel Massey: "I left Toronto in rather a mad rush last night to arrive here in Sherbrooke today. I do, however, want to take the opportunity of writing you as soon as possible to say how extremely sorry I am His Excellency's name should have been dragged in by the United Church in its publicized criticism of a letter I wrote in April re Calvert's support to the DDF. When the reporters questioned me on that score I told them quite frankly I felt to bring in the name of the Governor General, an outstanding patron and supporter of the arts in Canada, was in extremely bad taste. To me, it's as bad as if I released names of United Church ministers whom I know take a drink. . . ."

On the eve of the 1956 Final Festival in Sherbrooke, DDF executive officers and governors quaked as the typhoon swirled around them. The Archbishop of Sherbrooke, Monsignor Georges Cabana, had already been of two minds about attending the *theatre* because he was then leading a Decency Campaign (women members of the DDF had been informed they would have to cover their shoulders at performances). Now the Calvert mess had him holed up, incommunicado, in his quarters. Reporters sprinted to interview Ongley on his arrival in town, but he refused to make any further statements. Well then, would the Governor General come to the Final? Ongley, in reply to both reporters and distracted DDF workers, merely shrugged.

After writing to Lionel Massey, Ongley decided the situation was serious enough for him to telephone Rideau Hall personally. He talked to the Governor General's son and asked whether it would be of any help if he travelled to Ottawa that night and met with Massey the following day. "I think it would be a useful idea," the younger Massey answered. "Father is in a very awkward position right now." Ongley agreed. If the Governor General came to Sherbrooke, it would mean he approved of the Calvert letter. On the other hand, if he failed to turn up, the DDF would receive a crushing blow to its prestige. Newspaper reports were already implying that Massey had threatened to withdraw patronage unless Ongley resigned or made a public retraction. Actually, though, all of the stories read that this was only "understood." The truth is that no comment of this kind came out of Government House at all.

Aware that even his executive would assume he was being summoned to Rideau Hall for a knuckle-rapping, Ongley slipped quietly out of Sherbrooke on the night of May 11, stayed at a Montreal hotel, then took a train to Ottawa the following morning. He read an editorial in the Ottawa *Journal* on his way to Government House: "The Toronto lawyer should have had his head read. On the other hand, if we are all accepting whisky money to build schools and hospitals and better babies through taxation, what is there so vile or wrong about the DDF accepting a bit of it to build better drama?" One columnist remarked dryly that the controversy had only served to make Calvert the best-known brand of whisky in Canada.

Vincent Massey met Ongley cordially at Rideau Hall. He told the DDF president that he appreciated the amount of work that must be hanging fire in Sherbrooke and was grateful for Ongley taking time to help sort out the problem. The two men walked into a library overlooking the garden and Massey asked Ongley if he would like a drink. There was a short burst of laughter and Massey added: "I'm a Scotch man, myself." He collected a decanter of sherry from a sideboard and placed it with two glasses between armchairs, and the agonizing over what both men agreed was "a tempest in a whisky bottle" began. What would be the best thing for Massey to do? Go to Sherbrooke or not go to Sherbrooke? Ongley got to his feet and paced thoughtfully. Massey also paced. Of course, the Governor General mused, scratching his head, he wouldn't expect Ongley to renounce or deny the letter. That would be too embarrassing. Ongley sipped his sherry. Well then, would it help if he *reworded* the letter, perhaps explained more clearly what he had intended to say? Massey said he thought it would be a great help if Ongley did that. "All right," said the lawyer. "I'll even clear it with you over the telephone."

Back in Sherbrooke, Ongley told his astonished executive he had been to see Massey about the Calvert Incident and that he was going to issue a reworded letter of explanation. The reaction from the DDF group varied. Some officers disagreed that Ongley should write a letter at all. Others insisted the president issue a full retraction but the lawyer said he would rether resign than do that. No, he thumped, the letter would be explanatory. Ongley shut himself in his hotel room and finally emerged with two hand-written pages which he showed to a small group of supporters then read to Lionel Massey over the telephone. "I wrote on April 13 last to the friends and families of the DDF concerning the question of our relations with Calvert Distillers," the note read:

> This letter raised some sincere differences of opinion among our membership. The DDF has as its objective the encouragement and development of theatre in Canada. The executive committee and I agree it is not a part of our function to promote the sale of any commercial product. The letter was written simply to acknowledge to our members the great debt we owe our sponsor who has made it possible for us to carry out our objective. I am sending this letter in order to correct a misunderstanding which has arisen.

Lionel Massey said he approved, but added he would have to check out the letter with his father. Everyone waited. After yet another conversation with Ottawa, Ongley – his affable, extroverted self again – released the letter to the press. Yes, Vincent Massey would come to Sherbrooke after all. But had Ongley retracted or merely explained? During that tense Final Festival week of 1956, opinions clashed within the DDF. "Maybe it was the perfect letter," Ongley has since decided. "People read what they wanted into it. As far as I'm concerned, I still think it was an explanation."

Vincent Massey himself was smilingly non-committal during his visit to Sherbrooke. Comments were, in fact, that the Governor General was proving what everyone had long suspected: that he was really a better actor than his brother Raymond. As usual, protocol was impeccable, the white ties were dazzling and the gowns brilliant (even though ladies wore stoles over their shoulders during a May heat-wave) and the Archbishop emerged graciously out of hiding to join in the festivities. "What was all the stuffed-shirt fuss about," wondered columnist Harold Weir of the Vancouver *Sun* . "Real royalty in London patronizes gin, whisky, ale, cigars and umbrellas. Are Canadians really that provincial?"

3.   The French are growing restless again.

Long after Lord and Lady Bessborough returned to England from Canada, the elegant, French-born countess confessed to an interviewer: "My husband and I insisted that the Dominion Drama Festival be bilingual, you know. Right from the beginning we felt we wanted to do something about unifying the two original cultures of Canada." The Bessborough dream had a lasting influence on the DDF. At one point in the corporation's history, in fact, the ideal of a fraternally bilingual-bicultural Canada became so overwhelming that the DDF seemed to be making national unification its top priority. Even now, the Bessborough philosophy clings to the DDF's successor, Theatre Canada.

Bessborough was firm about the fact that both French and English plays should have an equal chance of winning his gesso plaque and even before the first DDF Final in 1933, the top-echelon organizers sweated over details of competition that would satisfy French-speaking groups. Late in 1932, for example, Bessborough, Massey and Osborne decided it would be helpful to competitors if a list of suitable plays was distributed. Directors would not be handcuffed to the list but would be invited to choose from it if they wished. On December 3, 1932, Osborne wrote anxiously to Massey:

Last evening I had a message from Government House to the effect that H.E. wanted to know what about French plays. I explained that, as I saw it, we were under no obligation to supply any list of plays but were only doing it to be helpful. The French groups will receive the regulations which state clearly what may be played and it is for them to select and submit plays and scenes if and when we are able to get them together. So far I have received no co-operation from anyone on that point. The draft regulations had been translated into French but of course they have to be done over in view of the revision.

The question of the list plagued the DDF pioneers well into 1933. The English list was simple: the well-known classics, naturally, and Canadian plays by Merrill Denison (the playwright's *Brothers in Arms* enjoyed a small boom in 1933) and the somewhat untheatrical verse-plays of Marjorie Pickthall. But French plays? Well, there were Molière, Racine, Corneille, of course. The organizers scratched their heads over the rest. As it turned out, French groups entering the first festival of 1933 blithely ignored any necessity for a helpful list and picked their own plays or scenes. On the whole, in fact, their choices were far more original and contemporary than those of the English contingent. A run-down of the six French plays invited to the Ottawa Final shows no trace of Molière, Racine or Corneille. Le Cercle Dramatique des Etudiants de Laval brought a scene from Maurice Level's *Le Baiser Dans La Nuit*. Les Anciens Du Gesu de Montreal presented the first act of *Une Affaire d'Or* by Marcel Gerbidon. L'Union Dramatique de Quebec Enr. played a scene from de Erckmann-Chatrian's *Les Rantazau* (which won the prize for the best presentation in French). Le Rampe d'Ottawa came with a comedy in four short scenes by Jean Variot. Martha Allan's Montreal Repertory Theatre's French Section played a scene from Leopold Houle's *Matines et Laudes* and Le Conservatoire National de Musique de Quebec presented Charles Mere's short play *Les Trois Masques*.

In a way, it was no surprise to the 1933 festival organizers that the French Canadians were being so co-operative and amiable. After all, they had leaned over backwards to make sure this would happen. That first year of the DDF, there was

162

no flack about regional adjudicators because each area had been asked to approve its own. French Canadians – pleased, no doubt, about the way they were being painstakingly included in a dramatic festival spawned by English vice-royalty – agreed without comment to run their regional playoffs apart from English Canadians in areas where both groups were contesting. Eastern Ontario unquarrelsomely split into an English sub-regional in Kingston linked with a French sub-regional in Ottawa. Western Quebec held both English and French playoffs without incident in Montreal. Eastern Quebec posed a small problem at first. W. P. Percival, Deputy Minister of *Protestant* Education had been picked to organize the regional playoff in Quebec City, probably because he had been at the October, 1932 meeting. When Percival discovered that all of the twelve plays entered in the regional were French, however, he threw up his hands and smilingly turned over the show to a local French Canadian theatre enthusiast, Col. G. E. Marquis.

The politics of bilingualism at the 1933 Final were a little stickier because of adjudicator Rupert Harvey's fractured French and the need to seek the aid of Professor St. Elme de Champ of the University of Toronto. However, even in this instance, the founders of the DDF were certain they had preserved and even nurtured the Bessborough ideal of unity right down the line. Actually, a note of subdued astonishment runs through DDF correspondence and minutes of meetings during the 1930's whenever dissatisfaction among French groups from Quebec and later from around Winnipeg and Edmonton is mentioned. In a polite attempt to head off trouble, French advisors and translators were retained at DDF expense when the regional festivals were handed to a single adjudicator – Rupert Harvey – in 1934. Later, Osborne was dispatched to England and letters beseeching help were mailed off to DDF supporters abroad so that truly bilingual regional and final judges could be shipped to Canada.

But flack from the French grew thicker all the time. To the dismay of the DDF executive, the Eastern Quebec region began to lose interest in a regional festival and in 1935 it was noted with some embarrassment that no French-language play was entered in the French section of the Western Quebec regional in Montreal. The Eastern Ontario French section retained some muscle, though, and the DDF executive sighed with relief when *L'Innocente* by H. R. Lenormand performed by L'Ecole de Musique et de Déclamation de l'Université d'Ottawa walked off with the 1935 Bessborough Trophy with the blessings of British adjudicator Alan Wade.

Apparently, Wade's judgement failed to impress the French. When the DDF announced that the British judge would return to Canada in 1936 to adjudicate the regional playoffs across the Dominion, groups in Montreal threw a tantrum and asked regional representative, Martha Allan, to insist they wanted Wade to be assisted by a French-speaking aide or else they would find their own adjudicators. The DDF executive harumphed and said no. After all, what on earth did the French want? They had their own plaque for the best play in French. The executive was turning cartwheels to dig bilingual adjudicators out of the woodwork. In 1937, for example, the DDF begged the influential Harley Granville-Barker to comb Paris for a top-notch *French* adjudicator who could also speak fluent English, and the corporation finally grabbed the brilliant young director, Michel St. Denis as judge for the Final.

That year, though, puzzled DDF policy-makers did get some insight into the reasons for French-Canadian restlessness when regional adjudicator George de Warfaz stated to the press that he had heard no cultured Parisian French in Quebec but that individuals in the province spoke the language of the sixteenth century. After the hurricane of protest from French-Canadian regions died down a little, the highly-upset DDF executive wiped its collective brow, then thanked its lucky stars that at least the shambles might be straightened out by Michel St. Denis at the spring Finals. Perhaps, indeed, M. St. Denis might even repeat Alan Wade's "political" ploy in 1935 and award the Bessborough trophy to a French-Canadian play. Unfortunately, the adjudicator from Paris had few French entries to choose from that year. Only three short plays were entered for the Final (the French regionals were shockingly sparse): Jose Germain and Emmanuel Bourcier's *L'Absolution*, presented by the Renaissance Théâtrale of Montreal; Sacha Guitry's *Françoise*, staged by the staunch Le Caveau of Ottawa; and Jean Sarment's

Le Voyage à Biarritz, played by Le Cercle Molière of Winnipeg. The three 1937 French entries were all presented on Monday evening, April 27. M. St. Denis awarded the Bessborough Trophy to the Toronto Masquers with their production of Canadian playwright John Coulter's *The House in the Quiet Glen*. Le Caveau got the French award.

No one could blame St. Denis for his decision, of course. But it was obvious now that French-Canadian relations with the DDF were strained to breaking point. But why? Well, the executive argued among themselves, it was obvious the selection committee would have to be far more cautious about the choice of adjudicators. The French *must* be satisfied with the regulations. "The bilingual character of our country is part of our national inheritance," Col. Osborne reminded the DDF's inner circle at a 1938 meeting. He shook his head sadly and the executive, aware they were listening to a man who still had the ear of Bessborough in England, stared silently back at him. "Our festival," Osborne added, tapping the desk with gentlemanly restraint, "will lose tremendously if we do not encourage both languages."

But 1938 was also the year the Final moved from Ottawa for the first time – "to the people," as Osborne explained – and to Winnipeg, headquarters of the persuasive Lady Madge Tupper. It was also a city, the DDF noted, with a percentage of French-speaking ticket buyers. In memoranda of the 1930's, Col. Osborne agreed with members of his executive that Toronto would clearly be a washout as far as French plays were concerned and that Montreal audiences might stay away in droves because of the overwhelmingly large number of English plays always entered. It was at a Winnipeg meeting, though, that the DDF was again shocked out of its wits by the extent of French-Canadian disenchantment with Bessborough's lovingly-planned filial fling. A young Montreal director named Herbert Whittaker (who would later become theatre critic of the Toronto *Globe and Mail*) brought a message by proxy from DDF governor Prince Paul Lieven which suggested it might be time for the DDF to split itself into two separate Finals, one French and one English.

Whittaker explained that Prince Paul (a White Russian with little theatrical background who had quickly jumped on to the DDF social bandwagon) believed the subject of separate festivals had become important in Montreal and that if it were shoved aside, the festival in the region would be injured. Prince Paul also felt that French groups could not make progress until an adjudicator could be found who could speak French fluently. This nugget of information floored DDF volunteers who had worked tirelessly to make sure the adjudicators they were now hiring were indeed fluent in French. After some collective spluttering, a Winnipeg representative spoke up and said that of course the Final should not be divided but perhaps the DDF might assign special French judges to the regionals. It would be expensive, of course, the Winnipegger agreed. But if the French groups felt that way, that was that. After all, the DDF stood for bilingualism and fair play. The meeting agreed the whole matter was something that had to be examined. Not now, of course. "You know," mused a harassed Col. Osborne as the discussion concerning the French dragged on, "Eastern Quebec has never made an attempt equal to the importance of the region. Montreal hasn't, either. Ottawa is definitely doing better and so is Winnipeg and Northern Alberta. There are some bright spots, I suppose. Some are pretty bleak. But we have to remember, you know, that this is a bilingual festival."

Prince Paul Lieven turned up at a June 1938 meeting of the DDF at which he brought up the subject of the French groups in person. The problem of satisfactory adjudication was particularly acute in Montreal, complained the Prince. In Ottawa, which had a relatively happy French Section within the Eastern Ontario region, most people were more or less fluent in both languages. In Montreal, this was not the case. The DDF officers present dutifully chewed over the problem and assured the ruffled White Russian that the door was open to all suggestions. In the end, Prince Paul agreed to drop the matter for the present while he consulted the French groups "with a view to submission of a plan."

The conversation then turned somewhat gloomily to the coming 1939 Final in London, Ontario. "There won't be much of an audience for French plays there," someone muttered. The meeting unhappily agreed. At other festivals it had been the tradition to lump the participating French groups into a single evening. Or, if enough turned up, an evening and a matinée. It was suggested that it might be a strategic move in London to scatter the French plays throughout the week's program. That way, audiences who came to see an English production would be sampling one of the French entries as well. The executive stole a cautious glance at Prince Paul and Judge Constantineau, a representative of the Western Quebec regional committee. The Prince was silent but the judge commented mildly enough that he was sure this would be agreeable to any French-speaking groups who were invited.

In 1939, however, there were just two French plays available to scatter: Jean Jacques Bernard's *Martine* presented by the persistent Le Caveau group from Ottawa and Charles Mere's *Les Trois Masques* staged by those other French-speaking stalwarts from the west, Le Cercle Molière. In a gesture that smacked somewhat of despair, the festival committee threw up its hands and simply staged them both together at a Wednesday matinée. It was a tossup for the adjudicator to award the Best-Play-in-French plaque, and he gave it to Le Caveau. The Ottawa Drama League clinched the Bessborough Trophy. Ironically, the League had chosen to present Terence Rattigan's *French Without Tears*.

The French question within the DDF simmered on the back-burner during the Second World War but, inevitably, it flared up again to plague the inner-circle idealists (most of them from Central Ontario) when the DDF was revived in 1947. Echoes of times past reverberated around a preliminary meeting of "persons interested in the DDF" which was held at the Chateau Laurier in Ottawa during June, 1946. Asked about how drama groups in Montreal had fared during the war, A. H. Rowland of Montreal (representing the Montreal Repertory Theatre and other local drama groups) told the meeting that many of the groups which had taken part in the seven former DDF festivals had now disappeared. However, he felt that those who were still producing plays were in a healthy condition and that English non-professional theatre, particularly, was showing improvement. That sounded mild enough. But later in the meeting Florence Castonguay of Ottawa wanted to know how French entries in the 1947 regionals would be judged. Rowland shrugged his shoulders. He suggested there should be a separate regional in Montreal for groups from Ottawa, Quebec City and Montreal. "Groups in St. Boniface and Edmonton," he added, "will have to make their own arrangements as in the past." The officers of the DDF nodded their agreement. It was thoroughly understood that the organization would remain steadfastly bilingual. No one could shake that.

In 1947, though, a new theatrical element from Quebec entered the DDF: professionalism. Well, semi-professionalism, anyway. Just before the outbreak of the Second World War, an energetic priest named Father Emile Legault of the Congregation of the Holy Cross had founded a Montreal group which he dubbed Les Compagnons de St. Laurent to stage religious productions. By 1947, the group – which lived as a kind of theatrical commune – had branched out into Molière Anouilh, Giraudoux and Pirandello and were junketing around the province and to Ottawa with their plays. There was nothing in the DDF regulations which barred professionals or semi-professionals from entering the festival so Father Legault's Compagnons (together with the perennial Le Caveau) turned up in London to represent French-Canadian theatre with a smooth production of Molière's *Le Médecin Malgré Lui*. Canadian adjudicator Emrys Jones – awed with the group's expertise – awarded Les Compagnons the Bessborough Trophy. "We came back from the Festival, very happy because we had won," Father Legault has since admitted. "Recognition outside the province helped our publicity and our prestige." Certainly other groups at the 1947 Final must have been impressed with the theatrical superiority of Les Compagnons. On awards night, Father Legault was hoisted onto the shoulders of admiring French and English-speaking competitors and paraded triumphantly around the theatre.

Still, groups from Quebec – which were acquiring professional status at a faster rate than those in English Canada – held back from throwing their full weight behind the DDF French regionals. Le Rideau Vert, for example, a company formed in 1948 by members of an earlier group called L'Equipe – and L'Equipe itself – were both conspicuously absent at that year's Final in Winnipeg. Instead, the French showing included only those now-familiar names: Le Caveau, Cercle Molière and, for a return visit, Father Legault's strong Les Compagnons.

Actually, the 1948 Festival could have turned out to be a murderous blow to French-English relations within the DDF if it had not been for the level-headedness of Father Legault himself. The script of Les Compagnons' entry, Anouilh's *Antigone* had been prudishly pruned on orders from the Roman Catholic Church in Quebec and adjudicator Robert Speaight was openly critical about it. "I was divided as to whether to give the Bessborough Trophy to *St. Joan* from London or Les Compagnons' *Antigone*," Speaight wrote in his memoir *The Property Basket*. "However, I found one place in the text where Antigone had been bowdlerised and I ruled this inadmissable. I gave the trophy to *St. Joan*. Luckily, Father Legault was quite indulgent about the whole thing and told me that if what I had said would help create a saner and more Christian spirit in Quebec, it would be well worth while." Later, Father Legault and Speaight became firm friends.

The old pre-war mutterings from Quebec were beginning to trickle in again, however. Regional adjudicators were not fluent enough in French and neither were – according to the French Canadians – the Final judges. And when was the DDF going to hold a Final in La Belle Province? Would the organization always concentrate its efforts and draw its main representation from the centre of the Dominion? Again, DDF officers shook their heads in stunned amazement. Quebec had always been represented on the DDF executive – that had been the express wish of the founder – but unfortunately, French Canadians seldom turned up for meetings. Playoffs in the French-Canadian regions were still thinly attended. Sometimes, in fact, it scarcely seemed worth while to send an adjudicator. And about those adjudicators. Did the French Canadians realize the endless expense and trouble the executive took to find experienced, bilingual theatre people who would be acceptable to both cultures?

After 1949, when British adjudicator Philip Hope-Wallace actually judged three French-Canadian newcomers at the Final, Le Conservatoire Lasalle of Montreal, La Comédie

Nouvelle of Ottawa and Cours François Rozet of Montreal, the DDF planners gritted their teeth and set out to please the French. Michel St. Denis (surely no one in Quebec could quarrel with his appointment) was brought back in 1950 for the Calgary Final. There was a scramble in 1951 to find someone equally as attractive to the French and English, but the frantic DDF finally had to settle on Jose Ruben, a European actor then living in the United States whose chief claim to fame was that he once played opposite Minnie Maddern Fiske. Ruben was not popular but he awarded the Bessborough Trophy to Father Legault's Les Compagnons for their production of Martens et Obey's *Les Gueux Au Paradis*.

At that time, the influential priest was considering the possibility of disbanding his group because, as he once told an interviewer, "my strength was leaving me, my heart was not in it as it once had been." The breakup came in 1952. But the success of Les Compagnons at the prestigious DDF Finals was already creating ripples in French-Canadian theatrical circles. Actors and directors who had tasted the headiness of national exposure were forming new groups and confidently plunging into professionalism. Jean Gascon (who would later become artistic director of the Stratford Shakespearean Festival) and Jean-Louis Roux of Les Compagnons formed Le Théâtre du Nouveau Monde. Guy Hoffman, who acted in *Les Gueux Au Paradis* quickly became a star. Others who had been with the group in its hours of DDF glory – Yves and Jacques Letourneau, Gilles and Denise Pelletier, Denis Vachon, Guy Provost – were all adding new muscle to the theatre in Quebec.

Aware of what was happening, the DDF executive itself tried to keep on its toes as far as the energetic French Canadians were concerned. Beseiged now with complaints of "non-communication" and "English-oriented festival" from Quebec and even from French groups in the middle west, the DDF executive literally begged the popular St. Denis to return for the 1952 Final in Saint John, New Brunswick. The organization then clinched what it believed was a perfect bilingual, bi-cultural coup by persuading a St. Denis disciple, Pierre Lefèvre to judge the year's regionals. From the French point of view, however, the hopeful 1952 Final was a disaster. Just one French-language play, a piece by Quebec playwright Marcel

Dubé called *De l'Autre Côté du Mur* got to the Final. For the first time in festival history, there was no award for the Best French Presentation, though Dubé would win the top Festival trophy for his play *Zone* the following year in Victoria.

Could it be that the French adjudicators were too harsh with French plays? And English adjudicators too soft? Could it be that French groups actually disliked judges with Gallic background because in many cases they were actors or directors not much different from themselves? Certainly, it was grimly noted at DDF conclaves that imported judges never received the adultation in French-Canadian areas that they did in English regions. Even back in the nineteen-thirties, it was remembered, the great men of the theatre from abroad had occasionally been *hissed* at by irreverent French-Canadian drama enthusiasts. And did the French Canadians have a valid point when they complained the Final had never yet moved into Quebec?

In 1954, Guy Beaulne, chairman of the Western Quebec Region of the DDF and a frequent participant in the festival, read a report which referred again to "a lack of firm organization" within the DDF because of "difficulties in contact between English and French groups." He then brought up that long-festering complaint about a Final in Quebec and said there was a growing feeling in his region that the festival should soon be held in Montreal.

Well, there it was out in the open and memos began to fly between executive secretary Richard MacDonald at the DDF's Ottawa office and influential members of the executive. MacDonald felt it would be a good idea for the Final to go to Montreal in 1956. But because of the weakness of regional organizations within Quebec and the overwhelming percentage of English plays always in competition, he advised careful consideration be given to the plan. Perhaps it might be better to wait a year or two than to stage a Final in Montreal that would flop financially. "However," he continued in one 1955 communiqué, "perhaps our executive would be prepared to take a chance and break even. Montreal, after all, is Calvert's home district and we might be able to get some additional support from them."

During talks with Western Quebec regional representatives in Montreal, MacDonald found there was indeed a strong undercurrent from both English and French groups that it was about time the DDF sortied into Quebec and he reported this back to the executive. Still, there was hesitation about the fact that Western Quebec could swing a successful show. Wasn't there somewhere else in the province, a smaller town with a good percentage of English-speaking residents, where the DDF could make its important Quebec début?

"I think we should go to Sherbrooke instead of Montreal in 1956," MacDonald wrote to incoming president David Ongley. "We would have a reasonably successful festival there, I'm sure. And even if it does not come up to the highest standard it should be as good as any we've had in places like St. John's or Victoria." Ongley agreed. "We should certainly go to the province of Quebec as soon as possible. And because of language difficulties and so on, Sherbrooke is really the only available place. The main hotel, even without turning over all the available space, can handle 200 people."

The DDF made the supreme effort to emphasize its bilingual character in Sherbrooke. The masthead of the program read: *"Programme du Festival National d'Art Dramatique et de la Conférence sur le Théâtre."* Underneath, relegated to second place, was the English translation: "Program of the Dominion Drama Festival and Theatre Conference." Even the date on the program was in French: *14 au 19 mai 1956*. Inside, there were messages in English and French from Governor General Vincent Massey and descriptions of Le Festival/The Festival in both languages. L'Index du Programme was in French with English subtitles. To round out the determinedly Gallic mood of the show, the DDF executive engaged Madame Françoise Rosay, the French actress, as Final adjudicator.

Unfortunately, Madame Rosay had been badly briefed in France and was not at all sure about what she was supposed to do. Apparently the Canadian Embassy in Paris had given the impression there would be other adjudicators and that all kinds of well-paying assignments had been lined up for her in Canada. She was demanding (a DDF female staff member had to lace her into her corsets every evening before the performance), apparently at sea and temperamental in a bewildered kind of way. No matter, reasoned the DDF executive. Madame Rosay was French and the Final was at last on French-Canadian soil. Luckily, two of the eight Festival plays were in French: Le Cercle Molière's production of Molière's *Les Fourberies de Scapin* and La Compagnie de Montréal's *Les Insolités* by local playwright Jacques Languirand.

The adjudicator from France picked Patricia Joudry's *Teach Me How to Cry* for the top trophy (could it really be that French adjudicators tried to favour the English just to show their objectivity, wondered the DDF). But La Compagnie got the Plâque du Festival for the best French production and also the Sir Barry Jackson Trophy for the best Canadian play. So would the Sherbrooke experiment be a turning point for French and English-Canadian relations within the DDF? And would the occasion in Quebec even help bridge the gap between the two founding cultures, a byproduct of DDF work once envisaged by Lord Bessborough? Certainly there were some changes in the French-Canadian picture from the mid 1950's on. For the first time in the organization's history a French-Canadian representative, Yves Bourassa of Montreal, actually began attending DDF meetings on a regular basis. Bourassa was apparently hooked on the bilingual-bicultural dreams of the DDF and quickly introduced other Montrealers to its ranks, notably television director Jean Pelletier and Judge Edouard Rinfret, both of whom would figure significantly in the DDF's future. He was also clearly determined to head for the Top, an ambition that most members of the old-guard DDF executive seemed to approve. After all, a French-Canadian president could surely help squash rumours that the corporation was in the iron grip of an English cartel.

During the late 1950's and early 1960's too, there was a shift in attitude among French-speaking theatre groups concerning DDF participation. English-language professional companies such as Canadian Players, the Crest or the company at Stratford, Ontario, would rather be showered with rotten tomatoes than perform at an "amateur" Dominion Drama Festival. Not so the Quebeckers. DDF victory meant hard cash as well as hardware and they knew they could almost always outclass the English entries.

173

Besides, they had also discovered that the hierarchy of the DDF quickly crumbled under any show of hard-nosed professional conduct. After festivals, French groups had no hesitation in sending off bills for all kinds of extra expenses to DDF headquarters in Ottawa. Confronted with such Gallic brashness, the organization invariably paid up without protest.

French groups began to get touchy about DDF playing dates, both at regional and final festivals. Many of the performers were now working in radio or television and insisted on appearing on nights that would not interfere with their other acting assignments. The final night of the festival, too, was prime time (the adjudicator's enthusiasm always seemed fresher for the play he had just seen) and the French Canadians argued strongly for choice positioning. DDF planners listened patiently and – true to polite Bessborough tradition – always tried to please.

In 1961, French-Canadian interest – both participatory and voluntary – was so strong that it was decided that now was the time to take the plunge and stage the Final Festival in Montreal. Artistically, though, the Big Show was an embarrassment and adjudicator Michel St. Denis (who else could be booked for Montreal?) indicated his disappointment by observing that "the DDF has not improved since 1937." Montreal critic Lawrence Sabbath commented after festival week: "Never did an adjudicator dispense with more unwillingness the largess of trophies than did Michel St. Denis on closing night. Typical of the prize-giving was the reluctance, amounting to sadness, with which he handed out the Best Actress award, noting as he did so that the standard of female performance was considerably below the male level." Later in his article, Sabbath wrote: "The DDF is badly in need of quick and drastic shock treatment if it is to continue as the effective instrument for which it was created in 1933."

But under the firm organizational hand of regional chairman Judge Edouard Rinfret, the 1961 Montreal Festival was a stunning success financially. After the bills were paid – including Western Quebec's mandatory contribution to the national office – it is now legend within the DDF that profit from the festival helped underwrite the region's operations for the next few years.

Later in the 1960's, French-Canadian groups, heavily loaded with young professional talent, continued to clean up at festivals. Two stunning grand slams were in 1967 and 1968 when French-Canadian playwright Robert Gurik's Le Théâtre de la Mandragore and Pierre Voyer's Les Enfants de Voiture walked away with most of the cash and trophies in Saint John's, Newfoundland and Windsor, Ontario respectively. (Interestingly, Quebec's best-known professional groups such as Le Théâtre du Nouveau Monde, Le Rideau Vert and l'Equipe never entered the festivals under their own names as their predecessor Les Compagnons de St. Laurent did. The names of the strong French-Canadian groups were constantly changing though the same professional actors, directors and playwrights turned up for several Finals).

But the tides of separatism were running strongly in Quebec and French Canadianism now clashed badly with what Quebeckers were later to dub "the DDF of sinister memory." English groups still at the amateur level began to resent the easy polish of the French contingents and – even though DDF Control still argued the old cliché that bilingualism was essential for the corporation's character and there was nothing in the Royal Charter to forbid professionals from competing – the French began to get the message. In 1969, the Western Quebec region decided to split its English and French regional playoffs. Only one French-language play, L'Angoisse d'une Jeunesse Partisane by Yvon LeLièvre was entered in the entire zone. Zone Three, Eastern Quebec, held no festival at all. The two French-language troups present at the 1969 Festival at Kelowna, B.C., were Robert Gurik's La Troupe Universitaire de la Laurentienne from Sudbury (which won two awards) and the perennial Le Cercle Molière from St. Boniface (which also won two).

In 1970, Eastern Quebec was again conspicuously absent from DDF competition, though the French in Western Quebec were more active than the previous year (Canadian playwright Robert Tembeck brought Théâtre 1 of Montreal to the 1970 Winnipeg Final with his production of Survivants). But the writing had long been clearly on the wall. "Everyone in Quebec hated the way the DDF was operated," Robert Gurik told critic Lawrence Sabbath in a 1968 interview. "I didn't feel so strongly about it as many others. I guess it did serve me well. But we spent an enormous amount of energy on it, probably far too much. I suppose the general reaction to the organization in the 1960's reflected the political indecision of the province itself."

One reaction was the setting up of a separate, non-professional or non-union theatre organization by former DDF governor Guy Beaulne – then a member of Quebec's Ministry of Cultural Affairs – called L'Association Canadienne de Théâtre Amateur or L'ACTA. The Association first held joint meetings under the wing of the DDF (which did nothing to discourage it) and sent groups to DDF regionals. Later, however, it began organizing its own festivals and meetings. Beaulne once commented about L'ACTA and the DDF in an interview which, in many ways, reflected French-Canadian attitudes toward the corporation since 1933. "There was always the problem of communication," he said. "The DDF tried to be a melting pot, a Tower of Babel. It simply couldn't be done. The French groups always felt lost at the time of the Final Festival. They were simply not in their own environment."

CHAPTER SIX

Finances

1. Well, we've created the thing how are we going to pay for it?

Vincent Massey's prompt $2,500 donation to the Dominion Drama Festival in 1932 was sent directly to DDF treasurer Sir Charles Gordon, president of the Bank of Montreal, with instructions to open the festival's first bank account. The balance began to dwindle almost immediately. A few days after the cheque was cleared, Massey wrote to Sir Charles asking that $500 be transferred to Col. Henry Osborne in Ottawa to help with current expenses.

In the first months of the DDF, Massey was pleased but not unduly astonished to find others shared his practical view of the infant organization. Lord Bessborough sent a $500 cheque to Montreal in early November. Sir Charles himself donated $250, then scribbled a note to Massey: "Sorry, it isn't large but too many calls." Montreal financier J. W. McConnell unexpectedly chipped in with $1,000, a generous gesture which prompted Bessborough to ask Massey whether they should make McConnell an honorary vice-president. McConnell clearly wanted to be helpful – after all, even millionaires appreciated a nod of approval from Rideau Hall – but active participation was not on his mind. He did write to Osborne, though, suggesting names of other possible donors including Frank Meighen, Col. Herbert Molson, Sir Joseph Flavelle, Lady Flora Eaton, Lord Atholstan, Mrs. Jesse Dunlap. Osborne checked out the list with Massey and the chairman replied that Flavelle and Eaton were both good bets but that Mrs. Dunlap seemed to be concentrating her financial interests on a new observatory at Richmond Hill, Toronto. Letters requesting donations winged their way to the entire group, however, and Sir Joseph Flavelle responded with $200 and Col. Molson sent $250.

Osborne himself was sensitive to the fact that he would have to be careful with cash. The first accounting of expenditures of the Dominion Drama Festival suggests that he must have noted the pay-out of every penny with Scrooge-like precision. The account is dated January 23, 1933, and reads: "Disbursements to date total $150.14 for stenographic services, stationery and postage, printing, telephone. I have $349.86 in the Bank of Montreal, Ottawa."

By the following month, however, most of this money had been spent and Massey again wrote to Sir Charles authorizing him to send yet another $500 to Ottawa. In March, Osborne was begging for still more and in early April he wrote an alarmed letter to Massey saying he was now receiving requests from groups concerning their promised advances for half transportation expenses to the Final. Massey instructed Sir Charles to transfer $2,500 to Osborne at once. The festival, it seemed, would not cost peanuts though there was much optimistic talk of it eventually becoming self-supporting. Yet even if it failed to pay for itself, the early organizers reasoned, so worthy an enterprise – backed by celebrated names across the land – would surely open the billfolds of all Canadians who understood the crying need for a national culture.

The fact is, the first festival of 1933 made a small profit. After all expenses were paid from the sale of tickets and private donations, Osborne found there was $419 left over. He immediately communicated the cheerful news to Massey and enclosed details concerning income and outflow of cash. Ticket sales for the first DDF Final brought in $2,472. Regional adjudication expenses siphoned off $1,013. Adjudicator Rupert Harvey was paid $955. The bill for half travelling expenses came to $3,272. Billeting and theatre rental cost $1,732. Provincial amusement tax gobbled $224 and administration expenses came to $637. There were serious consultations about Ways and Means. Osborne suggested it might be better to make a flat grant to Final Festival groups in 1934 that would be based on the distance they had to travel. He also suggested that groups be asked to pay an entry fee at regional level which would help with adjudication expenses. "If there were 100 entries," Osborne pointed out, "that would give us a fund of $2,000 right there!"

Massey agreed with the honorary director about these changes in DDF policy, then instructed the Massey Foundation to send another donation to the Bank of Montreal. This time, the cheque was reduced to $1,000. Lord Bessborough again contributed $500, and in December 1933 Osborne was able to report that with other small gifts dribbling in from around the nation, the DDF pot now contained just over $2,000. By the time of the 1934 Final in Ottawa, the picture had somewhat improved. Private gifts were up another $950 and the new entry-fee brainwave strengthened the festival fund by $1,789. After all the 1934 book-keeping was completed, it was found the Final had earned a net profit of $1,309. "Private subscriptions were way down last year," Osborne reported to Massey. "But the decrease in donors was slightly more than made good by an increase in ticket sales and the entry fees. You'll see our largest item of expense is $2,441 for Harvey's regional adjudication."

By November, 1934, though, increasing DDF expenses had whittled the Montreal bank account to a mere $275 and the billfolds of culture-conscious Canadians were obviously not flying open as readily as the DDF had expected. On paper, it seemed as though the 1935 Final had netted a profit of $1,303 but other expenses had rolled in and the DDF executive faced the unpleasant fact that it would need $750 to balance that year's books.

And 1935 was an important year. After all, Lord Bessborough, the DDF's founding father, would be completing his term of office as Governor General in the Fall and Massey — always conscious of doing the right thing — felt it would be unseemly for His Excellency to leave Canada with his theatrical godchild wallowing in the red. In July of 1935 he decided to write to Col. R. S. McLaughlin of General Motors Canada asking for the $750 and explaining that this was Bessborough's last year in Canada as representative of the Crown. He also outlined the achievements of the DDF and how it had already contributed

179

enormously to the cultural development of the nation.

McLaughlin took a few days to reply, and his letter sounds suspiciously as though he took time in composing it. To begin with, wrote the chief of General Motors Canada, he was indeed honoured to hear from such a distinguished personage as Vincent Massey. "It is easy to understand why you and His Excellency are so deeply interested in affairs of this nature," the letter continues, "But how you could even guess that a country boy like myself living away out in the suburbs would be much, if any, interested in an affair of this kind requires some imagination. However, if you think I should make a contribution, call on me for anything within reason. Say $100?"

Clearly startled by McLaughlin's caustic response, Massey sent the letter on to Osborne with a short memo: "Please return when digested." Then he wrote politely to McLaughlin thanking him for his reply and assuring him that he would "be content to leave the amount of the contribution to you." Osborne was also startled by the McLaughlin communication. "That was a curious letter McLaughlin wrote," he replied. "Nothing has come in yet and as matters stand I think the only thing to do is to let it ride." The matter, apparently, rode on indefinitely.

By the time the December 1935 executive meeting under the new Royal Charter rolled around, both Massey and Bessborough were in England. Lord Tweedsmuir was now patron of the DDF and no one wanted to embarrass the new Governor General with anything as crass as money. Nevertheless, the inner circle of the DDF forced itself to peek into the corporation's moneybags in relation to the Final planned in Ottawa for April, 1936. The minutes of the meeting concerning finance sound as though the officers tried to shove the nasty subject under the rug as expeditiously as possible. "The requirements under this head were explained to the committee," the hired stenographer recorded:

> A conservative estimate of the amount necessary to be found, over and above the normal net receipts from the Final Festival, the entry fees from groups and other sources of income, was between $2,500

and $3,000. Towards this the Massey Foundation had contributed $1,000 and Mr. H. S. Southam $500. The honorary director would exert his best efforts to raise the additional amount required. The meeting expressed its grateful appreciation of the generosity of those who had so kindly assisted the Festival in this manner.

A year later, financial matters within the DDF looked a smidgen brighter. At a November 1936 executive meeting, secretary-treasurer John Aylen cleared his throat, smiled mildly and announced that the corporation had actually accumulated a surplus of $1,400. The executive smiled back and there was an appreciative thumping on the table. But hold on. There would be some deductions from this amount to cover administrative expenses between then and the following April. It was sincerely hoped, though, to add something to the surplus from year to year. Any donations? Well, Aylen replied, Mr. H. S. Southam of Southam Press (who had become the DDF's chairman now Vincent Massey's name had been moved up to vice-president) had promised to contribute a steady $1,000 to the corporation "for a period of years" and the Massey Foundation had also agreed to grant an annual $500. "With this assured support and other prospects or possibilities, it was felt that the financial position was secure for the time being and gave promise of being even more so in the future."

It was the kind of rosy optimism that was to be characteristic of DDF thinking even during its most precarious years to come. Extinction was unthinkable for such a high-born, high-minded enterprise. The scanty discussion concerning finance at a 1937 executive meeting, for example, illustrates the fact that the DDF always firmly believed that something would turn up to rescue the corporation from ruin. "The financial position was considered satisfactory and it was *expected* that the season would close with a moderate surplus on hand," read the minutes. "The assurances which had been given justified the hope that sufficient funds would be available for the next season."

In Winnipeg during the 1938 Final, the subject of

finance was not waved off quite as airily, though the optimistic, forge-on spirit was still there. "Colonel Osborne briefly explained the present financial position of the corporation, stating that the books were carefully audited each year and that there was approximately $670 on hand at the end of 1937," the minutes tell us:

> The organization is small, the only sources of revenue being three: entry fees, the net profit from the final festival and supplementary private donations. He pointed out that the entire organization was voluntary, the only person being paid was the office stenographer and that this year the Central Committee had been able to effect a few more economies and obtained a few more donations. He said that his aim was to build up a reserve and that if any Governor or Regional Committee could assist the Central Executive in this it would be appreciated.
> Answering questions, Colonel Osborne said that the balance in 1936 was $1,094.38 and in 1937 $670. This year, $3,125 had been given in grants-in-aid of the travelling expenses of groups competing in the Final Festival. The cost of regional adjudication was $2,257.43. This year the cost of the final adjudication was somewhat smaller on account of the distance travelled by the Final Adjudicator [Barrett clark from New York] being less than in previous years. Mr. MacTavish gave a short summary of the financial result of the Winnipeg Festival and said the only figure he could give at the present time was that the net profit would not be less than $1,000. He pointed out that Winnipeg had already sent to Ottawa by way of donation a further sum of $1,000.

Well, that wasn't too bad, was it? Could it be that the Dominion Drama Festival really was guided by some divine force? DDF officers nodded without too much surprise when Col. Osborne reported in June, 1939 that the corporation's surplus of $270 had grown to $2,000 by the end of 1938. This

182

announcement could have been yet another example of the DDF's apparent belief that surpluses were magically exempt from the invasion of expenses. An Ottawa *Citizen* report of April 14, 1939, hinted, in fact, that the DDF was in dire financial straits and Col. Osborne himself admitted to the executive that the corporation was not proving to be self-supporting and that "we are seeking ways to remedy the situation." Perhaps the finals and regionals could be held in alternate years to save money. Or perhaps it might be time to ask the federal government for help.

But the June 1939 meeting would be the last time the DDF executive would get together before the outbreak of the Second World War. It was planned then to hold the 1940 Final in Ottawa in the spring. But long before the first crocuses were up in the capital's flower-beds, it had been decided to haul down the DDF curtain. And no one – not even the ever-optimistic Col. Osborne – would predict if and when the glitter, glamour and the well-bred shenanigans of the past seven DDF Finals would ever dominate Canada's theatre scene again.

2.   **It started all over again,
        but money migraines remained.**

Even during the Second World War there was speculation among former regional respresentatives that the DDF had decided to abandon its festivals because it was financially strapped. This speculation smacked somewhat of heresy, of course, because it was surely unthinkable that such middle-class problems as deficits and possible bankruptcy could ever be associated with an organization loaded with Class. But there were critics, too, who loudly complained that the DDF had run out on community theatre at a time when interest was increasing and also when Canada needed to organize entertainments for troops and war charities. Much of this work, incidentally, was left to the regional drama leagues to handle alone, and many continued to organize festivals right through the war years.

The DDF executive itself scattered (though many kept

183

in touch with each other), went into hibernation or passed away during the Second World War. There was family mourning for Nella Jefferis of Toronto and Martha Allan of Montreal. Vincent Massey stayed on in London during the blitz. Col. Henry Osborne and John Aylen worked on wartime projects in Ottawa. There was a brief flurry of interest in the revival of that old dream of a national theatre when the federal government formed a special committee on Reconstruction and Re-establishment in 1944. The idea was that the creative arts stood in a key position as far as the national economy was concerned and the government was thinking of setting aside $10,000,000 to encourage architecture, music, drama, literature, painting and crafts, perhaps through the building of community centres.

The projected plan excited Osborne enormously, and he asked Edgar Stone whether he would represent the DDF at meetings attended by such groups as the Canadian Guild of Potters, the Royal Architectural Institute of Canada, the Canadian Authors' Association, the Canadian Group of Painters and various sports organizations. Stone, apparently, was not impressed because as he reported to Osborne, "each group seems to be approaching the nebulous bait of $10,000,000 of Government appropriation with wide open mouths for their particular interests." Dutifully, he also turned up at a sub-committee meeting to discuss the possible building of community centres and also at another chaired in 1945 by English actor-producer Earl Gray (not to be confused with Canada's ninth Governor General) at the Arts and Letters Club which wrangled over how the acting profession could claim a slice of that $10,000,000.

"Matters are in abeyance," Stone wrote to Osborne. "The meeting at the Arts and Letters Club was opened by John Coulter on the basis of a professional National Theatre with buildings – professional casts – scenic shops etc., including schools of drama and travelling companies. All again focussed on the responsibility of the government footing the initial bill. The meeting see-sawed back and forth between the amateur and the professional point of view. A representative of each group was asked to speak. They were all in favour of some development – the amateurs so long as it protected them and the professionals likewise." Later in the letter he referred to the Toronto Conservatory of Music, which had been approached by the government to take in veterans for a rehabilitation drama course. This it had flatly refused to do "as they claimed it was taking money for preparing veterans for an industry that did not exist. In my opinion, before government or assistance from any other source can be expected, it is up to those who believe a Canadian professional theatre is feasible to prove it by actions first and words afterwards." The $10,000,000 idea never got off the ground.

There were other stirrings on the Canadian drama scene in 1945, however. For one thing, the proposed federal government plan had started Osborne thinking about a possible renaissance of the DDF and the honorary director admitted to a reporter from the Ottawa *Citizen* that various individuals were already giving the idea "serious consideration." For another, two Torontonians, John Adaskin and Arthur Gelber, decided that with the Second World War coming to an end, the time was now ripe to revive the legitimate stage in Canada. The two entrepreneurs formed a company to present a production of *The Hasty Heart*. The play opened in Toronto and Pauline McGibbon (who was to become an active volunteer for the DDF in 1949) was sent as advance agent to book theatres across the country from Winnipeg to Montreal. The project died miserably in Niagara Falls.

The following year, Dora Mavor Moore's New Play Society began staging professional productions in Toronto, then the DDF formed a committee to decide whether it was possible to breathe some life into the organization and perhaps even get a festival under way in 1947. It was a nostalgic meeting. Col. Osborne was older and less energetic but he was as courtly as ever and his very presence recalled the great days of Bessborough and Massey and the carefree fun and games of Festival. Yes, of course the DDF must live again. And of course there must be a festival in 1947, this time under the patronage of Canada's new Governor General, Viscount Alexander of Tunis. All right, so everyone knew His Excellency was more interested in tennis and private parties than culture. But the patronage was traditional, wasn't it? Surely Colonel Osborne could persuade Lord Alexander to follow in the hallowed steps of Bessborough and Tweedsmuir. As for the site of the revived festival, why not make it London, Ontario, where the DDF was suspended in 1939? There was a touch of romance in that. And financing? Well, something would turn up, even if everyone connected with the corporation had to shell out from their own pockets.

Costs were cut to the bone for the Bargain Basement DDF show in 1947. Regions held their own playoffs and selected and paid their own adjudicators. No grants were made in aid of travelling expenses for invited groups. The cost of importing a final festival judge from abroad seemed prohibitive and besides, things were still pretty unsettled in Europe. It was unanimously decided by the new DDF executive committee to hand the prestigious job to Professor Emrys M. Jones of the University of Saskatchewan, a Welsh-born Canadian who happened to be on the 1946–7 executive committee anyway. The main thing, everyone agreed, was to get things swinging again. After all, Bessborough and Massey wasted precious little time after the October 1932 meeting, didn't they?

Surprisingly, the DDF made some money on the 1947 London Final. Interest in the revival was so high in the city and surrounding areas that the Grand Theatre was packed for most performances. Just as surprisingly for the traditionalists, the Canadian adjudicator was as much of a hit with audiences as pre-war luminaries such as Barrett Clark and Michel St. Denis. "Now, having successfully stirred itself up, dressed itself up and stepped out again," wrote John Coulter in *Saturday Night*, "the Dominion Drama Festival seems little the worse for its long sleep. The Festival has come back strongly. It is again a Canadian institution, perhaps the greatest artistic institution in the country."

But even great artistic institutions had to be nourished. Executive pockets were again emptied to help stage the 1948 Final in Ottawa – where the DDF returned to its expensive pre-war tradition and imported British actor-producer Robert Speaight as final adjudicator – and the committee was able to raise $2,350 with that invaluable old brainwave, entry fees. But in 1949 when the festival shifted to Toronto, new avenues of income had to be explored. One plan, which produced instant bleats of agony from across the country, was a decision to levy "contributions" from the thirteen regions which then made up the DDF. Prince Edward Island and Eastern Quebec were let off the hook relatively lightly with a hundred-dollar levy each, because the DDF rationalized that entries from these areas were generally low. Western, Central and Eastern Ontario – then the three busiest and most prosperous regions in the festival – were expected to chip in with the highest levy of $1,500 apiece.

In 1949, too – as it had in Winnipeg during the 1930's – the corporation unashamedly canvassed Toronto for program advertising. Those approached could scarcely refuse. The Robert Simpson Co. took a full page and so did that other old friend from the past, the Bank of Montreal. Mona Coxwell, chief of Samuel French's Toronto office (who had staunchly supported the DDF in her own publication *Curtain Call* during the 1930's) bought half a page to plug her company's stock of plays. Birks Silversmiths – surely a high-toned enough firm to be associated with the gilt-edged DDF – co-operated by taking a full-page advertisement and, not surprisingly, so did the T. Eaton Co.

That year in Toronto was traumatic in many ways for the Dominion Drama Festival. The Saskatchewan Incident was rumbling over the heads of the executive. Chairman D. Park Jamieson and his trusty aide, Dr. Alan Skinner, were growing restless about their heavy load of responsibilities. Then there was always that unpleasant subject, money, money, money. The regional contribution idea was unpopular, of course, but it had to be tried. At the executive meeting in Toronto, Jamieson passed a tired hand over his bald head and got down to further brass tacks. The finances of the corporation, announced the chairman, were "in an extremely serious situation." Future policy would depend largely on the profit from the Toronto Final which, he sighed, would cost the DDF $25,000 in expenses. Right now, the DDF had managed to harvest $9,000 from private subscriptions. The Province of Ontario had given $2,000. The City of Toronto had donated $1,500. Simpson's and Eaton's had both paid in $1,500 and other individual contributors had been worth $500 apiece. Fun and games, eh? Even with the prospect of the Governor General's arrival, private

187

parties and full-dress balls, Final Week loomed gloomily. After it was all over, Jamieson acted swiftly and asked two influential DDF supporters, David Ongley and Charles Band, to look into the creaking machinery of the corporation and come up with some helpful suggestions the following year in Calgary. Obviously, things could not go on this way.

At that time, there was only one ray of hope. Vincent Massey was back in Canada after his long stay in London and had been asked by Prime Minister Louis St. Laurent to head a Royal Commission on National Development in the Arts, Letters and Sciences – a possible spin-off from the ill-fated Re-Development idea of 1944. The DDF, scenting the possibility of federal government support for the cause at last (and surely Massey of all people would thump the DDF drums), prepared a detailed, 39-page brief concerning the corporation which was presented to the Commission by D. Park Jamieson and H. Alan Skinner in July 1949 after the depressing Toronto Final. Massey had been kept in touch with DDF affairs by Osborne, but he clearly needed to be filled in as far as recent events were concerned. He listened attentively to the DDF brief, even parts of its history that he must have understood better than the current chairman of the corporation.

"Much is left to be done," Jamieson read:

> The progress of the DDF has been hampered because from its inception it has not been financially self-supporting and has had to rely on yearly donations and on volunteer help. New fields of work are continually opening up. . . . The DDF has now a difficult problem on its hands. With its present recurring and increasing deficits to be met by private donations each year, it is not in a position to adequately carry on its present task, let alone undertake the great volume of additional work and services which are required if the future of community drama and national drama in Canada are not to suffer. The Festival must find some assured means of continuing financial support, sufficient to meet the yearly deficit and establish a permanent headquarters and office

with a small paid staff if it is not to cut its activities back to a size where they can again be taken care of by volunteer help.

Massey was finally to admit when his report was tabled in June 1951 (the Canada Council, recommended in the report, would not be born until 1957):

> Nothing in Canada has done so much for the amateur theatre as the Dominion Drama Festivals which, apart from the war years, have been held since 1933. To make its work fully effective, however, the DDF needs help in meeting recurring and increasing deficits (now borne by private donations) and in extending its activities. . . . Drama groups have pointed out to us the impossible financial problems involved in sending a company of players over great distances to compete. In 1950, only two groups in Nova Scotia expressed any interest in the Calgary Final Festival and no company east of Quebec City was in fact represented.

(Massey apparently overlooked the fact that there was more involved in this lack of French-Canadian co-operation than paucity of travel grants from the DDF). "We are informed," continued the report, "that many local drama societies are now reluctant to enter the festival since if they win their regional they cannot attend the national competition. . . . We found widespread agreement that it would be a serious setback to our national understanding if for financial or other reasons acting groups in Canada are compelled to abandon the Festival or if it must restrict its further development."

Massey asked journalist and playwright Robertson Davies (already an active supporter of the DDF) to write a section on Drama for his report and Davies decided to design the piece as a dialogue between two traditional English theatrical characters, Lovewit and Trueman.

Trueman says angrily: "The Dominion Drama Festival is one of Canada's cultural glories, but Canada characteristically does not know it. The Dominion Government is indifferent to it and hundreds of thousands of citizens either know nothing of it or are profoundly misinformed about it. It receives no penny from the public purse. And yet it engages the attention of much of the ablest artistic talent of the country and it provides in its final yearly festival a week of drama which has won the sincere admiration of extremely able professional men of the theatre who are brought here to judge it. I cannot think of any other country in the world where a comparable effort would be so persistently snubbed by the Government. Even on the lowest level, its publicity value to the country is enormous. The libel that Canada hates the arts is more strongly supported by the resolute slighting of the DDF than in any other single matter." Well, the Dominion Drama Festival still had friends in high places, it seemed. Perhaps something would turn up after all.

3.   Think commercial.

The Band Report, as the reorganizational study tackled by Charles Band and David Ongley was dubbed, reached the ears of the assembled governors of the Dominion Drama Festival at the Calgary Final of 1950. It was obvious the two men had heeded the complaints of Jamieson. One of the report's strongest recommendations was that the DDF should open a permanent headquarters in Ottawa and hire a secretary-treasurer and a stenographer. At a time when the DDF had less than $100 in its bank account, this seemed like a cavalier gesture but the Band Report was promptly accepted. At the same meeting, the corporation agreed to a suggestion that Father Emile Legault of Les Compagnons de St. Laurent should launch a national magazine for the DDF, to be called *Theatre Canada*. The magazine made its appearance for one glossy issue in 1951 – though it was revived in several forms during the next two decades – and lost the hard-pressed DDF $2,500.

The staff idea turned out better. Secretary-treasurer Richard MacDonald, a handsome, huskily-built Englishman who was lured from his job as Co-ordinator of Cultural Activities for the Government of Alberta, would eventually become better-known across the country than the DDF's presidents.

Other financial matters were thrashed out in Calgary. Ongley and Band asked for – and got – an honorary treasurer with administrative ability (Donald Kerlin of Montreal Trust accepted the voluntary job), a finance committee and a nominating committee. The probers said they felt the beefed-up organization could struggle through the year on a budget of around $12,000 and Jamieson personally signed a note with the Royal Bank of Canada for an overdraft of $11,000. Floyd Chalmers of the Maclean-Hunter Publishing Company – who had been an honorary patron at the 1949 Final – contributed $1,000 and the executive promised to hustle around and liquidate the bank debt as soon as possible. Chalmers' $1,000, though, was the only hard cash ever to go into the DDF pot at that time. As David Ongley was to remember wryly years later: "So there we had hired Dick MacDonald from Edmonton as our secretary-treasurer, our bank balance was flat and we were carrying an $11,000 overdraft. Incredible optimism." One other thing the Band Report had to say about DDF finances was that it would be impossible for the regions to carry the corporation and that split financial responsibility was unfeasible. "Your committee recommends that financial responsibility for the DDF must rest with the executive," the report read. It was the beginning of the corporation's divorce from its long-standing dependence on private patronage and its growing determination to think commercial.

The Dominion Drama Festival's eight-year association with Calvert Distillers Ltd. began in a casual way. Not long after the meeting in Edmonton, a group of DDF executive officers met to discuss the problem of ways and means at a downtown Toronto hotel. David Ongley, who seems to have taken charge of the DDF's financial headache at this stage, mentioned it was too bad the age of aristocratic patronage was dead. But surely there were some foundations or business corporations that could be tapped for funds? Murray Wilson, a member of the Central Ontario Drama League and Toronto manager for Calvert's, spoke up at this point and said that perhaps his company might be interested. After all, Seagram's was dabbling in the art-exhibition field. He volunteered to call head office in Montreal and arrange for a meeting with Ongley and Jamieson the next time top Calvert executives were in Toronto. Well, it was a hope, anyway. The DDF officers agreed to the plan.

The first contact between the DDF and Calvert's was at the company's Toronto office a few months later. The Calvert contingent was headed by M. M. Schneckenburger, advertising-sales manager for the company. Ongley spoke for the DDF. Schneckenburger was sympathetic but it was obvious he was not sure it was politic for a whisky distillery to become promotionally involved in the cultural field. Could there perhaps be a backlash? Ongley pressed on, however, producing facts, figures and arguments. Schneckenburger continued to be cautious and suggested further meetings. The meetings continued, on and off, for months. Jamieson attended some, but finally asked Ongley to carry the ball, together with another emerging personality in the DDF, Pauline McGibbon. The back-and-forth discussions between the DDF team and the Calvert squad between 1950 and 1951 must have been nerve-wracking. Calvert's clearly wanted to help, and were even becoming convinced that the tie-in with the DDF might actually enhance their status in the eyes of a public still persuaded that booze and tobacco were the agents of Satan. But still, the odds were tricky. The DDF, on the other hand, was aware it was involved in a life-or-death struggle for the organization. Yet the negotiators also knew there could be outraged protests, both from DDF supporters and the public, once the news was out.

At the time of the London Final of 1951, matters had jelled to the point where the DDF liaison men could test the mood of the corporation's inner circle concerning the proposed Calvert sponsorship. As predicted, there was some shock. But after all, nothing was at all definite and the financial situation within the organization was as gloomy as ever. Amidst collective signs and nods of approval (the staunchest DDF backers of the plan were Catharine Brickenden and Fred Phelps of London and Dorothy White of Ottawa), the negotiators were authorized to carry on. They did. Prospects for an agreement began to look so bright, in fact, that Ongley and Mrs. McGibbon began thinking about what the new trophies should look like.

Certainly it seemed as though the possiblity of a bail-out by Calvert Distillers would be in the nick of time. Early in 1952, Jamieson (who had by then decided to "retire" after twenty years with the embattled DDF) wrote a depressed memo to all governors of the corporation. "At the present time, we owe the bank over $8,200," read the memo, "and we must provide for general and festival expenditures of $9,500 up until the the of May, 1952. Our probable additional receipts from entry fees are $1,700 and we hope to receive at least $3,000 profit from the final festival. This means we will conclude this year's festival with a deficit of approximately $13,000 unless further financial contributions are received in the meantime. It is obvious that unless substantial contributions are immediately forthcoming no grants in aid of travelling expenses can be made in 1952 and the question of the continuance of the festival after this year and its future must be considered."

Not that DDF supporters were unaware of the continuing emergency. "Honorary governors" had made an appearance within the corporation, a title which could be bought (working governors were elected) for the sum of $100 a year. In the beginning, contributions were voluntary and many of the honoraries were bona fide governors of the DDF, anyway. In 1953, however, policy-makers of the corporation made their first desperate move to set a regional quota of honorary governors, a ploy which failed miserably from the beginning.

In the meantime, though, talks with the Calvert people were beginning to sound serious. But what if there were a slip-up? Late in March, 1952, a self-appointed DDF committee which included Pauline McGibbon, David Ongley, Murray Wilson, Roy Stewart, Fred Phelps and Richard MacDonald sat down to talk about the Calvert deal and what would happen if the plan was rejected in Saint John, New Brunswick, during Festival Week that year. Ongley and Pauline McGibbon began the discussion by reporting on their long negotiations with Calvert's. If the deal was completed, they told their colleagues, it would mean the DDF would receive an injection of $15,000 or even more for a minimum of two years. Calvert's seemed willing to sign, seal and deliver. So should the DDF accept the offer? If the organization turned it down, it would clearly be necessary to look for another sponsor or throw in the towel. Even if the DDF did accept the Calvert offer, in fact, another $10,000 to $15,000 would have to be found in order to carry on. Travelling grants had been an on and off policy and that, of course, was a bad thing.

The committee began to kick the financial gong around still further. It was agreed, somewhat wearily, that the regions had always been "spoon-fed." They had not been meeting their set "contributions." Well, perhaps the levies were too high. After more discussion, the list was revised with Western and Central Ontario at the top of the levy heap with $750 each. Prince Edward Island and Eastern Quebec came last with annual contributions of $100. If all regions co-operated, levies could bring in a total of $4,250. A jacked-up scale of entry fees would syphon another $3,750 into the DDF fund and, together with levies, this guaranteed the DDF an annual $8,000. Honorary governors? Definitely. The regions should be made aware of the fact they were morally responsible to flush out honorary governors. If the regions met all their obligations, the committee felt the DDF could count on an income of $37,000 a year. Provided the Calvert deal was accepted, of course.

The April 1952 Canadian Press story concerning Park Jamieson's departure from the DDF chairmanship that also contained hints about distillery sponsorship sparked an angry telegram to Vincent Massey – who had then been appointed Governor General – from Aba Bayefsky, chairman for the Assembly for Canadian Arts. "Urge you request Government to take immediate action to help finance Dominion Drama Festival," read the wire. "Sponsoring of festival by advertisement minded commercial interests would make Canada laughing stock among nations and seriously undermine our cultural prestige stop all Canadians would applaud Government backing of festival." Bayefsky's appeal was answered by J. F. Delaute, administrative secretary to the Governor General. His wire read: "Representations submitted in your telegram April 20 re Dominion Drama Festival have been brought to attention appropriate authorities of Government of Canada."

Rumours were already flying about "a distillery paying for the DDF" by the time governors and invited groups arrived in Saint John later that month. Was it really true? Well, everyone would know when Governors' Court convened during the week. At Government House, Massey was at the receiving end of more complaints. "Urge Government financial support of Dominion Drama Festival," wired one DDF governor, William B. Watkins. "Meeting Thursday noon to consider the sponsorship of festival by Calvert Distilleries stop some of committee think this solution of financial problem in bad taste stop please help." Massey wired back: "Very sorry to hear about financial problem stop you will understand that in present circumstances I am unable to be of assistance stop have sent your telegram to the Prime Minister's office."

Massey was true to his word. Watkins' telegram was shuttled to Louis St. Laurent with a covering memo from Lionel Massey to the Prime Minister's secretary, Ross Martin. "Naturally we can take no action here and I have, therefore, sent the attached telegram in reply. I spoke to Jack Pickersgill this morning on the telephone and told him I was sending it down." As it happened, the gesture was unnecessary. William Watkins had already sent a duplicate telegram to St. Laurent. Ross Martin replied on behalf of the Prime Minister on May 1:

> Mr. St. Laurent wishes you to know His Excellency the Governor General has informed him he received a similar message to the one you sent to this office. As you know, the estimates for the expenditures of the Federal Government have already been prepared for the current fiscal year and, in making them up, the Government had to take into account the very heavy outlays that must be made by national defence. Mr. St. Laurent wishes me to assure you he is not unaware of the valuable work being done by the Festival. At the same time he feels sure you will realize that what you have suggested is something which cannot be considered on the spur of the moment and that it is related to the whole series of matters referred to in the Report of the Massey Commission. The Government has been giving consideration to all the recommendations of the Report

195

and, once decisions have been reached in respect to the various matters connected with it, the appropriate announcement will be made.

Pauline McGibbon and David Ongley stopped over in Montreal on their way to New Brunswick and met again with Schneckenburger. Yes, the deal was on, but Calvert's said they would pull out without any problems if the DDF itself decided against the plan. Ongley said he would call in again on the way home from the Final and let Schneckenburger know what went on at Governor's Court. As it happened, the meeting was noisy but capitulation was definitely in the air. It had been a hectic year for the DDF, a tired-looking Jamieson told the governors, then he said the words everyone had been waiting to hear: that Calvert Distillers and the executive had a proposal to place before the meeting. There were mutters and a scraping of chairs but Jamieson plunged on. Together with the cost of designing new trophies, donating cash prizes, helping with advertising and programs plus a grant to the DDF's national office, the distillery would be spending around $25,000, explained Jamieson. More mutterings. The retiring chairman added that the present proposal would in no way affect any possible future grants from the Federal Government. Then he sat back and listened silently to the arguments, pro and con. Some governors simply threw up their hands and admitted they had no idea what to do. There were problems about proxies. Should those acting for absent governors vote for or against the plan? Finally, Jamieson urged the meeting to get down to the nitty-gritty of the question at hand. Would the current board of governors allow Lord Bessborough's dream to die or not? Without too much more discussion the motion to accept the Calvert offer was moved, seconded and carried.

A jubilant Ongley flew to Montreal a few days later and completed details of the Calvert sponsorship with Schneckenburger. The financial troubles of the Dominion Drama Festival, the lawyer felt, were now surely over. He was not worried about comments and complaints. Apparently there was insurrection in Manitoba and representatives of the region were threatening to pull out of the DDF. In Winnipeg, Lady Madge

Tupper had written a letter to the editor of the *Free Press* protesting the "unbelievable" plan. In the House of Commons, Member of Parliament Joseph Noseworthy asked if the government was considering any action to prevent the "substitution of a distillers' trophy for the Bessborough Trophy as the top award in the Dominion Drama Festival" and Louis St. Laurent replied almost word for word as he did in his letter to DDF governor William Watkins. The *Ottawa Gazette* published an editorial headed "Let's Hang Our Heads In Shame" which mourned: "Let's not blame the distillers or the governors. Let us blame ourselves and hang our heads in shame as a wanting people. Better to have drama supported by somebody who thinks enough of drama to support it than to have no drama at all." Dozens of editorials urged the federal government to implement the recommendations of the Massey Commission.

One of the last letters received by Park Jamieson as chairman of the DDF concerned the Calvert controversy, and it must have confirmed his decision to sever connections with the corporation he had helped since 1932. On May 12, 1952, an officer of the Royal Bank of Canada wrote:

> As you know, the governors of the DDF are presently indebted to us to the extent of $10,400 which is secured by your personal guarantee and, when the matter was last discussed with you, we pointed out that we expected to have the obligation taken care of by June 1, 1952. As we have recently been reading with a great deal of interest the newspaper reports and publicity which you have been receiving in connection with the new sponsorship and the success of the Festival at Saint John, we shall appreciate it very much if you will let us know as soon as possible when and from what source the loan on our books is to be liquidated.

4.   Whisky and Broadcasting

Calvert Distillers made it quite clear to the executive of the Dominion Drama Festival that the firm would not be responsible for any previous debts incurred by the corporation. But after the Saint John Final, the company pitched in to honour the two-year agreement its officers had worked out with David Ongley and Pauline McGibbon. Fourteen handsome trophies, carved in wood by sculptors Frances Loring, Florence Wyle and Sylvia Daoust, cost Calvert's almost $8,000. The company sent the DDF's national office a cheque for $15,000. This included a grant of $12,600 toward national office expenses and $2,400 to be paid out in cash awards to regional and final festival winners. Money was also made available to help print festival programs.

Perfect. But there was still the nagging question of whether the DDF's financial angel would flap away after the two-year agreement expired. Ongley, who was then acting chief of the DDF because of president Dorothy White's illness, obviously believed Calvert's would renew. In 1953 he wrote an anticipatory memo to members of the DDF executive outlining the current financial position of the corporation and revealing the demands he planned to make when the distillery's two-year partnership with the DDF came to an end. The memo began with a complaint:

Since the sponsorship of Calvert's, revenue from other sources, such as honorary governors and smaller donations, has dropped an estimated $4,000. Operating expenses have increased, even though the sponsors have helped with such things as the DDF newsletter. But the cost of mailing has doubled as it has been sent out with a Calvert booklet. The director's travelling expenses have increased, partly because of increased hotel and railway costs, but he has had to entertain more frequently and because of the Calvert association, guests seem to think refreshments are part of the whole thing.

Ongley told the executive that when time came to ask for a renewal he was going to suggest Calvert's increase their grant by $10,000, partly to employ a full-time theatrical director (to be known as the Calvert Drama Adviser) who would circulate around the regions. He pointed out that next time a deal was negotiated, Calvert Distillers would not have to shell out any more cash for trophies.

The Calvert company did renew their agreement with the DDF the following year but there were no extra bonuses at that time. Apparently the distillery believed they were getting good value for their patronage, however. For one thing, the name Calvert was always prominently mentioned when the top DDF trophy was awarded at the Final. Richard MacDonald, the DDF's director, always pointed out during press interviews and broadcasts that Calvert's were behind the DDF all the way. Ongley reported meticulously to Schneckenburger concerning the number of times he had dropped the Calvert name at public gatherings and even at meetings of the Canadian Bar Association. "The Regina Festival was a success as far as theatre was concerned," read an Ongley communiqué to Schneckenburger in May 1955. "Publicity was difficult due to the damned Saskatchewan liquor laws."

Renewal time was coming up again in 1955, though, and this time Calvert's not only planned to continue with the DDF deal but also to become more generous. For one thing, the company agreed to pay an annual $1,500 toward an insurance and pension policy for DDF director Richard MacDonald. For another, Schneckenburger told Ongley the distillery was planning a national advertising campaign to inform Canadian readers about how whisky was boosting culture. The expensive layouts, which appeared in every major newspaper and magazine across the country in 1955 and 1956, featured line drawings of rehearsals in progress and other theatrical goings-on, garnished with the slogan: "Calvert helps build a living Canadian theatre." The DDF was naturally ecstatic at this turn of events. "Our executive is concerned in only one thing," wrote an impressed Ongley to Schneckenburger. "They feel that more publicity should be possible for Calvert's and are extremely anxious that everything be done as far as we can on our side to assist in this end."

Ongley continued to be zealous in his personal publicity campaign for the DDF's sponsors. Even he agreed, though, that perhaps he had gone somewhat overboard with his celebrated "buy Calvert" letter before the 1956 Sherbrooke Festival. The Calvert company itself stayed quietly out of the picture during the raging controversy, but when the DDF again approached the firm in 1957 with renewal proposals for the following year, there were signs that the distillery was beginning to feel it was plunging too deeply into the sponsorship game. In March that year, MacDonald was asked to meet with Schneckenburger to discuss possible ways of saving on Calvert's DDF spending. Schneckenburger pointed out that during 1955-56, ending with the Sherbrooke Final, the company had actually paid out $36,812.96 on DDF activities and he wanted to slice this back to $28,000, including the straight grant. It was decided to save $4,000 on program covers. Press receptions paid for by the distillery were to be chopped and the $2,500 Calvert Ball – a feature of the Final – would be trimmed to cost no more than $1,500. Schneckenburger also indicated there would be a cut in publicity services.

It was a blow, but the DDF continued to believe that underneath the bluster, Calvert's was all heart. After the 1957 meeting with Schneckenburger, MacDonald was authorized to write to the distillery requesting an additional $5,000 to the usual $15,000 straight grant at renewal time. The letter included such phrases as "we are in a serious situation financially" and "we are making a drive for funds from our sources, although there is the usual opposition because of present corporate support" and "people approached also think the Canada Council will take care of us, but there is no guarantee of this." The letter must have struck a chord. The extra $5,000 came through.

But two years later, when Col. Yves Bourassa was president of the DDF, indications were that Calvert's heart was hardening. The plan at the end of 1959 was not only to seek a renewal in 1960 but to beg for more money as well. Bourassa decided he would try for an interview at the top, with Samuel Bronfman, president of Distillers Corporation, the parent company of Calvert's, Adams and Seagram's. He asked Schneckenburger if he could arrange the meeting. In a September 1959 letter to the inner-circle group called the Calvert Liaison Committee, Bourassa wrote: "Schneck, of course, guessed that the purpose of the proposed meeting was to ask for greater financial assistance from Calvert, so he probed a little. I did not say very much but I did say our situation was becoming impossibly tight. He is obviously very sympathetic. He realizes that our organization is growing fast and that while many new activities are added to our program we get no help whatever for administration. I am sure that with a proper presentation of our case we can reach our objective of $30,000 a year from Calvert in the future."

Nothing came of Bourassa's move to confront Bronfman (or Mr. Sam, as the industrialist was popularly known) in 1959. Instead, the Liaison Committee worked at a new draft brief which Bourassa intended to drop on Schneckenburger's desk in the early new year. Calvert's advertising manager proved to be elusive in 1960, however. In February he called Bourassa at his office in Montreal and asked him to come to Calvert's headquarters. The meeting was a shock to the DDF president. The Calvert company, Schneckenburger announced, had decided to drop its sponsorship of the DDF but the distillery was willing to try and help the corporation find another patron. If no one turned up by the end of the year, Calvert's would see what could be done to provide some temporary financial relief.

Stunned by the news, Bourassa returned to his office, then later telephoned Schneckenburger and asked if Mr. Sam knew what was going on. Schneckenburger admitted he had no idea whether Mr. Sam knew or not. Well then, decided Bourassa, he would let Bronfman in on the news. He did it, he believed, as subtly as possible. Governor General Georges Vanier – then vice-regal patron of the DDF – would attend Awards Night at the 1960 Final in Vancouver, and Bourassa wrote Bronfman inviting him to attend as the DDF's guest. "The Governor General will be presenting the Calvert Trophy," read the letter, "and, of course, this will be the last occasion of this kind because of Calvert's decision to end its sponsorship." To MacDonald in Ottawa, he wrote: "If Bronfman did

201

not know we were being dropped, he knows now. Let's wait and see."

Bourassa waited and waited. He petitioned everyone who knew Mr. Sam to plead the DDF's cause. He knew that DDF executive officers Vida Peene and Father Levesque – and also Sam Bronfman – were members of the Canada Council and Bourassa asked Miss Peene if she would tackle Bronfman on the question of Calvert's sponsorship at the Council's meeting on April 11, 1960. Bronfman did not turn up at the meeting because it was Jewish Passover.

Finally, Bourassa's well-known temper bristled. He marched to the head office of Distillers Corporation and asked to see Sam Bronfman. Bronfman received him. Well, thumped the DDF president, had Mr. Bronfman received his invitation to the Vancouver festival? No, Mr. Bronfman had not. Well then, did Mr. Bronfman know that the Calvert company was dropping its sponsorship of the DDF? No, Mr. Bronfman did not, and besides he was becoming very angry. Leaning across his desk he told Bourassa that he had no intention of interfering with a decision made by the head of one of his companies and that he would not lift a finger to do anything about it. Bourassa was obviously dismissed. "The bridges are in flames now," he wrote to MacDonald after the disastrous interview. "In the meantime, I don't mind telling you that when I next have a drink of Seagram's, Calvert's or Adams Gin it will be a frosty Friday." At the same time he wrote politely to a badly-ruffled Mr. Sam: "Thank you for throwing light on a move which has puzzled all of us." He added that the DDF was grateful for Calvert's contribution to its work.

But what about another sponsor? In July, 1960, Bourassa called a meeting of the DDF executive to "discuss specific details for sponsorship with representatives of a large national corporation." The corporation turned out to be that old ally of the DDF, the Bank of Montreal. There was a flurry of negotiations then the bank backed out in August. At the end of the month, the executive sat down again to think up some new ideas. Roy Stewart, the DDF's incoming president for 1961 suggested that Bourassa approach Vincent Massey. There were clucks of disapproval. Hadn't Massey done enough already for the Dominion Drama Festival? Well, how about the O'Keefe Brewing Co.? They had just made a big splash in Toronto with their new theatre, hadn't they? MacDonald had some good news. He had been talking to Jim Allard, a vice-president of the Canadian Association of Broadcasters who seemed to think there was a fair chance his organization might be interested in joining up with the DDF. He had sent out letters to CAB members concerning the idea. There was excited response which MacDonald cooled as quickly as possible. Allard was holidaying somewhere on Prince Edward Island and would not be back in Ottawa until the end of August. In any case, the feelers Jim had sent out to CAB affiliates would not be in until then. In the meantime, it was suggested that *The Case for Sponsorship*, a DDF handbook which had been prepared for prospective donors, be sent to Fred Mendel, president of International Packers in Saskatoon. Someone remembered Mendel was interested in the arts.

MacDonald had a long session with Jim Allard early in September. Allard assured the DDF director that he would have an answer concerning possible CAB sponsorship by the end of the month, but by September 13 Allard was telephoning the DDF's office with the news that the CAB executive had approved the principal of sponsorship. "Jim has directed a letter to all the affiliated station managers to get their approval of the sponsorship and acceptance of the amount which each would have to contribute," MacDonald wrote to Bourassa. "Jim has assured me he will have a definite decision for our next executive meeting in Montreal, October 15." He added that Allard had mentioned a contribution of around $150 per affiliate station. There were 200 members of the CAB, so this would mean a grant to the DDF of $30,000 per year!

The suspense dragged on. There was no definite decision by October 15 but by October 28, Allard reported to MacDonald that sixty per cent of the CAB's members had approved and forty per cent had not. "It's hard to say whether we're winning or not," MacDonald complained to Bourassa. At the end of November, the DDF director was writing to Roy Stewart: "Jim Allard advised that to date $17,000 has been guaranteed by CAB affiliates. His directors are now meeting in Ottawa and he says he is sure that $3,000 will be added from national CAB funds to make up $20,000. After checking with Yves [Bourassa] and Don [McGibbon, then treasurer of the DDF], I told Allard we would gratefully accept $20,000. Thank goodness we are now virtually assured of CAB sponsorship. McGibbon points out it will be much easier to approach other corporations now for additional donations. Because of the nature of CAB business there can be no question of competitive conflict."

The early weeks of 1961 were stirring times for the Dominion Drama Festival. The Canadian Association of Broadcasters agreed to a five-year sponsorship of the ailing corporation. Then, Baxter Publishing Co. of Toronto suggested it might be a good idea to revive the *Theatre Canada* magazine idea and circulate it as a national theatre arts publication. The DDF was to supply copy concerning community theatre, and the Canadian Theatre Centre was to handle news of the professional stage. Only two issues were ever published. As MacDonald told the sad tale to Guy Beaulne in June 1961: "*Theatre Canada* has been discontinued after two editions. A little more than 15,000 copies of the second issue were distributed by mail across Canada but only 84 new subscribers were secured. Three hundred and fifty came from our own list, so this makes a total of only 434 subscribers. The publisher lost $1,000 on the first issue and more than $800 on the second. He is now adding a section on theatre to his established publication *The Canadian Commentator*. We are continuing and expanding the bulletin we started a month ago. . . ."

But cheer up. The CAB had come through, hadn't it? Something always turned up at the last moment. And before long, contributions from CAB's member stations were arriving at the DDF's office in Ottawa and spot announcements were winging across the airwaves: "The Little Theatre in this community is a springboard for dramatic talent. This station, as a member of the Canadian Association of Broadcasters, contributes to the support of the Dominion Drama Festival, the *ultimate* in Canadian Little Theatre."

5.   The Nervous Sixties.

With the Canadian Association of Broadcasters safely in the sponsor's chair for at least five years, the Dominion Drama Festival checked out its financial resources. The Canada Council was helping to underwrite travel grants and adjudication expenses. The Province of Quebec was contributing $8,000 a year to provide a bilingual assistant to DDF director Richard MacDonald (plus a $3,000 scholarship to be awarded at the Final) and the CAB itself had promised to approach other possible benefactors such as the Marconi company, RCA Victor and General Electric. It was a tempting moment to hope the DDF's financial crisis was over, but there were other bleak clouds on the horizon.

Quotas for honorary governors and regional levies, for example, continued to ooze into the national office as reluctantly as molasses out of a can. If all the regions co-operated it was estimated that income from these two sources alone would total a helpful $14,800 a year but in 1961, just $8,800 had been harvested from around the Dominion. During a finance committee meeting at Winnipeg's Fort Garry Hotel in 1962 (chaired by the DDF's treasurer, Donald McGibbon), it was decided to elect a representative in each region who would keep a watchful eye on the financial responsibilities of the area. It was also agreed to create a brand-new category of governors. These would be called "sustaining members" and would be asked to donate $25 each a year to the DDF. McGibbon warned representatives "to be careful not to approach anyone who might be expected to become an honorary governor at $100." He did introduce an extra ray of hope at the meeting. As treasurer of Imperial Oil Limited, he boasted influential contacts with top corporations and with the conflicting Calvert sponsorship at an end, he felt it was time to pass the DDF hat around Toronto's boardrooms as soon as possible.

There were some smiles around the committee table. The DDF badly needed a moral lift as it entered the 1960's. Lack of cash had been an embarrassment in more ways than one. Apart from handcuffing the corporation as far as internal expansion was concerned, money problems had been the direct cause of the DDF abandoning its dream of establishing a National Theatre School and reluctantly passing the ball to the professionally-oriented Canadian Theatre Centre. Everyone connected with the DDF knew the organization had discussed the possibility of such a school as long ago as 1952 and had been active in bringing director Michel St. Denis (the founder of the Old Vic school in London) to Halifax as guest speaker at the 1958 Final. The DDF, with the help of private donors, had also persuaded St. Denis to boost the idea in Quebec City, Montreal, Ottawa and Toronto – a journey he made on his way to establishing a theatre school at the Juilliard School of Music in New York. But where would the money for the Canadian school come from? After an endless succession of committee meetings between 1958 and 1960 – during which there was a running battle as to whether the French-English school should be established in Toronto or Montreal – the DDF backed out as active organizers, a Theatre School "blueprint" was prepared under the leadership of professional director David Gardner, and the CTC swung into action.

In 1962, the DDF was still smarting over the fact that the CTC would always get the credit for founding the National Theatre School. Former president Yves Bourassa, in fact, continued to shake his fist over the sad chain of events, insisting it was he and DDF colleague, Jean Pelletier, who had persuaded the government of Quebec to fork over $50,000 to get the school going in an office at the Théâtre du Nouveau Monde in Montreal. Jean Gascon, who then ran the theatre and had been appointed head of the Theatre School as well, conducted his first classes in the Legion Building at 1191 Mount St. And the "DDF's" Michel St. Denis remained on friendly call as the school's artistic advisor. Oh well, at least the corporation was represented on the board of the National Theatre School – and on the board of the CTC as well. It wasn't as though the DDF's long association with Canadian theatre was unrecognized.

In the meantime, though, the thirst for recognition had to take a back seat to the pressing problem of survival. At a 1963 finance committee meeting in Kitchener, Ontario, treasurer Don McGibbon announced with only a trace of an optimistic grin that excess of expenditure over revenue the previous year totalled $516.83. Well, that was definitely better than the $4,477.53 gap of 1961-62. Those sustaining members? Thoroughly disappointing. They had brought in just $510. But he had successfully persuaded a few national corporations to shell out a total of $3,300 for the DDF coffer. The following year in Charlottetown, P.E.I., the news was somewhat brighter. Excess of expenditure over revenue was down to $104.06. Sustaining members were chinking in $850 and national corporations had contributed $8,000. But hold on. Deficits were still blooming, even though revenues seemed higher. In 1965, the DDF deficit was $1,867.09. By 1967, it had ballooned to $9,700.40.

It was between 1965 and 1967, though, that the DDF began to feel the effects of their latest disaster: the discontinuance of the Canadian Association of Broadcasters as major sponsors. There were many postmortems as to why the CAB disappeared after their five-year partnership with the corporation. Perhaps the Association felt the overall publicity was not worth the $21,000 a year which affiliate stations were eventually contributing to the DDF. Perhaps the CAB had made up its mind long ago that a five-year agreement would be a five-year agreement. Or perhaps the DDF executive had taken the CAB too much for granted. Did anyone remember how tardy the inner circle had been in inviting representatives of the Association to the presidential suite at the Finals? The Calvert people, of course, wandered in and out as they pleased. The CAB representatives waited politely to be asked and too often during the hectic week of festival, the DDF forgot they were even there. Another story was that the CAB had once indicated they would pull out of the sponsorship if Richard MacDonald decided to retire. And MacDonald retired in 1966. Oh well, the CAB was still providing $1,000 in prize money. The Canada Council's Centennial Year travel grant brought in $8,000 and the Province of Ontario Council for the Arts kicked in $30,000 in 1967.

By 1969, Don McGibbon (who was outgoing president that year) was writing a memo to governors which produced groans wherever it landed:

A summary of our budget for the year ending March

31, 1969 shows a loss of at least $9,200. Combined with the loss of $5,000 for 1968 and $9,700 for 1967 the current year's forecast is more than can reasonably be accepted. Anticipated income for the current year for operating purposes is not likely to exceed $48,250 as set out on the attached budget. Our minimum operating expenditure will be $51,950, which automatically creates a deficit of $3,700. We have in the past received certain support for regional adjudication fees and travel. We will not get this in 1969, so it is a matter of charging these expenses to designated purposes without a corresponding increase in income. The result is a loss of $5,000 in this area which, combined with our ordinary operating loss of $3,500 produces a total deficiency in income of $9,200 for the current year.

If that news wasn't bad enough, the memo became even gloomier. "The number of honorary governors is decreasing. In 1968, there were only 40 of them. Should we drop the category altogether and ask regions to find more patrons? Regional contributions totalled only $3,250 in 1968 and a notice of motion has been given that this amount must be increased by $2,000. We must have a pattern of increased revenue supported by regional representatives." McGibbon mused over other ideas. How about approaching the *working* governors for $100 or $50 contributions? Would it be an attractive carrot to honorary governors and sustaining members if they were recognized at both national and regional levels? Could participating drama groups be persuaded to pay a membership fee if they were represented by an honorary governor of their own?

The following year, with McGibbon back as chairman of the finance committee, the financial situation of the DDF was as critical as it had been when Park Jamieson was talking of throwing in the towel twenty years before. Wrote McGibbon to DDF governors:

At a meeting of officers on Saturday, January 3, 1970, the financial position of the corporation was shown to be extremely dangerous. We now have an accumulated deficit of $30,000, covered by an unsecured bank loan and it is clear we must take strong action to help matters immediately. A donations campaign to business firms is being prepared with all haste by the finance committee, the members of the national executive are being asked for financial contributions and the honorary governors are being asked for assistance too. Support is needed now for essential operating expenses – salaries, rent, adjudicators, etc. The regional fees have been set for the year 1969/70 and so no increase can be legislated. However, I am appealing to each region to make a voluntary contribution this month. The list of regions is attached showing the amount of financial help we hope from each. Improvements in our financial position must be made on a long-term basis, of course. Income must be increased and expenses decreased. This appeal is to help the emergency situation now.

The regional levies quoted in the memo produced further moans of protest from around the country. The four regions of Ontario (which now included one called Quonta) were expected to pay $4,000, or forty per cent of the total national contribution of $10,000. Prince Edward Island got off with $50.

Alvin Shaw, then Dean of Romance Languages at the University of New Brunswick and DDF president in 1970, stood as unflinchingly as possible in the front of the firing line. "I met with Mr. LeJeune, an assistant bank manager this morning," wrote the DDF's 1970 director, John Hill, to the president. "On a personal level, we are most friendly. Two facts emerged. One was that the level of our loan appears to be out of the local level league through the lack of liquidity in funds. Two is that the manager appeared to have no knowledge whatsoever of our function or purpose or achievements. He wanted to have our 1968/69 financial statements, list of grants promised, list of donations expected, list of officers and their occupations. Even if we make deep cuts in operation, if we are to maintain the tempo and methods and style of service, costs should still be more than last year. . . ." Protests from the regions were also beginning to shower in. "Unfortunately we will be unable to meet our assessment of $1,250," complained B. A. Sully, regional chairman of the Western Ontario Drama League. "We're having financial problems too. In any event I would be remiss even if we were financially solvent to ask our region to support the DDF until there is some indication there is truly a new purpose for this organization."

"We reluctantly advise you that it will not be possible for Newfoundland at this present time to pay the assessment," wrote John C. Perlin, chairman of the Newfoundland Drama Society. Meanwhile, in the Fall of 1970, John Hill prepared a new financial statement which was released to the DDF executive at a meeting in Montreal. The news was far from cheerful: "An audited balance sheet shows an accumulated deficit of $27,808. If we add this figure to the total of deferred expenses, $8,036, we arrive at a figure of $35,844 for accumulated deficit." In an attempt to encourage regional representatives to pull up their socks, Shaw wrote a letter later in 1970 which expressed hope for the future and outlined some of the plans the DDF was making for re-organization. One letter of reply set him back on his heels. Wrote Mrs. K. Caple, Chairman of the DDF's British Columbia Region:

> At a recent meeting here, the governors of the B.C. region expressed their concern about the mounting debt and continuing lack of a clear statement of the financial position and the unsuccessful efforts, for several years now, to balance expenditure with income. They see no basis of fact to support the optimism of the officers, expressed in your letter of November 9. They feel there must be some factor, some opportunity for successful expansion, of which they are ignorant. If there is such an opportunity, or a firm indication of it, the executive committee is entitled to know, because they and the other governors share the responsibility of finding a viable function and for balancing the budget. At the executive

meeting in Montreal it was made clear by the fund-raising and the financial reports that the DDF was heading for bankruptcy. The officers offered no alternative. We must pay our bills, even in bankruptcy. The debt is increasing at an alarming rate each month, the support is diminishing. In view of this, the B.C. governors made the following motion at their meeting an November 9: Moved and seconded that a letter should be written to the president of the DDF stating that the B.C. governors feel that steps should be taken to close the national office on or before March 31, 1971. Mrs. Caple will draft the letter. Passed. Since all arrangements for the coming Showcase Festival will be looked after by the National Arts Centre this motion will affect only DDF's communications with zones and regions in which B.C. would be happy to play a major part.

Alvin Shaw replied quickly:

My letter was not necessarily optimistic but a calm assessment of our present position and a suggestion that optimism and defeatism are totally incompatible. I do not agree with your comment that fund-raising and financial reports offered at our last meeting indicated we are heading for bankruptcy. But regions must accept the responsibility to discharge the obligation to raise $10,000 for debt retirement . . . an obligation which they decided to undertake some eight months ago. This obligation is far from having been discharged. Our debt is not increasing at an alarming rate each month and support is not diminishing. No national arts-oriented organization is ever in a sound financial position. For almost 40 years we have operated on the knife edge of disaster. We are no different than other such organizations. The accumulated debt of the National Theatre School, after 10 years, is approximately $150,000. Our position is relatively comfortable by comparison.
        We cannot entertain a motion to close the

211

National Office. We have major responsibilities to the Government of Quebec, POCA, the Canada Council and the National Arts Centre. The national office must remain open. The alternative to bankruptcy is hard work in terms of a dedicated fundraising campaign. The chief cause of our financial and spiritual bankruptcy – or a state approaching it – is our narrow regionalism. With few exceptions, we have been unable to adopt a truly national viewpoint, one which will allow us to act as a unit in the face of adversity or felicity. This country must have a theatre organization which is capable of such an attitude. I hope it will be the DDF. We have reduced costs from $82,000 to $42,000. The DDF must continue to fight its internal and external enemies – defeatism and insolvency, respectively.

Shaw continued to argue with his discouraged regional representatives, insisting that if the DDF folded, amateur theatre would disintegrate into isolated pockets of narrow regionalism. He preached that standards would fall "and the inevitable inroads of television and strong professional regional theatres" would eventually destroy the community theatre that Lord Bessborough helped put on its feet. Not everyone in the corporation was throwing up their hands in despair. In March, 1971, past president Vida Peene sat down at her desk in Toronto and wrote the ailing DDF a cheque for $500. Vincent Massey, H. S. Southam and even J. W. McConnell would have applauded the practical gesture. Volunteer Jeannie Hersenhoren, who had been helping Don McGibbon with the DDF's financial appeals, wrote to Miss Peene immediately. "For some time I've felt so depressed about the lack of response within the DDF executive itself to the need for help to the deficit fund. I've also been depressed about my own lack of success in appealing for such help. So your letter this morning with its extraordinarily generous cheque has done a great deal to 'lift my morale and I know it will do the same for Alvin Shaw and John Hill." Perhaps executive officers of the past had been right after all. Something would always turn up.

CHAPTER SEVEN

Adjudicators

1. But where do we find the judges?

Governor General Lord Bessborough solved the problem of finding an acceptable adjudicator for the Dominion Drama Festival's first Final in 1933, simply by importing his old friend Rupert Harvey from England. There were adjudication headaches for Vincent Massey and Col. Henry Osborne at the regional level, of course, but in that first year of Festival, no one could ever have predicted the agonies the DDF would suffer in the future as they searched frantically for qualified judges.

The first hint of trouble was in mid-1933 when the DDF's organizers began to think about an adjudicator – bilingual, naturally – who could handle the Final in the spring of 1934. But who? Partly because of press comment and partly because of the difficulty in tracking down enough qualified Canadians, it had been decided to hand the job of regional judging to a single adjudicator. Bessborough argued that Harvey was clearly the perfect man for the cross-country marathon and in August 1933 Col. Osborne was shipped to England to offer the assignment to the British producer and also to ask his help in choosing a celebrated "name" to judge the Final.

Harvey agreed to accept the regional job for a fee of 225 pounds plus expenses. As for the Final judge, he told Osborne quite frankly it would be difficult to pin down a man who was both bilingual and a theatrical luminary. A few names were mentioned. There was Henry Oscar, the West End actor-director. But after meeting Oscar, Osborne wrote to Massey reporting that "his French is about the same as Harvey's," and, after observing Harvey's performance at the 1933 Final, Massey knew what Osborne meant by that. There was actor-producer Allan Wade, a man who had worked with the great Harley Granville-Barker. But the word from contacts within the British Drama League was that Wade had been known to break contracts as an adjudicator if a more lucrative job turned up in the meantime. Then there was J. T. Grein, the well-known essayist and theatre critic. No decision was made about a 1934 Final adjudicator before Osborne left London for home.

In October, however, Harvey wrote to Osborne:

> I ran down Allan Wade and put the proposition to him. He isn't as impressed as he ought to be, but he's keen and willing. I also got hold of J. T. Grein who is full of enthusiasm. He said in fact "if they do me the honour of asking me I shall accept at once in principle." In principle means he is getting on for 70 and suffers from a weak heart. He can't walk any distance. I assured him that every time he rang a bell a fleet of motors would dash up to the door. He wants his wife to come and look after his creature comforts. He would naturally expect to pay her expenses but I have assured the men I've talked to they would receive hospitality at Government House or elsewhere. I would choose Grein. One thing against him is that although he is a Dutchman he looks slightly Jewish and I don't know how that would go down with either French or English Canada. But that is a point on which you will be fully informed. Wade is younger, about 50, I should imagine and also speaks French though with nothing like Grein's perfection. I find, indirectly, that Oscar's French is not as good as my own. I do so wish actors wouldn't lie so fluently.

Rupert Harvey arrived in Ottawa in time to direct Viscount Duncannon and Julia MacBrien in the Christmas production of *Romeo and Juliet*, then set out on his regional voyage of discovery to pick the productions which would be invited to the prestigious DDF Final the following May. Almost immediately, letters complaining about Harvey's incompetence began landing on Vincent Massey's desk.

"This, of course," Massey wrote somewhat tiredly to Osborne, "is at variance with his reputation. People apparently in Kingston disagreed with his having placed the Cobourg entry third – a trifling little piece, apparently – but the markings seem clear enough." Osborne replied soothingly that Duncan Cameron Scott of the Ottawa Drama League had told him Harvey was not well when he went to Kingston and was therefore not at the top of his form. "In 1933, Kingston people criticized Sterndale Bennett, particularly his award to three Ottawa teams," Osborne reminded Massey. "This year they criticize Harvey. In spite of what was said about the merits of *Ebb Tide*, I'm sure that if it, as well as *Marco Polo* had been placed – thus giving two plays to Ottawa – we should have heard about that. Particularly as before the festival they were already criticizing Harvey in advance as an adjudicator because he had produced the [Christmas] play in Ottawa. That little coterie in Kingston is hard to satisfy. Mrs. Fyffe who played in the Scotch play done by the Faculty Players showed no such feeling. As for the Scotch play itself, everyone agrees it was quite inaudible, apart from the accent."

Harvey also ran into a storm of criticism in Toronto, and Henry Button, Canadian director of J. M. Dent and Sons Limited, who happened to be a friend of Massey's wife, Alice, decided to address his complaint to her instead of the DDF's beleagured chairman:

> Whatever happened to Harvey? Why the sudden change of front? How can he reconcile his findings on the final night with his findings on Monday and Tuesday? As luck would have it, a friend had the wit and wisdom to take down what he said about each play and he was kind enough to give me his notes. They are enclosed. If the others are as accurate as the *Tintagiles* report ("a most impressive and

215

imaginative production by Nancy Pyper of an extraordinarily difficult play"), then it would puzzle a
Philadelphia lawyer to get at the reasons for Harvey's
final decision to give first prize to Edgar Stone's production of *Michael*. Anyway, all those with whom
I have talked are frothing at the mouth and this
includes people who do not know Mrs. Pyper. If
Tintagiles doesn't get to Ottawa then I at least foresee
the end of the Drama Festivals. They wouldn't
deserve to live. The big question is, when did Mr.
Harvey change his mind? And, of course, why? He
would have great difficulty in explaining satisfactor-
ily who he placed what he called on Monday "a good
custard pie comedy" (*The Devil Among the Skins*)
ahead of a most impressive and imaginative production as *Tintagiles*. Such is life.

It was a frigid week in Ottawa that May of 1934.
J. T. Grein, who turned out to be a small, balding man who
one journalist described as "a gentleman who looks like Punch"
was installed with his wife (who wrote cinema criticism for
the *London Sketch*) at Government House. His favourite comment to reporters was that the May tree in his London garden
must now be very much in bloom. As Harvey had promised,
hospitality and adulation were showered on the couple as lavishly as if they had been visiting heads of state.

Nancy Pyper's *Tintigales,* incidentally, did get to
Ottawa (some who remember the formidable lady still say she
transported the play to the Final by sheer personal force) but
Grein upheld Harvey's controversial decision at the Toronto
playoff by awarding the Bessborough Trophy to Edgar Stone's
production of *Michael*, a mystical Russian play by Miles Malleson. *Michael* was presented on the closing night of the festival
and Grein announced his decision almost immediately after
the curtain came down. The production, he decided with an
eloquent wave of his hand, was "marvellous, wonderful, beautiful." The audience applauded its approval. "Then, as it died
down," wrote an Ottawa reporter, "Mr. Grein with that smile
which had endeared him to every audience throughout the

week, said it had been the most interesting week in his very long life. He was not sorry he had crossed the waters. 'You are the finest audience I have ever had in my life and now I have to say farewell.' He paused. 'Shall I say farewell or au revoir?' he went on. 'Au revoir,' came back the reply as the whole house, including the Governor General, rose to its feet and sang with full-throated sincerity, 'For he's a jolly good fellow'. Mr. Grein stood with his hands resting on the table in front of him. His eyes shone with gratification and his smile became brighter. Then it died away and he made his way to the wings amidst prolonged cheering and with tears of pride and joy streaming down his cheeks." Grein never did return to Ottawa, though it is likely he would have been invited after his success in 1934. He died not long after returning to London and his May tree.

So whom could the DDF persuade to judge the 1935 Final? After a conference at Government House it was decided to follow up on Rupert Harvey's suggestion and try for Allan Wade. All right, so there had been warnings about the chap's lack of responsibility. But there was that prestigious tie-in with British actor-producer Harley Granville-Barker and Bessborough reminded Massey and Osborne that Wade had introduced Pirandello to the English-speaking theatre. Another thing, Wade had translated many *French* plays into English. Well, that was the clincher. A formal letter of invitation was sent to Allan Wade in the summer of 1934 and the producer accepted almost immediately. The next thing to do was to flush out a regional judge and Harvey and his contacts suggested Malcolm Morley, a director who was somewhat less known around London than Wade. By then the heroic job of cross-country adjudication in Canada had captured the imagination of the British press and Morley – who snapped at the newsworthy assignment – was waved good-bye as excitedly as if he were about to climb Mount Everest. Later, on his return to London, he was beseiged with requests for interviews and one, published in the *Observer* in June 1935 must have made him the talk of theatrical circles:

Mr. Malcolm Morley, a distinguished English theatrical producer, has just come back from Canada after travelling a fantastic number of thousands of miles (15,000 or 16,000 in all) as regional adjudicator at the Dominion Drama Festival. The figure of miles travelled is not an exaggeration. Entries to the Dominion Drama Festival were to be found in all parts of the country and Mr. Morley went from coast to coast, and into small towns in search of them. He saw more than a hundred companies perform and recommended sixteen for the finals in Ottawa. He comes back with a great deal to say about the state of the drama in Canada.

"In the first place, it has to be grasped that the professional theatre in Canada is almost on its last legs – on its last toe, one might say. Toronto used to have five theatres. It now has one and performances are given there roughly at the rate of three performances every three or four weeks. One month it may happen that an American company (the Lunts for example) comes up there for three days in a classic. The next month it may be three days of a pointless American farce. And that is almost the entire extent of the professional drama in Canada. I have been in Montreal three times and have never caught a play there. I talked to a man in Nelson, British Columbia, who had never seen a play himself and had never spoken to anyone who had ever seen a professional show. Yet a natural instinct for living drama is growing fast. It has been greatly encouraged by the retiring Governor General, Lord Bessborough, who instituted a Dominion Drama Festival for amateurs. With him in this are associated other men, Col. Henry Osborne and the Hon. Vincent Massey – our own Raymond Massey's brother and, incidentally, so good an amateur actor as to be a rival to Raymond. Vincent Massey gave Hart House to the University of Toronto, with its own private theatre. It was in Hart House that the Toronto competitions for the Drama Festival were held."

Morley seems to have encountered little real criticism during his regional swing, though those who remember him say that as the pace began to erode his nervous system he often relaxed – before performances, unfortunately – with a drop too much of alcohol. Like many other adjudicators Morley also quickly became intoxicated by overdoses of adulation. At one regional festival he was commenting on a scene from Jane Austen's *Pride and Prejudice* and arrogantly remarked that the actresses who had played the Bennett girls seemed to be drawn from a much higher social level than the actress who had been cast as their mother. The husband of the lady concerned rose from the audience and offered to fight Morley then and there. There is no record that the adjudicator apologized. Morley, too, like Harvey and regional judges who would follow him, encountered the endless jockeying among groups to pick a play that would be sure to impress. Before the producer arrived in Toronto, for example, word got around that he had a marked preference for farces. Morley's list of winners from Toronto that year was headed by four comedies.

The DDF executive waited nervously in the first months of 1935 to see whether Rupert Harvey's gloomy warnings about Allan Wade's reputation were true. Letters to Wade, however, continued to be answered promptly and the adjudicator himself turned up, complete with mandatory white tie and tails, for the Final. It was as though he knew his blue-ribbon employers had put him on probation. During Festival he said all the right things ("actors, like poets are born and judging by what I have seen this week the birthrate must be high in Canada"), his "engaging smile" was commented on by the press and he even explained his methods of adjudication to interested reporters: "I try to understand exactly what each group is trying to do and then make up my mind how far they have been successful. It has been said that I didn't like certain types of plays and it may be that I have a preference for certain styles and types but this factor does not enter into judgments." A pleased DDF invited Wade back to Canada the following year to handle the long regionals.

Although the organizers of the Dominion Drama Festival admitted the job of choosing good adjudicators was proving to be tougher than they thought, Bessborough's enormous influence plus the DDF's growing web of contacts in England paid off for the first three festivals. Optimism concerning the DDF's far-flung prestige was so high, in fact, that the executive – even with Bessborough and Massey no longer in the picture – decided to aim for the top when the 1936 Final was being planned. Why not invite the celebrated Harley Granville-Barker? The name was so awe-inspiring that two letters were sent from Ottawa to the actor-producer-playwright's home in Paris. One was from Osborne, the other from Canada's new Governor General, Lord Tweedsmuir. To Osborne's delight, Granville-Barker replied:

> Many thanks for your letter. I have received His Excellency's too, and answered it. You do me much honour by your invitation, and if it would not inconvenience you unduly to wait a few weeks for a definite answer, my hope is that I could accept it. But if it would, I shall of course understand. My immediate difficulty is that I have in hand long-promised work which must be finished before I allow myself to leave Paris for more than a day or so. I should also have to fit the Canadian visit with one which my wife and I must make if we can to the United States. But if you could wait – say until Christmas for my definite answer I ought by then to be able to see my way clear. I could cable.

The letter went on to say that Granville-Barker had heard of the good being done in Canada and was glad the authorities had recognized the value of it, "a favourable contrast to the lamentable lack of official care for the drama in England." On the last day of 1935, there was jubilation in the DDF camp when Granville-Barker wired Lord Tweedsmuir: "Have cabled committee undertaking to adjudicate."

Granville-Barker's acceptance of the DDF's final festival offer caused as much excitement in the capital itself as it did at both Government House and in the DDF's corner of John Aylen's office. "The Drama Festival directors are to be congratulated on securing the services of a man whom historians of the British drama rank with Shaw, Barrie, Galsworthy, Jones, Pinero and Wilde," editorialized the Ottawa *Journal* in January, 1936. "From 1915, Granville-Barker has lived quietly, mostly in Paris, his time engaged in translation. He is an expert linguist." In another article the *Citizen* did some digging and found some overseas clippings which gave Festival fans a clue as to the great man's philosophy concerning the theatre. At Cambridge, revealed the newspaper, Granville-Barker once stated that the physical conditions of the Greek theatre were so far outside modern experience that he doubted if any one could appreciate more than dimly the emotional effect of poetry in the Greek drama in its own time. Granville-Barker apparently felt that much Restoration drama had a peculiar snobbery about it "and swaggered about its little nastiness as good style and freedom from the prejudices of the vulgar." He also stated that "the reason we have progressed so slowly of recent years is that there is hardly a theatre in the world equipped to portray the literary and technical advances of the last two decades." Heady stuff. Ottawa could scarcely wait for a man of such impressive intelligence to arrive. The DDF executive itself preened at the attention Granville-Barker was already receiving in the press. With popular Allan Wade already on his way to judge the playoffs, it looked as though 1936 – Lord Tweedsmuir's first Final as patron of the DDF – would turn out to be a banner year.

Reporters crammed the railway station in Ottawa when the adjudicator arrived on the evening of April 19, 1936. The *Citizen* told the whole story the following day:

> Keenly interested in anything and everything concerning the theatre in Canada and anxious to assume his duties as adjudicator of the finals of the Dominion Drama Festival, Harley Granville-Barker, noted British playwright, author, critic, actor and director arrived in Ottawa last evening accompanied by his no less famous wife, Mrs. Helen Granville-Barker. The tall, handsome, dark-haired festival judge was in the best of spirits when he descended from the

Canadian Pacific transcontinental train and greeted Col. H. C. Osborne, honorary director of the festival, John Aylen, K. C. hon. secretary-treasurer, Allan Wade, regional adjudicator, and many others who were on hand.

As soon as he had disposed of the matter of baggage to his satisfaction, Mr. Granville-Barker crossed over the platform to where newspapermen awaited him. During a walk, Mr. Granville-Barker where the chauffeur from Government House awaited him. During a walk, Mr. Granville Barker discussed various aspects of the theatre and when questioned by a reporter as to what play of his own he liked best he stated in his own inimitable way: "Why the one I wrote last, of course," and then added, as if in after thought, "that is, provided that I do not have to read it again. Yes, the last one is always the favourite."

Queried regarding amateur dramatics in France, where he now resides, he pointed out that there was a great deal of interest being shown there, especially by students. "The Boy Scouts have been putting on a large number of plays. There have also been quite a few put on for children. These plays of course have been especially written for the youngsters." Young people who are anxious to do something in the theatre were told to do the best they could. Mr. Granville-Barker, who has had a varied and successful career in the theatre, would give no advice beyond that. This is not his first visit to Ottawa. He said he well remembered his previous visit some time after the end of the war when he came out to lecture, he was not quite sure of the date but thought it was around 1920. He said that he was looking forward to renewing acquaintanceship with a number of people whom he had met in the capital at that time.

The good press continued, with coverage of

Granville-Barker's remarks after every play. "The remarks of the adjudicator were eagerly awaited," reads one report. "Large audiences always turn up at the Little Theatre to hear him and he is frequently applauded for his terse and to the point and always constructive criticisms."

Granville-Barker tried to be scrupulously diplomatic. He paid tribute to individuals "behind the scenes" for their help in staging so many smooth performances. "I have little to say about the play," he remarked on one occasion. "That seems to me to be what acting and good acting is. We see the ideas of the author made flesh, made human." Yet he could also be critical. Adjudicating a performance of *The Old Trouper* by Charles Brooks from the Theatre Guild of Saint John, New Brunswick, Granville-Barker rapped: "This was a futile and clumsy play. The actors were frankly wasting their time and yours when they produce such a play. It was not like anything on heaven or earth. They plunged themselves into something and there was nothing to be done." But then the balm: "I'm so sorry, because the four people in it played with sincerity."

The Little Theatre was "packed to suffocation" on the final night of the festival. Clearly impressed by the status of community theatre in Canada, Granville-Barker commented on the prestigious audience. The Governor General and Lady Tweedsmuir were there. Prime Minister Mackenzie King sat in the front row and so did Sir Robert Borden, several members of parliament and the Hon. Norman Armour, the U.S. minister to Canada. "The drama is in a happy position in Canada," gasped the adjudicator. "It has such strong supporters!" In another move that could be construed as both diplomatic and an encouragement to Bessborough's much-publicized vision of a national drama for Canada, the British producer awarded the Bessborough Trophy to a play called *Twenty-five Cents* written by W. Eric Harvey of Sarnia, Ontario. The play was directed by DDF supporter Catharine Brickenden and staged by the London Little Theatre. Granville-Barker liked a *Canadian* play! The applause was deafening.

The experience of adjudicating the Dominion Drama Festival made a deep impression on Harley Granville-Barker. Nothing of the kind had ever happened to him before. He was frankly astonished that the *amateur* theatre movement was attracting such devout interest from vice-royalty, leaders of government and the social elite of Canada. When he could escape from the fawning press, gushing hostesses and receptions at Government House, he had serious talks with Col. Osborne about the future of the festival. Later, after his return to Paris, he wrote letters to the DDF director which Osborne read aloud to the executive committee. "I think you should introduce three-act plays into the festival," one letter advised. "You have to go forward. You can't be static."

Granville-Barker also offered to help the DDF in finding top adjudicators in France and promised to contact Jacques Copeau, director of the Comédie Française, who he knew spoke fluent English. Osborne was delighted at the suggestion. What a superb way of reviving the flagging interest of French-Canadian groups! That summer, during an official pilgrimage to Vimy Ridge (he was still working with the Imperial War Graves Commission), he first talked about adjudication assignments with actor Miles Matheson and director Tyrone Guthrie in London then went to Paris where Granville-Barker introduced him to Copeau. The French director was interested but said he was not at all sure that the date of the 1937 Final could be wedged into his schedule. Actress Yvonne Arnaud was mentioned as an alternative, also Copeau's nephew, Michel St. Denis, who had his own Compagnie des Quinze in Paris as well as the St. Denis London Theatre Studio.

Copeau later confirmed that it was impossible to accept the Canadian job, so Osborne extended the invitation to St. Denis. It was one of the most brilliant choices of adjudicator the DDF ever made. St. Denis would judge a record of five Finals (Philip Hope-Wallace came next with four invitations) and exert an influence on DDF development well into the nineteen-sixties. In 1937, the director was forty years of age, tall, broad-shouldered and already celebrated in theatre circles on both sides of the English channel. It was clear, even at his first Final, that the DDF had scored a tremendous coup. Unlike his predecessors, adjudicator St. Denis was not prepared to be diplomatic for diplomacy's sake. Neither was he unkind. Those who remember his comments at Festival now describe him as "the teacher" though this aspect of his character was to grow somewhat crusty as the years went by.

One performer who probably learned a great deal from St. Denis at the 1937 Final was a student actor named Lorne Greene, who appeared in a Queen's University Dramatic Guild's production of the Spanish play *The Secret* by Ramon Sender. Greene played First Prisoner in the production and was also co-director. It is interesting to re-read what St. Denis had to say about the play. It had some good points, he said, but "I don't find it horrible enough." He added that the actor who played General Gallofa was "not terrible enough" and that the prisoners "talked too loudly." The lighting, he concluded, was not effective.

The DDF executive committee had trouble locating suitable regional and Final adjudicators for its 1938 Festival which finally – because of sharp proddings from an insistent Lady Madge Tupper – moved to Winnipeg. When representatives from Montreal and Toronto asked why those bustling centres of community theatre were being bypassed, Osborne remarked with a wry smile that Winnipeg was a compromise between the "immoralities of Montreal and the unpleasant virtue of Toronto." Officially, he told reporters that the Festival "was moving out of Ottawa to meet the people." Several likely judges were approached in London and Paris for the Winnipeg festival, but only one man – Malcolm Morley – could see his way clear to take on the back-breaking job of judging the regionals. The matter of a Final adjudicator plagued the executive for months until DDF supporter Mona Coxwell suggested Barrett H. Clark, a Toronto-born author and critic (his father was American) who was then working with her parent company, Samuel French, in New York.

Clark was scarcely a Granville-Barker or a St. Denis, but the executive agreed that they had to come to a quick decision. With a pleased Malcolm Morley already on the road, the DDF wrote to Clark, inviting him to adjudicate the 1938 Final. Clark himself was somewhat surprised at the offer, but he had a deep interest in the theatre and had naturally heard of the Dominion Drama Festival from his friends and relatives in Toronto. He accepted. "After his opening bow," wrote the Winnipeg *Free Press* of the adjudicator, "Mr. Clark made an unorthodox move in going to sleep with some of his thoughts so that he could obviously give a more considered opinion the night after of what he had seen the night before. It is an excellent practice. It demonstrated both his sincerity and implied his reaction to our Canadian effort – that it was often worthy of so much more than a swift or snap judgement. . . . When he decided to expand his comments, as he did after Monday, he added immeasurably to his adjudicatorial stature, becoming more truly himself. By the expression of his human foibles and prejudices he exposed the chinks he admitted in his critical armour. Is that kind of adjudicator preferable to the hypocrite who might profess to be a miraculous combination of Aristotle, Lessing and Granville-Barker?"

Clark also endeared himself to community theatre enthusiasts and also the DDF itself – which was beginning to feel the weight of its own importance on the Canadian arts scene – by coining another word for *amateur*. "Barrett H. Clark has a new term for the theatre," wrote Frank Morris in the *Free Press* during the festival. "It has been called a number of things in Winnipeg, many of them not printable, but the most popular title to date has been 'the living drama.' The word amateur is only mentioned behind closed doors. Mr. Clark's title is the 'non-professional theatre', as neat and diplomatic a way of putting it as we've ever heard."

Clark's success in Winnipeg set members of the DDF executive thinking about sources of adjudicators. Was it always necessary to import them from England and France? Lady Tupper certainly thought not. "I see no reason why we have to drag people all the way across the Atlantic to do the job," she snapped during a meeting at the Fort Garry Hotel. "Why don't we ask Mr. Clark to approach suitable men in the great American theatre? At least they could act as *regional* adjudicators." There were some nods of agreement and some shakes of the head. Individuals from abroad had prestige. They added colour and publicity value to the Festival. Lady Tupper harumphed and tried to push her point home. Significantly, though, the DDF seldom looked to "the great American theatre" for adjudicators in the future.

The following year, in fact – when the Festival moved to London, Ontario – the DDF was again scratching around in London to find regional and Final judges. It was a nerve-wracking job, which had powers within the DDF – at that time, Col. Osborne, John Aylen and D. Park Jamieson – wheeling and dealing with everyone who had the slightest connection with the theatre. Lord Bessborough and Vincent Massey were both contacted by letter and so was Michel St. Denis and Harley Granville-Barker. Names were flung into the air, then invariably plopped out of sight like so many pebbles into deep water. Finally, a regional possibility loomed into view, an English actor named George Skillan. George who? Well, the fellow could boast a quarter century of experience on the English stage. He was a student of Shakespeare. And he was *available* for the long hike across Canada. Interviewed on his arrival in the Dominion, Skillan told a reporter: "No, I have no preconceived notions about Canadian acting. I might have some difficulty with Canadian performances in French, partly because of my limited familiarity with the language and partly because of the different accent in Canada." However, the hearty thespian added with a wave of a hand, he wasn't worrying about that. If the acting was right, the play would get across, anyway. When the report reached the DDF executive, there were shivers of apprehension.

Skillan, though, managed to plow through the regional playoffs without too much complaint from either French or English groups. Perhaps his unquenchable jollity saved the day. The Final adjudicator for the DDF's last Festival before its suspension during the Second World War also completed his assignment without undue complaint from either the press or the public. DDF contacts in London, England, had managed to persuade S. R. (Robin) Littlewood, then dean of the city's theatre critics, to accept the 1939 job. Littlewood was not a well-known name in Canada, but he unquestionably had experience and intelligence and, to the DDF's relief, influential members of the Canadian media agreed.

Wrote the often highly-caustic Hector Charlesworth in *Saturday Night* after the seventh Dominion Drama Festival:

From the standpoint of the public, the nightly adjudications of S. R. Littlewood, dean of the British critical fraternity, were the most entertaining heard in connection with any of these festivals. In candor it must be said that discourses of adjudicators in the past have not infrequently been tedious. Mr. Littlewood, who (shades of J. T. Grein) looks like Mr. Pickwick, and like him breathes the spirit of brotherly love, has the gift of ironic humor. Beneath his kindly persiflage was a stratum of very sound criticism. He was trained in the 'nineties under the great critic A. B. Walkley on the long defunct *Star*, whose misfortunes form the theme of Philip Gibbs' best novel. He himself was for many years theatrical critic of the deceased *London Morning Post*, which maintained high literary and ethical standards. Mr. Littlewood pays more attention to what might be termed the 'public relations' of the theatre than most adjudicators and is indeed highly sensitive on that point.

Littlewood committed only one blunder according to press comment of the time. He criticized a play written by Brian Doherty (who was to become founder of the Shaw Festival at Niagara-on-the-Lake) called *Father Malachy's Miracle* as irreverent and said he thought its humour would wound the feelings of the Roman Catholic Church. As Charlesworth pontificated in his *Saturday Night* article, "this was a clear misconception." In any case, Doherty's play did not receive the Sir Barry Jackson award for the Best Canadian Play in 1939. The trophy went to *Divinity in Montreal* a play about Sarah Bernhardt's appearance in the city written by Janet Alexandra McPhee and directed by Herbert Whittaker.

At Governors' Court in London that year, there was the usual hair-tearing about the paucity of adjudication talent and someone even suggested it might be a good idea to dispense with imported celebrities and hand over the job to a board of three Canadian critics. As usual, the argument wheeled around to the fact that English or French judges carried more prestige and, in any case, were more experienced. At that time, no one was to know that the headache of tracking down a suitable duo of adjudicators for the 1940 Ottawa Festival would be conveniently avoided by the outbreak of the Second World War. There are indications that the problem might actually have stumped the DDF that year. Minutes of meetings show the DDF executive had no ideas about 1940 judges at all.

2.   Help!

The headache of finding suitable adjudicators continued to irritate the DDF executive until 1971 when the corporation abandoned its competitive festivals. Almost every Final produced its own brand of trauma, but letters and cables which flew between Ottawa and London during the 1950's show that next to shortage of funds, the search for adjudicators in those years raised more wails of anguish than any other DDF problem.

London's 1947 Final slid by without too much difficulty because it was the first DDF effort after the Second World War and everyone was prepared to accept Welsh-born Canadian Emrys Jones of the University of Saskatchewan (who had an impeccable English accent) as Final adjudicator. In 1948, the DDF was lucky to grab one of its most celebrated Final judges, author-actor Robert Speaight. Robert Stuart, an English actor, accepted the cross-country jaunt without too much persuasion that year and in 1949 the regional question sorted itself out nicely when Speaight agreed to return because he wanted to see more of Canada. That was the year the DDF tucked another well-known British name under its wing, drama critic Philip Hope-Wallace and in 1950, longtime friend Michel St. Denis came back for the Final with actor Maxwell Wray – only too happy to get the work – handling the regionals. But in 1951 the cupboard was bare and the executive was forced to settle for actor Jose Ruben at the Final, a gentleman who, it was later discovered, was almost completely blind.

The real drama of the DDF's struggle to employ prestigious adjudicators unfolds simply by scanning correspondence, particularly between the corporation's national director Richard MacDonald, Evelyn ("Bill") Williams, deputy director of the British Council's drama department (who

229

patiently tried to help the Canadian organization for years), and various candidates for the job. Communiqués of the mid-1950's, in fact, reveal moments of near-hysteria on both sides of the Atlantic!

June, 1953, Evelyn Williams to Dick MacDonald: "It's possible that Hugh Hunt of the Old Vic might consider the regional adjudication for 1954. His French is excellent but he certainly will not commit himself now. Free-lance actors are unable to accept engagements so long ahead. I don't think you realize what a difficulty it is to find adjudicators, especially those for the regionals. There is the strenuous travel and besides, they are almost killed with kindness."

October, 1953, cable from Williams to MacDonald: "Hunt regretfully unavailable please cable orders re further approaches."

October, 1953, cable from MacDonald to Williams: "Please approach John Allen (regional adjudicator for 1953) and see if he would recommend Eric Capon stop if his French is adequate there seems to be no specific reason why he would not be suitable."

October, 1953, Williams to MacDonald: "We're thinking of Evan John as regional adjudicator. He is a writer and an authority on sword-fighting. As a matter of fact, he has written a book on its history. Evan John would be my choice if he can stand the strain of it. He is highly strung and the pace is gruelling however much you try to protect the judges."

October, 1953, MacDonald to Williams: "Please approach André Van Gyseghem, the actor-producer. Then Evan John. But what about the French-language requirement there? Stephen Joseph has been suggested, but he is under 30 and I think that's a little too young."

October, 1953, Williams to MacDonald: "By the time you get this letter you'll have a cable saying all our current suggestions are unavailable. I'm asking for further suggestions because I seem to have exhausted all of my own. As you know from my cable, Hugh Hunt had to refuse because he could not be out of England for so long. I then tried Van Gyseghem and he seemed interested but yesterday he got a very good offer and had to refuse. I'm pretty sure I could find dozens who would be glad to go, but there's the problem of the second language. The number of people with fluent French is not large. I do beg you once again to get someone good from France with the co-operation of Michel St. Denis. The job is now on offer to Evan John but I'm not optimistic."

October, 1953, cable from Williams to MacDonald: "Evan John accepts stop letter and publicity following."

November, 1953, Williams to MacDonald: "You got my cable saying Evan John accepts, letter and publicity following. If expense was not a problem I would have added a heartfelt thank God, because of all the jobs I do, this is definitely the most difficult. I really don't think your committee understands the difficulty – the fact that so few actors are bilingual and so few are prepared to cut themselves off from work in this country for four months of the year. It's always an immense relief when I cable that I've succeeded in pinning anyone down."

December, 1953, cable from Williams to MacDonald: "Regret visit Evan John cancelled owing to death fatal accident stop cable your preferences substitutes."

December, 1953, cable from MacDonald to Williams: "Very shocked news Evan John cancellation owing to fatal accident. Try Stanley Hildebrandt, Graham Suter, Stephen Joseph or any other suggested by British Drama League stop how about Malcolm Morley stop have arranged to telephone you at nine a.m. your time tomorrow."

December, 1953, cable from Williams to MacDonald: "We and the British Drama League suggest Graham Suter, age 34, married, extensive repertory experience stop suggest you cable him directly."

December, 1953, cable from Suter to MacDonald: "Glad to accept job as regional adjudicator Dominion Drama Festival stop letter following."

December, 1953, MacDonald to Williams: ". . . and then there is the problem of the final adjudicator. I think I mentioned to you during the year that we'd like to have Robert Speaight back again at the usual fee of $500 and this time we'd like the final adjudicator to stay on for another two days to give a seminar for the directors of the plays."

January, 1954, H. M. Tennant Ltd., theatrical managers

231

to MacDonald: "Naturally we appreciate you are anxious to invite Robert Speaight to the Dominion Drama Festival at Hamilton, Ont. between May 10 to 15, 1954. But unfortunately at this moment, Mr. Speaight is appearing in Charles Morgan's new play *The Burning Glass* which will open in London in the middle of February. In the event of this play being successful it would be out of the question for us to release Mr. Speaight for the period necessary for him to attend the festival."

February, 1954, Williams to MacDonald: "I've approached Hugh Hunt again, this time about the Final and he has tentatively accepted the job. Hope I can cable you the good news about his definite acceptance."

February, 1954, cable from Williams to MacDonald: "Hugh Hunt accepts stop confirm directly with him at Brook Cottage, Brockenhurst Hampshire."

May, 1954, Williams to MacDonald: "Had lunch with Graham Suter on his return from England and he talked about the kindness he received on all hands. It would be immensely helpful you know, if you could report at first hand to your committee about the conditions in the theatre here which make the adjudicators, especially the regional ones who have to be out of the country so long, a major annual headache. This might sound selfish, I suppose. To some extent it is. But I do feel it would be far easier for you to convince them than for me to do so. I don't think many of them appreciate the difficulties. Not only is there the British system of runs which govern most theatres here, but they find it difficult to pledge themselves to be out of the country and unavailable to answer the telephone. The right kind of call, you know, could lead to another engagement which might have to go into immediate rehearsal and lead to a job for the next couple of years."

August, 1954, MacDonald to Williams: "My trip to Europe is planned for next month. I might even take a flying visit to Copenhagen to see about adjudicators. Maybe the Danes could give us the kind of adjudication we want and Lord knows what that is. I believe that Danish and Swedish theatrical activity has developed considerably during the past few years. Although Hugh Hunt did a creditable job, you know, he was not generally appreciated."

September, 1954, MacDonald to Williams: "My trip to Paris is turning out to be a flop. No one is keeping appointments. I have extended my stay here for two days, but nobody has turned up. I'm frustrated with French officials. They are most unsatisfactory and unproductive. They start work late in the afternoon then leave about five o'clock. I tried to get the co-operation of the International Theatre Institute but André Doucette, the director, did not keep our appointment. I had hoped to see Michel St. Denis. He said he would be here, but I've heard nothing. Right now, our adjudication problem remains unsolved, though I have one or two possibilities. This year I'd really like to get someone of French origin for the regionals. I feel the English adjudicators are sometimes a little easy on the French plays. I'd like somebody not too old, not too young. Between 35 and 40. Somebody who would be acceptable to our French groups in Quebec. We are prepared to pay $1,000 for the regional job. It's raining and raining in Paris. Let me know if you have any new ideas."

September, 1954, Williams to MacDonald: "Did I tell you how wonderful it was meeting you personally after all these years? How about Hélène Dast, daughter of Jacques Copeau?"

September, 1954, MacDonald to Williams: "I'm back in Ottawa and getting quite desperate again about the regional situation for next year. I'll be giving a very negative report to my executive on Saturday when they meet. But at least I can now go to the executive and report on personal observation about how difficult it has been for you to secure regional adjudicators in the past. But once again I must appeal for your help this year. I can only hope Lynn Oxenford, the director, will be available. As regards the Final adjudicator, this will confirm the conversations I had with you concerning George Devine who seems to be No. 1 on the list for this coming year. To his name, I'd like to add that of Anthony Quayle who I met in Stratford and who is very interested in final adjudication. He assured me that he spoke French fluently enough to adjudicate the Final and seems very anxious to come to Canada. He thought he would be free at the time of our 1955 Final."

September, 1954, MacDonald to Williams: "The executive meeting went off fairly well. I received approval of the idea of employing a woman as an adjudicator if one becomes available. This leaves the way open for two possibilities, Lynn Oxenford and Gerda Wrede. We were thinking of the job of regional adjudicator. However, a woman would also be acceptable for the Final, all things being equal."

September, 1954, Williams to MacDonald: "I think that Andre Van Gyseghem would be better for the regionals than a woman because the job is so strenuous. I don't feel it's a job for the gentle sex, if we're still allowed to be that. The more I know about the regional job, the more strenuous I realize it is. Lynn Oxenford is a good choice for the Final because she's had good experience directing in European theatres. Right now she is on the staff of the British Drama League."

October, 1954, Williams to MacDonald: "I don't think there is the slightest chance Gerda Wrede would do the regionals. In addition to being artistic director of the Svenska Theatre in Helsinki, she is a very busy producer. I don't think the theatre would release her for so long a period. Even if there were none of these problems, Tony Guthrie has asked her to produce *Julius Caesar* for him in 1955. If you get Quayle or Devine you would do better for the Final than Gerda, dear though she is."

October, 1954, Williams to MacDonald: "I was talking with Lynn Oxenford and she told me she was not completely bilingual though she would be prepared to adjudicate or lecture in French. She reported in French from The Hague Conference in International Theatre last year and would like to be considered."

November, 1954, cable from Williams to MacDonald: "Van Gyseghem accepts regionals contact direct 24 Knox St. London, W.1."

February, 1955, MacDonald to Williams: "Disappointing news about Tony Quayle. I do hope a miracle happens and that Devine is available. However, I do gather he is doubtful he will be available at the time of the Final."

February, 1955, Williams to MacDonald: "Devine is off. There is Marius Goring but I have no reason to believe he will be any more free this year than in the past. There is Gerda Wrede, of course. There is Austin Trevor; he has often been suggested before but he is not really in the star class. What do you think of Michael Redgrave?"

February, 1955, Williams to MacDonald: "Redgrave is off. Where do we go from here? I have no inspirations beyond Austin Trevor. As I've said before, he is not really a star but he has done some good plays and films. Perhaps you could think of asking someone who has done the job before. Redgrave says, anyway, that he doesn't think his French is good enough, so that it might have been a difficult job for him, anyway. Can't you think of a bilingual Frenchman? I fear you can't. I wish I could."

February, 1955, cable Williams to MacDonald: "Wrede accepts stop contact direct in Helsinki."

February, 1955, Wrede to MacDonald: ". . . you mention evening dress, but do please tell me what sorts of weather you have in May in Saskatcheware [*sic*]. I suppose it is colder than Finland. I am looking forward so much to coming. . . ."

June, 1955, MacDonald to Wrede: "I'm so sorry about all that stuff about your English that Herbert Whittaker wrote in the *Globe and Mail*. There was apparently a rumour around Regina that you had not been expected to give public adjudication. That was, of course, absolutely ridiculous. Herbert could have checked this with me before leaving Regina. He knew as a governor of the festival that we would not engage someone without establishing their duties. You know it was true at first in Regina regarding your English, but by mid-week audiences had grown used to your accent and approved of your adjudications. There are some, of course, who will not bother to listen to someone who speaks with an accent, anyway."

June, 1955, Wrede to MacDonald: "What a nice letter, Dick. No, I won't forget a moment of the festival, not even the scared moments. It has all been a wonderful experience. I'll always treasure it as a wonderful memory. Don't worry, I'm used to criticism. All theatre people are. It was only that Mr. Whittaker put the blame on you that worried me. Personally, I encountered so much kindness. I talk so much about Canada over here. You're going to have a flood of immigrants. God knows what would happen if I were a young woman starting a theatre somewhere over there."

January, 1956, MacDonald to Yves Bourassa. "As you know, we've been trying to secure the services of French director Pierre Fresnay through the Canadian Embassy in Paris.

Although he was interested and prepared to come, previous commitments are such that he would not be able to attend our Final in Sherbrooke. Apparently he's booked.

July, 1956, MacDonald to Pierre Lefevre: "The executive committee is endeavouring to bring back adjudicators who have previously been here, so we are making an early approach to you to adjudicate our regional festival for 1957. The honorarium has been increased to $1,500, incidentally, plus out-of-poçket expenses. We do hope you will be able to accept this engagement."

July, 1956, Lefevre to MacDonald: "So sorry, but due to previous commitments, regional adjudication is out of the question."

October, 1956, Dorothy White to MacDonald: "I received your letter, Dick and immediately got in touch with Cecil Bellamy as requested. As a matter of fact, I've seen him twice and like him very much. He said he hadn't adjudicated before but he says he thinks he can do it. He's a producer at the BBC, as you know, and he doesn't want to lose his job. If the BBC lets him go for the time he is in Canada, I think he will accept. I'll be home for the October 13 meeting and we'll discuss the whole thing then."

October, 1956, cable from MacDonald to Bellamy: "Happy to confirm offer your engagement regional adjudicator as advised British Council stop honorarium $1,500 less 15 per cent income tax stop please cable acceptance."

October, 1956, cable from Bellamy to MacDonald: "Delighted to accept."

3.   **But did the adjudicators enjoy themselves?**

Adjudicators assigned to judge either the regional or Final festivals of the DDF apparently tackled their jobs with mixed feelings of love, hate, exhaustion and an incredible sense of power. Asked how he had enjoyed his Dominion-wide trip in 1934, Rupert Harvey admitted that he never really knew which town he was in and that his most vivid memory of Canada would be that he had seen at least ten million Christmas trees.

Robert Speaight described his 1949 regional tour as "interesting, arduous and not always a very grateful experience." In his book *The Property Basket*, he admits it was always "an excruciating form of torture to watch incompetent amateurs at work." Letters from some of the regional judges to the Dominion office in Ottawa tell of personal irritations, stomach upsets because of over-indulgent hospitality and overwhelming weariness.

"With all the buffalo and antelope meat I am given," wrote regional judge Cecil Bellamy in 1957, "I am slightly upset. The worst of this job is the perpetual crowds and, of course they are like children about the theatre and I've been trying to get them down to terra firma about it all. They will never do any good until they do. I leave tomorrow for Calgary and then for Banff, which I look forward to enormously. I've had beautiful weather all the way." Wrote Philip Hope-Wallace to Richard MacDonald in 1958: "One small point. I do remember that I got most terribly overtired last time. While I want to pull my weight fully on the social side, would you be kind and avoid accepting for me any invitations which don't seem really necessary or accept them on an optional basis so that I can contract out if I feel all my energies are required for the main job."

The Dominion office was always warning regional organizers not to smother their adjudicators with hospitality but local hostesses found the chance to entertain a theatrical celebrity from abroad so irresistible, they clawed at each other's throats for the right to throw dinners and receptions. The floods of adulation and awe that greeted the visiting judges every-where often spilled over into the theatre. Maxwell Wray, for example, the English repertory actor assigned to the 1950 regionals, found the rapt attention of the Canadian audiences so heady, he almost forgot the job of adjudication and talked mostly about his own "fantastic career" on the stage. By the time he was approaching the end of his trip, he was making rambling speeches about his first appearance in the theatre as a boy and how he had been so nervous he had wet his trousers.

Actor Richard Ainley, who tackled the regionals in 1959, seemed to snooze through most of the plays. Yet after they were over, he unleashed dozens of chatty letters addressed to regional winners which suggest a different aspect of his character altogether. One, written to Bubby Brook of Simcoe whose production of *The Boyfriend* not only won the regional festival but the Final as well, reads: "When I look back over the pleasure you gave me that night I can't think of anything except the little recommendation that I humbly made at the time. They were Madame's terminal syllables and Hortense's ditto. I thought it would be fun if Hortense put both her legs in the air at the end when she spoke on the telephone in Act One and I think it would build the laugh enormously." Invariably, the letters ended with something like: "Richard Ainley signing off and I shall be with you in spirit if not in what Harpo Marx calls 'the flash.'"

Ainley was one of the DDF's most controversial judges. To this day, those who remember the highly-uneven 1959 Toronto Final swear the actor sabotaged the show by picking inferior plays from across the country. The legend is that the Final festival adjudicator, Michel St. Denis, had fired Ainley from the Old Vic Theatre School and the actor was out for revenge. More charitable observers of Ainley's adjudication point out that the man was a war casualty and was ill and mentally depressed during his Canadian visit. The DDF executive, Ainley sympathizers believe, should have understood his odd behaviour. Certainly, Ainley did not receive the deferential treatment that the DDF usually reserved for its imported stars. A transcript from a tape made at a 1959 Toronto meeting shows the judge was grilled about his regional award of the Bessborough Trophy for Best Classical Play. By then, of course, the Calvert Trophy had become the DDF's highest award at the Final. Part of the tape goes like this:

Bourassa: We have a play, a classic by Plaute in the Final, yet the winner of the Bessborough has not been invited.
Mutterings.
Ainley: I've lost the thread, the web and the woof.
Silly laughter.
McGibbon: They want to know why you decided to give the Bessborough Trophy to *Miss Julie*, the Port Arthur Mummers when you are putting another classic in the Final Festival.

238

Ainley: I felt it was a feeling of equity. . . . *(The tape runs out.)*

Ainley, though, did keep in touch with the Ottawa office during his travels across Canada. Some adjudicators did not (probably because they were too exhausted to sit down and write), a fact which irritated the DDF's director, Richard MacDonald, a good deal. Cecil Bellamy, for example, was a favourite with MacDonald because he was continually writing letters about his adventures. Richard West, who landed the regional job in 1958, was a perpetual thorn in MacDonald's side, not only because he failed to communicate but also because his handwriting was as unreadable as Arabic to a North American Indian.

"I trust you survived in Winnipeg," MacDonald wrote to West during his trip, continuing:

> So far we have not seen any release in the newspapers regarding your adjudication of the plays. I have managed to decipher your cryptographic writing and believe I have correctly interpreted your wishes. Note I have agreed to reroute you direct from Montreal to New York. We will not do this until your arrival back in Ontario. Sorry to hear you were so ill in Toronto, thus preventing your expected extra-curricular activities. Most concerned to hear you had trouble at the Park Plaza when they refused to cash your travellers cheques. This is completely unheard of. Canadian travellers cheques are currency anywhere in Canada, far more so than a cheque from the DDF. While you are relaxing at Banff, horizontal, you might be able to raise yourself on one elbow with appropriate pillows and outline your report to the executive up to that point on your tour."

Interestingly, the crushing prospect of the tour itself did not deter regional adjudicators. Before leaving London, for example, West received details of a crowded itinerary which covered just over a month of his trip. He – and other judges

239

– could have pleaded terminal illness there and then. None ever did.

London, Wed. Jan. 1, 7:30 p.m. BOAC 633.
Gander, Thurs. Jan. 2, 4:05 a.m.
Gander, Fri. Jan. 3, 3:30 a.m. Single drawing room.
Corner Brook, Fri. Jan. 3, 12 noon.
Leave Corner Brook Sun. Jan. 12, 1:01 p.m. Share drawing room.
Arrive Port aux Basques Sun. Jan. 12, 7:30 p.m.
Leave Port aux Basques Sun. Jan. 12, 9:30 p.m. Ferry. Share two-bedroom.
North Sydney, Mon. Jan. 13, 6:00 a.m.
Leave North Sydney, Mon. Jan. 13, 8:50 a.m.
Arrive New Glasgow, Mon. Jan. 13, 3:04 p.m.
Leave New Glasgow Mon. Jan. 13, 8:35 a.m.
Arrive Truro, Sun. Jan. 19, 10:20 a.m.
Continue in Sydney-Montreal sleeper.
Arrive Sackville, Sun. Jan. 19, 1:45 p.m.
Leave Sackville Fri. Jan. 24, 4:05 p.m.
Arrive Charlottetown Fri. Jan. 24, 9 p.m.
Leave Charlottetown, Tues. Jan. 28, 7:45 a.m.
Arrive Campbellton, Tues. Jan. 28, 7:20 p.m.
Leave Campbellton Tues. Jan. 28, 8:45 p.m.
Arrive Levis Wed. Jan. 29, 4:40 a.m.
Leave Quebec Sun. Feb. 2, 2:00 p.m.
Arrive Montreal Sun. Feb. 2, 5:50 p.m.
Leave Montreal Sun. Feb. 9, 4:00 p.m. (chair).
Arrive Ottawa, Sun. Feb. 9, 6:00 p.m.

Final festival adjudicators, of course, had only one week of judging to do, but they also had the responsibility of handing out the most coveted trophies. "And that," Professor Emrys Jones who adjudicated the 1947 Final has remembered, "was a really hopeless job. It was very much like going to an agricultural fair and being asked to say which was the best out of that pig, that cow and that chicken. There were always so many different kinds of plays it was difficult to decide which was the best." Philip Hope-Wallace, who adjudicated the Final in 1949, 1958, 1960 and 1964 has recalled his DDF experiences in somewhat the same way. "It was always extraordinarily difficult to compare one thing and another. If all the plays were by Barrie for example – perhaps the same play – then we would be able to separate the sheep from the goats. But to a certain extent we were being asked to compare an omelette with a piece of cheese or a bicycle with a cabin cruiser."

Hope-Wallace has also stated that despite their awareness of importance and power, the DDF adjudicators were often scared men. "Even if you're right, you're wrong. People like adjudicators who won't pull punches. You must be absolutely frank or they'll loathe you and feel you're trying to butter them up. Yet people are extremely sensitive when they've come all the way from Vancouver in a cattle truck to Toronto and give the performance of their lives." Then there was the human need to live up to the awesome image. "You come off a stage fishing for compliments," Hope-Wallace once told an interviewer. Playwright and novelist Robertson Davies who adjudicated a regional festival in 1967 has said: "The temptation to say something that will raise a laugh or be a smart aleck becomes very strong after a while. To exalt yourself above the job you are doing is very great. And this can be death."

But almost all of the adjudicators succumbed to the temptation to make themselves *liked*, even though they knew the cream of society was cooling its heels at the stage door for a chance to shake hands. "I'm happy to be here on a stage – the only stage on which I have ever appeared professionally in the Dominion of Canada," quipped Robert Speaight to roars of appreciative laughter. Smiled Rupert Harvey during his 1934 regional swing: "I live normally in London, England. I am now in London, Ontario. The only difference I can find is that London, Ontario is far friendlier than London, England." Gushed Malcolm Morley in 1935: "What a great experience this is for me. I am a great enthusiast of the theatre! I would go miles to see a play." And stated S. R. Littlewood with a touch of endearing nervousness: "This is my last appearance and this is the last performance. If you want to throw your hats, please throw them now."

But despite the stage-fright, the endless travelling for some, the conundrums of adjudication and the overwhelming hospitality, the consensus from most DDF adjudicators has been that the experience was worth it. "People were very nice to me," Hope-Wallace has fondly remembered. "Afterwards, of course, there were terrible post-mortems." Emrys Jones has agreed: "It was a lot of fun. I was treated wonderfully." Jones has also admitted that the lobbying from groups and the "frequent propositions" made to him as adjudicator at the 1949 Final was a fascinating sidelight of his assignment. Once, during his week in London, Jones was "kidnapped" by friends of a competing team and taken to a house in the country where he was offered all kinds of attractive distractions. "I told my hosts that if they didn't take me back to town immediately, I'd put on my hat and walk there." Jones, who attended many festivals during the 1950's, has said he knows the same kind of persuasion was used in most instances, however carefully the DDF executive tried to shield their top attraction from such unseemly goings-on. Those close to the DDF who remember past festivals will admit, though, there were times when the top attraction made a point of escaping the protective moral shield altogether. Well aware that a big name contributed to big box-office receipts, the DDF policy-makers – always discreet ladies and gentlemen, anyway – looked the other way.

As time went on, big names from abroad became more elusive for the DDF's hunters to track down. The use of Canadians as adjudicators had been talked about as far back as the 1930's, but it was not until 1960 that the Dominion Drama Festival actually allowed there were men and women in the Canadian theatre (which was beginning to develop professional muscle) who were qualified enough – and interesting enough – to work as DDF judges. Even then, the Bessborough-Massey-Osborne tradition died hard. 1960 was the year the corporation had to admit the job of cross-country adjudication by one man was really a tortuous task. It was decided that several judges should be retained to pick winners from the eight newly-created zones. Naturally it would be impossible for the DDF to afford such a crowd of imported adjudicators, so the executive looked around from likely candidates at home. The big Final? Oh, a man from abroad, of course. Philip Hope-Wallace, back for his third appearance.

The pioneer contingent of eight Canadian regional adjudicators were either supporters of the DDF or well-known professional and Little Theatre directors: James Dean of Toronto: Robert Gill of Toronto's Hart House; Eugène Jousse of Quebec; Dorothy Davies of Vancouver; Dr. Betty Mitchell of Calgary; Guy Beaulne of Quebec's Department of Cultural Affairs; Jean Béraud of Quebec; and Leon Major, who would become artistic director of the Neptune Theatre in Halifax. It was not until 1965 that a Canadian (except for Emrys Jones) was handed the once awe-inspiring job of adjudicating the Final festival. The DDF picked Guy Beaulne as top attraction at its Final in Brockville, Ontario. But the corporation cautiously looked to Europe again in 1966 when it assigned the Final adjudication to actor Marius Goring, a judge whom critic Herbert Whittaker described as "a frail ship on the waters of adjudication." Well obviously, imported adjudicators were not always a sure bet. Guy Beaulne was invited back in 1967 (the DDF badly wanted to nail such Canadian names as Jean Gascon or Gratien Gelinas for a Final but these men were always otherwise occupied) then in 1968, David Peacock, director of the National Theatre School was asked to judge the Final in Windsor, Ontario. French theatrical celebrity Pierre Lefevre made a second appearance at a DDF Final in 1969 but the DDF's competitive years ended in a blaze of Canadian nationalism when the durable Beaulne returned to preside over the Winnipeg Final of 1970.

There have been differences of opinion within the DDF as to whether the organization made the right decision to use Canadians as adjudicators. Some carpers have argued that imported men could always roast groups if necessary while local judges might try to avoid such discouraging confrontations. Others have said that Canadian adjudicators were always better than foreigners because they understood the theatre of their own land. David Gardner, former artistic director of the Vancouver Playhouse who adjudicated for the DDF, is one man who has said the switch to local talent was right. Even so, the Canadians discovered – together with their imported predecessors – that even limited regional adjudication was no picnic. Gardner tells in his own words what it was like to be a DDF adjudicator:

"I enjoyed it. I loved doing the research, I liked the communication with people. A great deal of lobbying went on, but one had to keep one's sense of humour about that and realize that such coercion goes on in the professional theatre as well. It goes on in any endeavour. How about government lobbies? But an adjudicator had to keep himself as pure as possible through all that and call the shots as he saw them. I was invited around a great deal but made it a rule not to attend a cocktail party before a play, though I'd be happy to attend the final night's party after it was all over. I was most interested to meet groups after each performance but that was after the fact. I didn't want to meet the performers before the play. That wouldn't be fair. I wanted to see the play with no preconceived ideas. If I met an actor at a cocktail party before I saw him on stage, for example, I could have said oh my gosh this man isn't acting at all. The man is simply being himself – though to be yourself on stage is to act rather well.

"Yes, there was sometimes coercion, but usually there was great kindness and warmth and people understood the attempt to keep one's integrity. I would want to read the play over during the afternoon of a performance so I often ate alone. But that was also because I wanted to keep myself as uncluttered and as well rested as possible. I would say it was tough work.

"I had some strange experiences, of course. I particularly remember my adjudication in Newfoundland in 1961. I arrived at some airport in the middle of winter with snowdrifts fourteen feet high, to be met by nobody. There was a call over the public-address system that a cab was waiting for me. I got into the cab and the driver said we were going to go to Corner Brook. We drove and we drove through a valley of snow. I saw nothing but snow for 50 miles. The taxi bill was $32. I had $35 in my pocket. I said, Jesus, what a welcome to Newfoundland. I was put up at the Bowater Hotel. Nobody met me in the lobby and there was no note in the box and I smelled sulphur in the air from the paper plant. Well, I thought this is a great welcome, I suppose someone will get in touch. I went to bed about 11:30 p.m. then suddenly the phone rang and someone said 'oh, you're here, we heard you've checked in, good, come over and have a drink.' I told the person I was in bed and he replied 'well, get your clothes on.' So I did. When I got to the room, the man who had been talking to me promptly handed me an envelope and said 'here's what you're supposed to say about this play on Thursday night.' I said thank you very much, took the envelope, put it in my pocket and said I would be very pleased to read it Friday morning.

"The man grinned and said 'oh, you're a fighter are you?' I said yes, I was a fighter. 'Oh,' replied the man, 'well, you're too young to be an adjudicator.' I said perhaps you're right, but I think you should decide after you've seen me adjudicate. Well, said the man, what do you think about this play and that play? I said I think that, that, and that. Why? Oh, then, you know what you're talking about. I hope so. Then I asked about the arrangements for adjudication. I wanted to see the theatre. The man said no, the first thing the next morning you get your photograph taken with the manager of the Bowater Paper Plant. I said, fine. But then I want to see the theatre and backstage and the arrangements for my little desk and I want to see the room I can write in. There would be no room for me to write in. I told them I wanted a room to write in. Would I have to write in the theatre with all those guys sitting around watching? Or have you got the whole week written out for me?

"Ha, ha. You're to have supper tomorrow with so and so from a group and we have cocktails every afternoon at four. I said thanks very much, I will turn down all those things. I will see you at the party at the end of the week. Oh. Well, who would introduce me at the theatre tomorrow night? Nobody. Go and introduce yourself. I said I would not do it. Why? Well, I said I wanted someone to go on and say this is Mr. Gardner. If I go on and say I am Mr. Gardner, who is to believe me? Okay, they would get someone to do that.

"Well, the festival started. The first night, it was J. M. Barrie's *Mary Rose*, not one of my favourite plays. I tore it to shreds. I had a heckler all through the adjudication, a man sitting in the front row who was very drunk. So I heckled back and said come on up and we'll all adjudicate together. It was a real battle. The entire week was a battle. The next day I was invited to lunch on a Bowater boat that was frozen into the harbour on an angle. I said I'd go to that one because I was supposed to meet all of Newfoundland's officialdom. I was the adjudicator, right? Well, there was a head table plus a lot of small tables and I was put as far away from the head table as possible. As a matter of fact, I was put at a table with my heckler, who happened to be a drunken millionaire who lived in Newfoundland. We had a marvellous luncheon. At the end of it we even liked each other.

"I said to him, shall we fight those bloody sons of guns up there at the head table and he said, why not. Give them hell the whole week. They've been used to running things here, so give them hell. And I did. Every night I gave adjudications as hard and as crisp as I could. But by the end of the week I think I had won people over. On the Thursday night, the group that had won the regional festival every year for the past six years came in that afternoon and went away that night. They didn't stay for the Final night, they were much too busy and confident. The performance was terrible and I said so. Also I learned they were all on pep pills. As a matter of fact, I mentioned in my adjudication that it looked as though the company was on drugs. Well, that was earth-shattering and at the end of it the man who had given me the envelope that first night said 'you can tear it up, you did it better than I did.' I said I hoped so.

"On the last night, I reviewed the final play then I went away and came back twenty minutes later and recounted my entire impression of Newfoundland from beginning to end. I talked about the insular attitude, the choice of repertoire which was entirely British repertory. That I would never have known I was anywhere near to the North American continent and so on. I asked them to join Canada. This, apparently, was all being taped. After saying all that I added that I was supposed to hand out some silverware. First award to this, so and so award to that. I give it to this company even though it doesn't deserve it. The standards were superb but the morality and intent behind the production and the creativity was nil. However, it was the best English repertory production of the week.

"Then the Lieutenant-Governor of Newfoundland got up to speak. He said he had a prepared speech but that he was going to tear it up. What was the point? Mr. Gardner was a courageous young man and it had been a most stimulating half hour. Straight from the shoulder you might say. So, straight from the shoulder back, he had to say he didn't agree with a lot of things that had been said. But Mr. Gardner had given everyone food for thought, so go in peace. That was Newfoundland. It was rough, but I remember it with a great deal of affection. It's interesting that the ones who told me to go to hell in the beginning were the ones who drove me to the airport."

CHAPTER EIGHT

The Social Side

1. "What do you do in the DDF besides putting on those plays?"

One sure way of getting a supporter of the Dominion Drama Festival really mad – or sad – is to mention the fact that the corporation was constantly criticized for its snobbish image, earnest socializing and hard-drinking bouts at Festival. If the crack about hard drinking fails to spark protests, a comment concerning the DDF's opposite image as a tea-and-crumpets group is guaranteed to do the job. Then, if you really want to go the whole way, simply add the words "mink-coated dilletantes."

Not that the governors and executive of the DDF (even those still active in Theatre Canada) were unaware of both the words and the criticism. Back in the 1930's, in fact, when festival audiences bristled with vice-regal, political and socially-prominent names, it pleased DDF supporters to know they were connected with such an elite organization. In later years, when criticism began to rankle, the DDF hastened to point out that the corporation's embarrassingly persistent image was inherited from the Bessborough days and besides, if it had not been for the support of important persons, the organization would not have got off the ground in the first place.

It took some time for Lord Bessborough's high-toned influence on the DDF to fade, however. And no wonder. At a time of bleak depression in Canada there could have been little social copy written that sounded as colourful as Adèle M. Gianelli's story of the 1933 Final in *Saturday Night:*

. . . Lady Borden's lunch for Mr. Rupert Harvey preceded the Saturday matinee and one of the guests was Lady Tupper who had come down from Winnipeg, the city which sent the first-prize winners, the Masquers Club in *The Man Born to be Hanged*. Afterwards, His Excellency entertained the Toronto and London players at Government House where they met, not only Mr. Ralph Alderson, His Excellency's cousin who is the foremost amateur actor in England, but that most important young leading man, Master George Ponsonby who, if not exactly a star, looked like a little ray of sunshine in his buttercup-yellow smock as he smiled cherubically and said "Mum" was coming home tomorrow. His Excellency received in the Chinese Gallery with Mr. A. F. Lascelles, Colonel Willis-O'Connor, Captain Stuart-French and Captain Tyron in attendance, all who have infinite tact in making guests feel *chez nous*. . . . Another Government House guest that day was that charming American woman, Mrs. D. P. Cruickshank, who came with her husband and received a warm welcome after a long convalescence. The French Minister and Madame Henry, Mr. Justice and Madame Rinfret and the Comte and Comtesse de la Greze were in His Excellency's dinner-party that night. . . . The newest form of *hors d'oeuvres* at Mrs. Black's cocktail party for the Vancouver Little Theatre was mermaidish, being *dulse* as the Maritimers call seaweed. This and other succulents were being offered with parliamentary persuasion by Colonel Coghill and Captain Ian Mackenzie and from the diplomatic set was that jolly couple, Mr. W. H. Beck, the American Consul-General and his pretty wife, both just back from holidaying in New York.

The handsome panelled room in the Speaker's Chambers was scintillating that day with its crystal chandeliers aglow; Mrs. Charles Camsell who had given a luncheon for her guest, Mrs. Wood, and some others came in from the House where they had been listening to Dr. Manion piloting his Railway Bill; the ADC's all came in after their tea at Government House. . . . David Drury arrives with Miss Catharine Dougherty's dinner-party and Mrs. H. A. K. Drury is looking just a trifle sad as that fascinating daughter of hers weds within a fortnight and goes to live in Liverpool . . . much stage talk . . . do you know that Mrs. Patrick Campbell takes only one lump of sugar in place of dinner before a performance?

With the newspaper headlines wailing about lengthening breadlines and continuing unemployment why should anyone carp about the fact that there was still some glamour left in Canada? After all, people were crowding into the cinemas to sample the tinsel from Hollywood, weren't they? But carpers there were. Roly Young of the Winnipeg *Free Press* wrote as far back as the 1936 regional playoff in Manitoba: "And now it is on to Ottawa. Apparently it will always be On to Ottawa, which is sufficient proof that in the long run the Drama Festival ends up as a society field day. Ottawa Society will go under martial law and bivouac the invading troops. They will be wined and dined, there will be pink teas and beautiful big receptions, everyone will have a grand time and they will take a few hours off to put on their plays. . . ."

Well, that was the way Bessborough shaped the Dominion Drama Festival. There had to be a spirit of fun as well as purpose. And, of course, a spirit of camaraderie. As festivals progressed in the nineteen-thirties, in fact, it seemed as though the DDF's hard core of regional supporters were becoming exactly what Bessborough wanted – one big, happy family. Soon, there were familiar faces (invariably WASP), all of whom owned the right clothes, knew the right people and who felt the somewhat arty character of Festival allowed them to celebrate a little more raffishly than they would at home. It became a giggly Festival expectation that some interesting love affairs would blossom during the week of the Final and that not everyone would stay entirely sober. After all, if was Col. Osborne himself who smilingly admitted that if the DDF turned out to be a success "it will have been founded on love and whisky." It was also Col. Osborne who mildly remarked at some festival that "in these days of cosmic research . . . and a planet is a hundred thousand miles away from another star and another star is a hundred thousand miles away from yet another star, what does it matter who gets into bed with who, anyway?"

The Happy Family Syndrome is illustrated in an article written by Mona Coxwell in her Toronto-based publication *Curtain Call* after the 1937 Final in Ottawa:

> Fun to be there, meeting old acquaintances! How is the Festival? Very gloomy answers. Nothing of any importance, with the exception of one or two of the French plays we are told, two of which are said to be excellent. At any rate, nothing has been missed by arriving late in the week. Nice to see so many familiar faces – Cizzie Brickenden from London looking lovely as always. Martha Allan from Montreal, sauve and distinguished. Nella Jefferis from Toronto, very charming and refreshed after a long holiday in the south. Sterndale Bennett is there and J. L. Robertson from Halifax. And there are Edgar and Agnes Stone from Toronto and Lady Tupper from Winnipeg. The slim pages in their red velvet tunics form a guard of honor. A little signal is given by Captain Leslie Chance, everyone rises and the vice-regal party arrives, passes down the aisle to reserved places in the front row. (What a pity they are always obliged to sit so far forward – we are certain they cannot see the actors' feet and a close-up in the theatre is so disillusioning!). Another little signal from Captain Chance – just a flutter of hands to the audience so it will be sure to do the right thing – and everyone sits again.
>
> How charming Her Excellency looks; they say she is shy and does not like people to stare at her. They also say she has attended the theatre every night of the Festival. For her sake we hope the plays

251

will be more cheerful tonight. Alas, more gloom! A fine setting, though, has been conceived for this play *Nocturne* by Harry Foster of the Little Theatre Guild of Charlottetown. But the play is absolutely without life and the actors carved out of a substance that has no relation to flesh and blood. The pace is painful and there is never any variation. The audience becomes politely restless. A certain well-known critic who has been sleeping quietly since the parting of the curtains, now begins a gentle snore. M. St. Denis, the distinguished adjudicator, turns and looks at him. Why wake him? No, he will simply move his small table further up the aisle away from the disturbed breathing. He probably envies the critic his ability to sleep!

While the society writers swarmed appreciatively to record the colourful goings-on at the Dominion Drama Festival, imported adjudicators themselves (some of whom remembered the drab attendances at British Drama League festivals) stared dumbfounded at Canada's fashionable audiences. As critic S. R. Littlewood was moved to comment in 1939 from the stage of the Grand Theatre in London, Ontario: "This audience is more brilliant than any I have ever seen in other than London!" That was the year Lord and Lady Tweedsmuir arrived at the festival in their private train, attended by uniformed squads of aides. Lady Flora Eaton motored up for the occasion, bringing her two dauthters, Evelyn and Florence. Toronto critic Hector Charlesworth held court in the foyer. Then there were the titles: the socially-smitten Prince Paul Lieven of Montreal and Baroness Helle Rosenkrantz of Denmark "who wore," according to a breathless *London Free Press* report, "a black accordion-pleated skirt and a chartreuse green lace blouse." After the final play on Saturday night, there was the usual parade of evening dress to a reception at the Hunt Club, then dancing at the armouries until dawn.

The 1939 Final, of course, was the last big show for the DDF until the Second World War, but the society-oriented image of the corporation persisted after it was revived in 1947.

One who helped perpetuate this public conception of the organization was its chairman, D. Park Jamieson, a man who had experienced the infectious sparkle of the early festivals and who had been thoroughly soaked in Bessborough tradition as well. Jamieson was celebrated for his rigid insistence on protocol, the proper clothes and his meticulously-planned dinner parties and receptions. The choice of guests invited to the presidential suite received as much attention from Jamieson as the perusal of DDF budget sheets. At the end of his chairmanship in 1952, agitation for a more relaxed festival had resulted in the creation of "green rooms" where participants from groups could not only meet each other (the early tradition was for local hostesses to entertain at their homes) but mingle with adjudicators and DDF policy-makers as well. In 1938 when Col. Henry Osborne suggested something of the kind, adding that "entertainments should be cut down so more time could be allowed," Jamieson was among those members of the Executive Committee who considered the idea to be pure heresy.

But even the cosy green rooms, and other attempts to democratize the DDF Finals as time went by, did little to erode the general belief that the corporation was merely a front for socialites out to have a good time. "Why, I once heard one of the governors remark that the DDF could be a really nice organization if only it didn't have to put on those damned plays," Toronto playwright Tom Hendry (a former director of the now defunct Canadian Theatre Centre) has remembered. In a 1971 issue of *Canadian Forum*, Hendry also wrote bitterly: "Historically here in Canada, outfits like the DDF developed the original arch-type, pre-war groupie species Cultural, subspecies Theatrical by providing periodic regional bacchanalia leading each year to a spectacular week at the national level of priapic and Dionysian mysteries cunningly designed to look like a competition between groups of amateur thespians. To them goes the credit of devising the inspired blend of devotion and debauchery which to this day is so much catnip to the groupie."

A letter from DDF director Richard MacDonald to incoming president Roy Stewart in 1960 indicates how the corporation itself felt about all the talk. The National Film Board had made a movie at the 1960 Vancouver Final called *Canada on Stage* and MacDonald enthused to Stewart that he had seen the film and enjoyed it. "And," he added, "the social side of the festival is played down, thank goodness." Yet in an interview, past-president Alvin Shaw once protested: "Yes, we've had our social moments. But it was unfortunate that our critics always looked in on us when we were relaxing with drinks in our hands. But to call us a dilletante organization only interested in drinking tea and liquor is ridiculous. People don't realize the amount of work done year round on committees."

In any case, DDF supporters have pointed out, Nonstop Socializing was not always at the command of the national committee. Regional representatives in host cities invariably went out of their way to make *their* chance to stage the Final the biggest, most lavish occasion of them all – especially when the DDF's annual culture-fest opened a new local auditorium. There was real cause for extra celebrations in Charlottetown, Edmonton and St. John's when workmen had scarcely quit the finished building before the festival's advance guard was setting up the registration tables. Then, of course, there were other reasons for throwing a special party. At the DDF's thirtieth birthday in 1962, the organization managed to persuade Lord Bessborough (Viscount Duncannon had succeeded his father by then) to come to the Winnipeg Final and this sparked some lively doings. Later, the corporation's excitement over its social coup was dulled when Bessborough sent the national office a bill for his travelling expenses.

When the Final at last got to Montreal in 1961, festival. chairman Judge Edouard Rinfret decided the occasion was so historic he would allow no one to forget what true French-Canadian hospitality was all about. Laurence Olivier was invited as a special guest, but he never did turn up. Who cared? There was a wine-tasting reception at the Botanical Gardens and the temperature soared to eighty-four degrees that day. There were jam sessions in the hothouses as the "tasting" degenerated into thirsty swilling. There was dancing, much Gallic embracing and vocalizing, then more wine in the buses which took the reeling guests back to the Mount Royal Hotel. The green room opposite Gratien Gelinas' Comédie Canadienne (where the Festival was held) swung noisily until dawn after each evening's performance. A mass was celebrated in Le Bon Dieu en Taxi, the cabbies' mobile chapel. Then, as a windup spectacular, a progressive meal at the leading Laurentian resorts in Val David, Ste. Marguerite, St. Sauveur and Ste. Adele was planned for the final Sunday of the week.

But the national office did make sure there was a sense of order and protocol at Festival, even amidst the partying. This persisted even into the 1960's, though there was one major effort to remove some of the starchiness from Final festivals in 1957. It was in August of 1956 that David Ongley – then president – wrote to Robert Speaight in London: "It's a great relief to have a final adjudicator for 1957 at such an early date. Just received word from Bill Williams that you're able to accept the engagement for our festival in Edmonton next May. Dress will be the same as when you last adjudicated the Final, that is, white tie and tails for the evening performances, matinees quite informal." But in April the following year, Ongley was writing to Speaight again informing him he would not have to bring tails with him that year. "I know how you hate the chore of carrying them. We're not even insisting that the executive wear white tie throughout the week, though they will probably turn up in dinner jackets." Speaight replied wryly: "Your letter shocks me deeply. I always thought Canada was the last stronghold of the white tie."

Some tradition-chained DDF supporters continued to wear full dress (and even decorations) at Festival, though, and there was always general approval of the national office's detailed program arrangements when vice-royalty planned to be present. At the Halifax Final of 1958 when Vincent Massey attended as Governor General, DDF governors were handed a fourteen-point procedure sheet which looked as though it had come straight from the secretariat at Buckingham Palace.

1.   6:00 p.m. The Governors and Dinner Guests assemble in the Bedford Room, the Nova Scotian Hotel.
2.   6:15 p.m. (a) His Excellency, the Governor General arrives at the Nova Scotian.
     (b) the Governors and guests are presented.
     (c) cocktails are served.

3.	6:45 to 8 p.m. Dinner in main dining room.
4.	8:00 to 8:10 p.m. (a) His Excellency retires.

3.   6:45 to 8 p.m. Dinner in main dining room.

4.   8:00 to 8:10 p.m. (a) His Excellency retires.
(b) Immediately upon departure of vice-regal party the Governors and guests proceed to the Queen Elizabeth High School Auditorium.

5.   8:25 p.m. (a) His Excellency arrives at Queen Elizabeth High School Auditorium.
(b) His Excellency is received by President and Mr. D. W. McGibbon, and chairman of Halifax festival committee, Mr. John Ellis and Mrs. Ellis, also House Manager Mr. David Zive and Mrs. Zive.
(c) Following reception, receiving party proceeds to their seats.

6.   (a) After receiving party is seated the House Manager announces from the stage in front of the curtain the arrival of His Excellency and the audience stands.
(b) His Excellency, accompanied by Mrs. McGibbon, Commander F. J. D. Pemberton, Mrs. Lionel Massey, Mr. D. W. McGibbon and aides de camp to His Excellency, Flight Lieutenant Ian MacMillan and Lieutenant Alan Henley and commodore D. Raymond proceed to seats.

7.   On His Excellency reaching his seat THE QUEEN.

8.   Performance by Coaldale Little Theatre of *All Summer Long* by Robert Anderson.

9.   Mr. Philip Hope-Wallace adjudicates the play and then withdraws to his retiring room to decide on the awards.

10.   Immediately following the adjudication there will be an intermission of 10 minutes during which the following action will be taken:
(a) the set will be struck and props removed. Drapes will be run in. Four suitable chairs will be set centre stage about 6 feet from curtain line. Two tables will be placed backstage left and right on which trophies will be placed. Lectern to be set just at curtain line in front of centre chair.
(b) When stage is set and signal given that adjudicator is ready for announcement of the awards, platform

party consisting of His Excellency, Mrs. D. W. McGibbon and Mr. John Ellis proceeds via right passageway to the stage. Position on stage facing audience: Mr. John Ellis, His Excellency, Mrs. D. W. McGibbon, Mr. Hope-Wallace.

(c) Audience will be given signal to return to seats.

(d) When all seated, curtain will be opened.

11.   (a) Mrs. D. W. McGibbon as chairman, expresses her thanks to local committee, followed by a short address by Mr. J. Ellis.

(b) Mrs. McGibbon presents His Excellency who will address audience.

(c) Mrs. McGibbon re-introduces Mr. Hope-Wallace and returns to her seat.

(d) Mr. Hope-Wallace announces the awards, concluding with the Calvert Trophy, asking each winner to come on stage. He will present each trophy except the Calvert Award and cheque for $1,000 which His Excellency will present. Trophies will be handed to His Excellency and Mr. Hope-Wallace by Mr. Richard MacDonald.

(e) Mrs. McGibbon makes presentation to Mr. Hope-Wallace.

12.   (a) Mrs. McGibbon requests that after the departure of His Excellency all winners will come backstage with their trophies for photographs. She explains all trophies must then be left with the national director for inscription and refurbishing.

(b) Mrs. McGibbon announces the departure of the vice-regal party asking the audience to remain standing until His Excellency and his party has left the auditorium.

(c) As His Excellency departs accompanied by Mrs. McGibbon, Commander F. J. D. Pemberton, Mrs. Lionel Massey and Mr. and Mrs. John Ellis, the official party and receiving line fall in behind the vice-regal party.

13.   Audience leaves the theatre.

14.   Festival is over.

2. Competition and awards are all part of the prestige.

Criticism of the competitive aspects of the Dominion Drama Festival began to reach Ottawa and Vincent Massey's cluttered desk at Batterwood House early in the history of the Dominion Drama Festival. "There is something childish about grownups competing for a prize," rapped Thomas Archer in a 1933 *Saturday Night* article. "In sport it may be permissible, but in art it is out of place and may very likely cause incalculable harm. Criticism is an excellent thing and let it be as severe as possible. But classification is a totally different thing from criticism and when that element enters, there is bound to be a certain amount of heart-burning."

But competition and awards were part of the Bessborough plan from the beginning and everyone connected with the DDF endlessly agreed that the most exciting moments of Festival were when the winners were announced. In the first years of the DDF, trophies were awarded at a Sunday luncheon but in the 1950's this was changed. The final night of Festival then became prize-giving time as well as the DDF's last social fling of the week. Interesting VIPs could always be counted on to hand out the hardware, and this enhanced the prestige of the corporation. As time went by the executive committee also discovered that awards themselves could be used to perpetuate the names of DDF notables and other important theatrical personages. By the end of the 1930's the Bessborough and Sir Barry Jackson prizes had been joined by mementoes to the best actor and the French Ambassador to Canada was offering awards for the top individual performances by a French-Canadian actor and actress.

The first backlash concerning competition and awards came after the Second World War at a 1947 executive meeting when Professor K. W. Gordon of the University of Saskatchewan "dropped what he admittedly considered to be a bomb" after the governors were asked for suggestions concerning an adjudicator for the 1948 Final. Professor Gordon urged that there should be a non-competitive festival in 1948 with no awards at all. "There is no reason that because we have trophies now we should continue to award them," Professor

Gordon told an astonished committee. "I have seen groups continue to direct their affairs long after they were dead just because at one time they won trophies at a festival." He emphasized that no matter how much fellowship had existed during Festival, an "unpleasant after feeling" resulted because of awards. "Trophies have an advertising value because we've conditioned ourselves to the idea," he added. But he believed the spirit of competition would still exist "through groups meeting to present their plays, even though awards are not granted."

There were varying reactions to Professor Gordon's unprecedented idea. E. G. Sterndale Bennett agreed that a non-competitive festival had worked well in his home province of Alberta but he wondered whether competition would discourage audiences who were anxious to know if their own teams would win. Chairman Jamieson was also worried that the abandonment of competition and awards might "seriously affect the revenue" of the festival. However, it was agreed the suggestion should be brought up for discussion at the following year's Final in Ottawa. Nothing really came of it then, of course. Noncompetitive festivals with perhaps some acting awards – just to encourage press coverage – were later suggested by governors, notably critic Herbert Whittaker. At the Victoria Final of 1966 it was actually voted to make the Centennial Year show in Newfoundland a non-competitive event but the executive backed down because regional representatives from St. John's howled in protest.

After all, awards were news. Awards were exciting. Awards had status. The arena-like atmosphere of groups locked in competitive combat created adrenalin at a Final. Above all, awards had social significance. The distinguished name of the DDF's founder, Governor General Lord Bessborough, still lived through his trophy. Sir Barry Jackson was remembered. Then, in the 1950's, other names associated with the DDF appeared on the list of awards. There was the Martha Allan Challenge Trophy for the best visual presentation. There was the Henry Osborne Challenge Trophy – the gift of Vincent Massey – for the best performance by a man at the Final. There was the Nella Jefferis Challenge Trophy – donated by the Heliconian Club to honour Toronto's late champion of community theatre

– for the best performance by a woman. There was the Louis Jouvet Challenge Trophy for the best director – a tribute to a great French actor and a nice bilingual touch as well. Then there were the *Saturday Night* Magazine plaques for the best supporting male and female roles at the Final, proof that the media had been staunch supporters of the DDF down through the years.

Awards really became an explosive issue within the DDF in 1952, however, when the corporation finalized its deal with Calvert Distillers and found itself with a major sponsor at last. According to David Ongley's recollections, the distillery was quite amiable about the DDF's ideas concerning awards. The festival organization suggested there should be thirteen trophies for each of the regions plus a super trophy to be presented to the winning group at the Final. The Bessborough Trophy? As far back as 1950 when talks with Calvert's began, the problem of how to dispose of the DDF's revered top award was tucked discreetly under the rug. It was finally dragged into the open early in 1952.

In the meantime, however, DDF negotiators had been making sure there would be Calvert trophies to hand out if the sponsorship plan finally germinated. Pauline McGibbon had talked with Toronto artist Cleve Horne and asked him to suggest someone who might prepare some preliminary designs. Horne in turn recommended sculptor Emmanuel Hahn who worked at the project for a few weeks then unveiled a clay model mainly composed of Grecian columns. "There was even a space for a whisky bottle," Ongley has recalled. "It was definitely not what we had in mind." Ongley and Mrs. McGibbon went back to Horne for more ideas. Medallions, perhaps? No, not impressive enough. Bronze and stone were heavy and plaques were too reminiscent of the old days. Perhaps, thought Horne, carved wood might be suitable? Both Ongley and Mrs. McGibbon agreed the idea sounded sensible so Horne sent the two negotiators to see sculptors Frances Loring and Florence Wyle, two Americans who had moved their studio to Toronto in 1912. Known affectionately as "the girls" (though the women were both in their sixties at the time), the celebrated artists listened carefully to the DDF's suggestions then submitted sketches. Those in the know – including Calvert's advertising department – were delighted with the results. Later, when work on the fourteen trophies actually began (using various woods such as mahogany, maple, tulip-wood, red birch, white-wood and sumach), "the girls" brought in Sylvia Daoust from Montreal to help with the job.

Behind-the-scenes financial dickering continued, however, and so did talks concerning the names of the trophies and their status within the DDF awards structure. Calvert's naturally wanted their prizes to be important features at both regional and Final levels but were somewhat reluctant to have all of them tagged with the Calvert label. Wouldn't this smack of blatant publicity? The DDF agreed that it might, then suggested that the regional trophies be given idealistic names such as *Meditation, Poetry, Wisdom* and so on. As for status, there was no question that thirteen trophies should go to the top regional performances.

The trophies finally finished, they were photographed, the stills mailed to Ottawa and at a special meeting of the executive committee, the disposition of the awards by region was decided by draw. British Columbia got *Meditation*. Alberta, *Truth*. Saskatchewan, *Music*. Manitoba, *Dedication*. Western Ontario, *Dance*. Central Ontario, *Tragedy*. Eastern Ontario, *Fawn*. Western Quebec, *Silence*. Eastern Quebec, *Love*. Nova Scotia, *Poetry*. New Brunswick, *Wisdom*. Prince Edward Island, *Invocation*. Newfoundland ended up with *Charity*.

The problem of what to call the super Final trophy was still unsolved. Calvert's continued to be unsure about whether it would be politic to name the Wyle carving after the distillery, but finally at an anguished meeting, Ongley thumped his fist on the table and decided loudly: "To hell with it! Why don't we go ahead and call it the Calvert Trophy, anyway?" Everyone present quickly agreed. But then the spectre again raised its embarrassing head: what to do with the Bessborough plaque? The best idea at the moment, the committee figured, was to strike a special committee of two – Robertson Davies and Herbert Whittaker – and ask the pair to devise some suitably distinguished way of disposing of Lord Bessborough's gift to Canadian culture. Should the plaque, for example, be given for something like lighting or imaginative staging? Bessborough was fond of that sort of thing. But then, that would perhaps downgrade the trophy too drastically. Maybe the gesso should be enshrined in a glass case as a permanent memorial to the DDF's founder.

Chairman Park Jamieson was asked if he would write to Lord Bessborough about the whole matter and in May 1952 he dictated a lengthy letter outlining the financial problems of the DDF, how the corporation had got backing from Calvert's and why it was therefore necessary to make the distillery's trophy the main award at the Final.

> The one matter which caused both the executive and the governors great concern was that, under the arrangement made, the trophy so generously donated by you would no longer go to the winning group at the Final Festival each year. As you were directly responsible for the inauguration of the Festival and its early success, everyone present at the meetings in Saint John was most desirous of having the Bessborough Trophy kept alive and form an important part of the festival awards. We realized, of course, that the disposition and future use of the trophy was a matter for your decision and I was instructed to get in touch with you and obtain your wishes in this regard.

The letter went on to say that a special committee had been formed and ideas were expected momentarily. "If on the other hand, you do not desire to have the terms of reference altered, it was suggested that, with your permission, we could have the trophy suitably mounted, framed and hung in some permanent place in Ottawa, such as the Ottawa Little Theatre." Bessborough promptly replied, thanking Jamieson for his letter and saying he wanted to ask Vincent Massey's advice in the matter. "I think you will agree it would be suitable that I should consult him as Patron and Honorary President on the subject before replying to you."

Davies and Whittaker chewed over the problem of

262

the Bessborough Trophy and finally emerged from their huddles with the brainwave that the award should be given for "outstanding achievement in the presentation of classical plays in the regional festivals of the DDF." A classic was understood to mean any play of recognized value, fifty years old or more. Translations of foreign classics would not necessarily need to be over fifty years old to qualify. The DDF liked the suggestion. After all, Bessborough was known to be addicted to Shakespeare and Molière and the word "classic" was dignified and had status. Davies and Whittaker were congratulated on their ingenuity.

Thunderclaps concerning the Calvert sponsorship were already echoing around the regions, but Lady Margaret Tupper zeroed in with a specific protest concerning the disposition of the Bessborough Trophy that must have shaken even Governor General Vincent Massey in Ottawa. In a sharp letter to the editor of the Winnipeg *Free Press*, Lady Tupper snorted:

> Although I have long since ceased to have any personal interest in the activities of the Dominion Drama Festival, I was a member of the original Board of Governors and organizer of the Regional Festival in Manitoba.
>
> I have read with indignation the Canadian Press dispatch from Saint John reporting that the Festival Committee has announced, apparently with much satisfaction that an annual grant for two years of $15,000 has been made by Calvert Distillers in return for which the honoured and much coveted Bessborough Trophy was to be arbitrarily discarded and replaced by a Calvert Trophy. It is unbelievable that this amazing arrangement for the deliberate, unvarnished and I would say cheaply-bought advertisement of Calvert Distillers' Canadian interests should even have been considered, let alone agreed to, by the Committee. Lord Bessborough, while Governor-General of Canada, founded the Dominion Drama Festival in the hope of establishing a Canadian theatre. It was, during his term of office, an

organization of which Canada was justly proud. That it has fallen so far below the hopes of its founder is deplorable, but at least it might have been allowed an honourable death rather than to be temporarily revived by a whisky transfusion.

An unpardonable insult has been offered not only to the founder of the festival during his lifetime but to a former Governor-General of Canada and it is sincerely hoped that some regard to decency will cause the members of the committee who were not present at the meeting at which this deplorable decision was made, or who voted against it, to register their disapproval by instant resignation unless the arrangement is cancelled immediately.

Massey observed the row over the Bessborough Trophy without official comment. Not long after Davies and Whittaker delivered their "classic play" idea to the DDF's relieved executive, he received a letter from his old festival colleague, Dorothy White, through his son Lionel:

In regard to the disposition of the Bessborough Trophy would you be so kind as to ask His Excellency to look over the enclosed recommendation from Robertson Davies and Herbert Whittaker. They were appointed by the executive of the DDF to make some suggestion for a proper and dignified use of the Trophy, subject, of course, to Lord Bessborough's approval. Mr. Park Jamieson has written Lord Bessborough fully on the subject and has had a reply saying he would like to consult His Excellency before making any decision. He has not seen the enclosed suggestions but we would like very much to have Mr. Massey's opinion and would be very grateful to you if you would draw his attention to it.

There was a personal P.S. from Mrs. White: "No one has asked my opinion but I would like to see the Trophy withdrawn from competition and hung in the National Gallery.

264

It is a beautiful example of gesso work by A. Scott Carter and there is no more space on it for further winners. I think it would be treasured now." Lionel Massey replied:

> Father wrote to Lord Bessborough about the future of the trophy and suggested that it should be awarded for some particular achievement. No doubt Lord Bessborough has now written to Mr. Jamieson conveying this general suggestion. Father has read the interesting proposal of Robertson Davies and Herbert Whittaker but, as he is Patron of the Drama Festival, he felt it would be advisable if their recommendation was taken up directly with the Chairman rather than himself. Naturally he now, as you will understand, has had to take a neutral position. I am afraid that this letter is not at all helpful but I know you will appreciate that it is preferable that Father makes no comment and that it rests with the Board of Governors. I would be interested to hear from you as to the ultimate outcome.

Even so, Vincent Massey's letter to Bessborough contained far more personal comment than his son had intimated. The communication, in fact, suggests that the entire incident was a shock for the Governor General. "I was glad to hear from you about the future of the Bessborough Trophy," he wrote to Stansted Park. "The matter has been giving me considerable concern. The published reports on this subject have given an unfortunate impression which is not borne out by the facts. This, I think, is made quite clear in Park Jamieson's letter to you, of which you were good enough to send me a copy."

Massey went on to say he felt that the Bessborough Trophy should continue to be awarded "as an encouragement and stimulus to amateur drama in Canada." Details would have to be carefully worked out, but under the altered terms of reference, the Trophy would continue to serve a very useful purpose in the field of amateur drama. The alternative of having the plaque enshrined, Massey thought would be "regrettable." If this suggestion were put into effect, the Trophy would be a

265

monument and nothing more. It would represent years of effort and achievement commencing with the imaginative beginnings of the festival under Bessborough's leadership. "If placed in the Little Theatre here or, indeed, anywhere else, it would be seen by a very limited number of people."

The first Calvert Trophy took its place as the premier DDF award at the 1953 Final Festival in Victoria, British Columbia – then still one of Canada's staunchest outposts of Empire. Ignoring the embarrassment he had clearly suffered over the awards outcry, Vincent Massey travelled from Ottawa to ceremoniously hand out the sculpture – a figure symbolic of the Greek contribution to theatre art but, unlike the regional trophies, bearing the less poetic name of Calvert Distillers. On awards night – a glittering social occasion despite the DDF's new commercial image – Massey bestowed his vice-regal blessings on the newly-financed organization with dutiful smiles and bows. It is still the opinion of DDF supporters who were there that the Governor General was genuinely sympathetic toward the corporation's woes and had decided to endorse the Calvert sponsorship even though he had been concerned about the squabble.

Objections from dissenters continued to plague the DDF's national office for some time after the 1953 Final. But as time went on, the Calvert Trophy (sweetened by the distillery's $1,000 prize cheque) almost, but not quite, achieved the cultural prestige that once surrounded the Bessborough Trophy. The gesso plaque itself was not always awarded in the regions during the years to come – a fact which may have helped it retain some of its former status. But perhaps it also became outdated. In the late 1950's and early 1960's, drama groups were becoming more adventurous in their choice of plays and Shakespeare, Molière and Corneille had less appeal.

The University Alumnae Dramatic Club of Toronto won the trophy for Checkov's *Uncle Vanya* in 1955. The Port Arthur Mummers earned it for Strindberg's *Miss Julie* in 1959. In 1960, when the DDF transformed its thirteen regions into eight zones, the Bessborough Trophy (or a reasonable facsimile) was still supposed to be awarded to the best classical production in each of the zonal areas, but few groups ever qualified. In

1964 the prize went to Toronto's Theatre Upstairs for its production of *Oedipus Rex*. There were two winners in 1965: La Troupe de l'Echiquier de l'Université de Sherbrooke for *Le Barbier de Seville* and The Xaverian Players of Antigonish for *The Wakefield Cycle*. There were just Canadian plays entered in the 1967 Final in St. John's, so no classics were staged at all. But in 1969 (when the DDF's national structure had again been changed, this time to four instead of eight zones) there were three winners: Mount Allison University's production of *Macbeth*, the Theatre Project of Saskatoon's *Woyzeck* and the Richmond Hill Curtain Club's *The Beaux Stratagem*. After that, the trophy was never again awarded and when Theatre Canada was created it was hung on the wall of the corporation's office in Ottawa.

Even though the debate raged on and on in Governor's Court during the 1950's and sixties as to whether the festival should be uncluttered with competition and prizes, the list of awards continued to expand. After Calvert Distillers abandoned its sponsorship of the DDF in 1960 and the organization came under the wing of the Canadian Association of Broadcasters, the "Calvert" trophies were kept but Florence Wyle's Grecian Figure became known simply as the "DDF Final Festival Trophy." The award still carried a prize of $1,000, this time donated by the CAB. Other prizes in the 1950's included the Massey Award for the best Canadian playwright at the Final (the Sir Barry Jackson Trophy remained as the prize for the best Canadian *production*, a splitting of hairs which caused adjudicators to wince in agony) and the Province of Quebec had added a $3,000 scholarship for the most promising actor, actress, director or set designer whose "mother tongue is French." The Canada Council was also contributing with awards of $400 for groups in zones presenting the best Canadian play, plus $100 to the playwright. The Council also gave $500 to the best Canadian playwright at the Final.

And still the parade of awards went on. The Social Register of Canada (recognizing no doubt that society and culture had been bedmates at the DDF's inauguration) offered a scholarship and maintenance grant of $2,000 to the National Theatre School to "a promising young actor or actress." La Fondation Les Amis de l'Art put up a prize of $200, also to some promising young French or English-language thespian. The Banff School of Fine Arts gave two scholarships of $300 and $150 each. In 1963 there were yet another two trophies offered by l'Association de la Radio et de la Télévision de Langue Française for the best male and female supporting roles at the Final. Then, in 1965, the DDF list expanded again to include the Strand Electric prize of four baby mirror spots awarded for the best stage lighting. In 1967, the CAB decided to celebrate Centennial Year by boosting its Challenge Trophy cash prize to $2,000.

By 1968, however, discussions at executive meetings were leaning more strongly toward the possibility of the DDF becoming non-competitive. But despite the talk, the Windsor Final that year saw more changes and additions in the traditional award structure. The CAB had pulled out as major sponsors but decided instead to donate a $1,000 Howard Caine Memorial Award to the author of a new Canadian play, as a tribute to one of the association's more active members. The DDF Final Festival Trophy was still the Florence Wyle sculpture, but now it was awarded without that handy cheque. On the other hand, the Canadian Broadcasting Corporation had entered the picture with a prize of $2,000 for the best presentation of a Canadian play and the Barry Jackson Challenge Trophy suddenly disappeared. To scramble the adjudicator's task still further, the Massey Award for the best Canadian *playwright* was retained. Inevitably the same writer managed to collect the majority of the festival loot.

As the 1960's drew to a close and DDF changes were in the wind, it was clear that awards had lost their original status and were becoming somewhat of a headache for judges to sort out in their minds. Besides, the governors general no longer arrived by vice-regal train or plane to hand over the prizes. VIPs from Ottawa were always far too busy to grace the official platform. Lieutenant-governors sometimes turned up, but even the old guard of the DDF no longer made the trip to Festival and some were electing to bow out of the aging organization altogether. The list of awards for the 1969 Final in Kelowna shows the struggle the DDF's executive must have had to lump prestigious DDF names, trophies and cash together in some kind of acceptable package.

Because the Canadian Broadcasting Corporation was still offering the fattest cash prize – $2,000 – its award came at the top of the list. But instead of the money going to the best production, the DDF committee upgraded the Martha Allan Challenge Trophy and awarded both the $2,000 and the trophy for "the best set designer at the Final." The CAB was still donating its $1,000 for the best Canadian play but to help out the confused adjudicator, the DDF linked the cheque with the Massey Award for the best Canadian playwright. The Sir Barry Jackson Challenge Trophy was brought out of mothballs and awarded – as it had been at various times in the past – to the best production of a full-length play written by a Canadian in each of the four national zones.

The DDF's last competitive festival in 1970 was a fascinating exercise in juggling names and priorities on the once prestigious list of awards. The Bessborough Trophy was listed beneath the Sir Barry Jackson Trophy in the zone lineup and actually appeared at the bottom of the page in that year's program. The Canadian Broadcasting Corporation prize of $2,000, still shackled to the Martha Allan Challenge Trophy was at the very top. By 1970, too, the Massey Award for the best Canadian playwright had lost some of its attraction because the CAB had dropped its $1,000 cash donation. But the Louis Jouvet Trophy was still there. Col. Henry Osborne was still honoured and so was Nella Jefferis. The last "name" to be entered on the DDF's roll of awards was nominated by La Fondation Les Amis de l'Art, which dubbed its special cash prize of $250 the Grace Elliott-Trudeau Award for the best actor or actress under twenty-six years of age. The DDF executive reminded itself that its first non-competitive showcase as Theatre Canada would be held in Ottawa the following year and perhaps Prime Minister Pierre Elliott Trudeau would turn up for the show.

3.   You mean it's old-fashioned to be dignified
          and socially acceptable?

One of the loudest public blasts at the Dominion
Drama Festival's interest in protocol, visiting "names" and
round-the-clock socializing came in 1961 after the Final cut a
boozy swathe through Montreal. "The DDF should be given
back to the actor and the theatre groups," complained John
W. Holmes, director of Toronto's Drao Players, apparently ignoring other critics who had long insisted the corporation had
never really belonged to performers at all. "When that happens,"
continued the director of that year's winning production,
Rashomon, "it will once more become significant in the world
of theatre and with the public. With all due respect to the dig-
nitaries called upon by the DDF, the performances should not
be encumbered by pomp and ceremony. Lights that should
have been used by the play are now taken over by television
floods. The emphasis on protocol and prizes has blunted the
purpose of the festival. It should be an unhampered meeting
of groups from across Canada."

Well, the DDF executive argued worriedly at meet-
ings and in private, the organization was *trying* to do just that.
The regions, though, were not happy about the prospect of
uncompetitive festivals because of that long-standing belief that
awards attracted audiences. Besides, would-be reformers were
constantly told, influential contacts were still useful to the DDF.
Honorary governors were sources of revenue that could not
be ignored. And although there were signs of professional
theatre growth across the country, the community theatre movement still needed strong support and that meant the DDF could
not be allowed to develop into an unstructured organization
run for – and by – irresponsibles.

It was in the mid-1960's, in fact, that the DDF elected
one of its most protocol-conscious leaders since the days of
Park Jamieson, the stately Vida Peene of Toronto. Those who
now reflect on Miss Peene's two-year presidency debate whether
she conducted her meetings with as much business-like efficiency
as old pro Pauline McGibbon. But the consensus is that Peene
conclaves were unequalled as orderly affairs and that she was

as aware of DDF custom of doing the right thing as she was about the nagging problems of financing, adjudication and bilingualism. Vida Peene bowed to the winds of change as much as she could but she clearly approved of members of the executive who wore white ties and lady committee members who swished to Festival in ballgowns. Since 1949 when she first rubbed shoulders with the dignified DDF brass (as a ticket-seller for the Toronto Final), Miss Peene considered Festival to be an occasion. Shenanigans – except, of course, for the usual DDF parties, banquets, balls and executive suite cocktail bashes – were simply not tolerated. No one quite like her would head the DDF again.

By the time Donald McGibbon of Toronto and Alvin Shaw of New Brunswick were installed as presidents during the late 1960's, it was obvious that unconventional lifestyles were invading doors which once seemed traditionally strong enough to resist them. At the Windsor Final of 1968, there was still an element of conservatism at Festival. But that was the year a DDF regional adjudicator picked a homosexual play, *Fortune and Men's Eyes*, to go to the Final and author John Herbert turned up for the performance dressed in cord slacks and sandals, a gold and velvet turtleneck sweater, a shoulder-length wig and a diamond stud in one ear. To add to the shock, Herbert stated flatly that "political manoeuvring behind the scenes of the festival invalidated the awards" (he has since charged that the regional adjudicator had been unsuccessfully pressured into changing her decision about *Fortune*), then labelled the DDF executive with that awful phrase, "socializing dilettantes."

At awards time, when Herbert refused to accept the $1,000 Howard Caine-Vincent Massey prize for the best Canadian playwright, there was more dismayed shock. Refused? A DDF award? Clearly the rafters were falling in, but as McGibbon, then president of the organization, has since remembered, "we kept our cool and decided to ignore the entire incident." It seemed to be the typically right thing to do so the entire executive agreed. Also typical of DDF fair play is that John Herbert's name is forever enshrined under the corporation's list of winners, accompanied by the words "not accepted."

Windsor was just the beginning of cataclysmic

changes at DDF Finals, however. At the Kelowna Festival of 1969, blue-jeaned, bare-footed youngsters from university campuses invaded the little British Columbian town and mingled unselfconsciously with the few regional and national representatives of the DDF who felt it was still important to turn up to performances in evening dress. But there was one individual among the participants who felt that blue jeans were not enough and that it was his moral duty to crack the high-society facade of the DDF once and for all. Director and playwright John Palmer had been invited to bring his zone's winning production of Slawomir Mrozek's *Tango* to Kelowna from Woodstock, Ontario. Kelowna – and the DDF itself – will forever remember that Wednesday evening in May 1969. To discourage ladies in long ballgowns, Palmer wanted to litter the lobby of Kelowna's Community Theatre with garbage, but was firmly discouraged by a now thoroughly-alarmed local committee. Instead, he installed a plastic wind tunnel from the front door of the playhouse into the auditorium which had playgoers squirming in their high heels and floor-length gowns until they entered the theatre. There they discovered another hazard. Each seat was occupied by a fully-inflated green garbage bag which somehow had to be disposed of before the ticket-holder could be seated. Some members of the audience – particularly the kids from other visiting groups – simply tossed the bags around or popped them with lighted matches. The less adventurous tried, unsuccessfully, to stash the embarrassing balloons under their seats.

The performance itself was a far cry from the likes of *Journey's End, Witness for the Prosecution* or the rash of Robert Anderson plays the DDF attracted in the 1950's and early sixties. There was some nudity. There was loud rock music. There were unmentionable words. But even before the audience was subjected to such untypical DDF fare, Palmer administered a prime insult. Someone struck up the first bars of *The Queen*. The audience rose to its feet, relieved that something at least had not changed. Then a slide of Adolf Hitler was flashed onto the Community Theatre curtain. The audience, torn between honouring Her Majesty and the greatest villain in modern history, tottered uncertainly.

In many ways, Kelowna was a turning point for the aging DDF. The Winnipeg Final of 1970 showed signs of creeping casualness. At Ottawa in 1971 and Saskatoon in 1972, just the vice-presidents wore black tie and then only on opening and closing nights. Long dresses were really comfortable hostess gowns. Adjudicators – now called animateurs – wore everything from sports clothes to ruffled-front shirts. The all-night parties, the inevitable love affairs and the jumping Green Room were still there. But the programmed grandness that was Bessborough, Massey, Jamieson, McGibbon and Peene had disappeared.

CHAPTER NINE

Players, Plays, Photographers and Professionals

1. **"I'll never forget the time I went to a DDF Final."**

The story of the Dominion Drama Festival during its four decades as Canada's annual cultural contest tends to be dominated by those who made it work, mark time or persuade its constantly-faltering body into renewed effort. In the early years, in fact, the individuals who manipulated the controls *were* the DDF. Actors, actresses, directors and playwrights – except for the celebrated few directly in contact with the policy-makers – were somewhat loftily regarded as temporary satellites who were billeted and entertained but, hopefully, seen and not heard in the presence of the great.

Even reporters who swarmed excitedly to the first festivals seemed to be more interested in the doings of high-society and the pontifications of imported adjudicators than in the personal experiences of visiting groups. This was a pity, because in the a time of gloomy depression, many players must have had stories to tell of their pilgrimage to Ottawa that were far more dramatic than the scenes they acted out on stage. Although the executive committee of the DDF first allowed groups half the cost of their travelling expenses then, later, scaled grants-in-aid, it was frankly recognized that it took considerable ingenuity for many participants to make the trip. And who were these people, anyway? What was their background? And what adventures led to their invitation to the Festival? Interestingly, it was Lord Bessborough himself who told one of the first stories about a group which came to a

DDF Final. After his return to England, he was asked to write about his work with the DDF and somewhere in the copy he included the tale of the Embassy Players of Vancouver who brought the Trial Scene from George Bernard Shaw's *Saint Joan* to the 1935 Ottawa Final. "The group did not have sufficient funds at their disposal to come by train," Bessborough remembered. "So they travelled 3,500 miles by bus. They slept in the bus several nights to keep down hotel expenses. In fact, the group travelled seven thousand miles to Ottawa and back to appear for thirty minutes on the stage." Happily, Bessborough was able to report, Brenda Fergusson of Vancouver who played Saint Joan in the production, won the Countess of Bessborough's memento for the best performance by an actress.

The little story is maddeningly sparse in detail. Did the bus ever break down? How were the roads across the country in those days? How and what did the group eat on the way? And what hotels were available for travellers in the 1930's? No one with access to a typewriter, apparently, ever bothered to ask. A more explicit account of a group's travels to Festival, however, comes out of the London, Ontario Final of 1939. That was the year the Nanaimo Dramatic Academy came from British Columbia with a gloomy verse play by Gordon Bottomley called *The Woman From the Voe*. There were twenty-three players in the group — some of them children — led and directed by a clearly formidable lady named Mrs. A. G. Graham. At that time, Mrs. Graham told an interested reporter, the population of Nanaimo was 6,000, and the entire town responded to a campaign backed by the mayor to send the group to Ontario.

"We cooked our own meals right in a kitchenette on the train," the director continued. "It wasn't canned stuff, either. We took fresh carrots and other kinds of vegetables and had good meals all the way. The railroad people were very cooperative. They supplied dishes and pans. The weather was another worry. When we left Nanaimo the daffodils were blooming, but when we struck the mountains there was ten feet of snow. In the prairies it was cold and at Fort William it was two degrees below. Now it's raining in London. We've been through all the seasons now, I guess."

The 1939 Final produced other stories that spotlighted

groups rather than DDF luminaries. One was later repeated in articles written by both S. R. Littlewood, the British adjudicator of the Final, and George Skillan, who had handled the regional judging. The tale concerns a group of four individuals – including the director – from the Clive Dramatic Society of Alberta who came to London with excerpts from Anton Checkov's *The Bear*. Clive was still a village of 250 persons in those days and the dramatic society had been formed to present concerts and plays that would produce enough box-office income to pay for a new community hall. The plan to enter a DDF regional excited Clive's small population enormously but there were problems to overcome. Director V. G. Duffy decided that he and his group of three actors – all of them farmers – needed some expert coaching before entering the playoffs. For almost a year, the quartet travelled two hundred miles to Edmonton and back to rehearse, logging at least 2,600 miles before they even appeared at the regional festival.

"Their performance was exceptionally good," wrote Skillan in England. "I talked with them afterwards and it was obvious they had analyzed their parts with the most searching care. I had thought that the leading man was an ex-professional on account of the sureness of his technique. I afterwards discovered that he was a farmer and that it was the second part he had played." Added Littlewood after adjudicating *The Bear* at the Final: "I was happy to award Lady Tweedsmuir's memento for the best individual performance by a man in the Festival to Robert Haskins of the Clive Dramatic Society. The three members of the cast had come nearly 3,000 miles in the face of every sort of difficulty."

Skillan's article also tells of how drama groups beat their way to the regional playoffs in the first chilly three months of the Canadian year. "We often had packed houses where the outside temperature was well below zero and the roads were tracks of ice and snow. It was under these conditions that a group travelled by road from Sarnia to Hamilton, some 150 miles, staged a very competent production of *Lady Precious Stream* then left for home at one o'clock in the morning. In Regina, the temperature was 43 below zero with 75 degrees of frost. The hall, holding 800 people, was in a remote part of the city and yet for three nights we had full houses and casts had come in from a radius of a hundred miles."

One well-known DDF personality did earn publicity as a member of a group rather than as a corporation executive that year. The Montreal Repertory Theatre had come to London with a production of Brian Doherty's play, *Father Malachy's Miracle*. The cast, though, was minus one player, an actor named Leo Considine who had become ill in Toronto. The London newspapers snapped at the story that director Martha Allan donned Considine's vestry attendant's costume and stepped into the role. Unfortunately, the Doherty play received blasts of criticism from adjudicator Littlewood.

Just about everyone at Festival knew the story of the MRT and its glamourous leader, Martha Allan, however. But who were the players who came with the Theatre Arts Guild of Kentville, Nova Scotia? Or the Beaux Arts Society of Victoria, B.C.? Or the Theatre of Action of Toronto, which staged John Wexley's somewhat radical drama, *Steel* in 1938? Or the Progressive Arts Club of Vancouver, which presented Clifford Odets' *Waiting for Lefty* in 1936?

The Progressive Arts Club did manage to gain some space in the Ottawa press, though the DDF executive was not at all sure that a play set in a labour union hall was quite suitable for vice-regal viewing. According to the newspaper report, the club was launched in 1935, and the twelve players and two directors – some of them unemployed – were able to reach Ottawa with the help of $500 raised through a tag day and the proceeds of twenty-five public performances in Vancouver and en route. The cast of *Waiting for Lefty* included a paper hanger, a carpenter, a waitress and a seventeen-year-old male dancer. Katharine Bruce, a clerk in a department store who played Edna, told an enquiring reporter:

> Garfield King, a Vancouver lawyer, and Dr. Murphy of Vancouver both put up $10 each and that helped us rent a small hall belonging to a division of the Great War Veterans. At first, we never thought of competing in any festival. We just went ahead and did the best we could for our own pleasure. This

is really all very unexpected. Our ideal is to present plays which more or less depict modern conditions and the striving for social justice. They must, of course, be good plays.

Director Guy Glover continued with the story:

> We chose a play that would appeal not only to those taking part but to a very varied audience. We needed no properties. A Vancouver taxi company loaned us the caps worn by the boys in the play. Our first performance was in the Ukrainian Hall but after three performances we were closed by order of the Vancouver Citizen's League who warned the owners of the hall they would do the same with any other play that had a similar plot. Luckily Police Chief Foster of Vancouver was vice-president of the Vancouver Little Theatre and right then they were rehearsing the Soviet play *Square in a Circle*. He used his influence and *Waiting for Lefty* opened again in a large downtown theatre.

Glover said that members of his group were hurt if people referred to them as "the unemployed Communists." Political discussions were discouraged at club meetings because the group had "too many nationalities and beliefs." It was the ambition of the club to help found a series of Workers' Theatres across Canada. "Workers who have never had time before must now have something to do with their spare hours. They can be led and educated to do really beautiful work." Adjudicator Harley Granville-Barker must have been impressed with the group's intensity. He awarded the Progressive Arts Club the trophy for the best performance in English.

Unusual groups of performers or newsworthy happenings concerning a group often managed to grab some press coverage at festivals, of course. A company which might have had a revealing tale to tell about the need of individuals to express themselves through community drama was invariably ignored for one which had been plagued with accidents or one which used, say, a dog or a parrot on stage. In 1937, the Strolling Players of Vancouver attracted enormous attention even before their play *The Barretts of Wimpole Street* got to Ottawa. At the British Columbia regional playoffs in March of that year, the players were performing before adjudicator George de Warfaz when someone yelled "fire!" in the theatre. A chair in one of the rest-rooms, apparently set alight by a dropped cigarette, was spotted by a member of the audience and within seconds many of the spectators were on their feet and stampeding toward the exits. For a moment, the play stopped, then actor-director Colin Laurence – then on stage – caught his cue and continued. Other members of the cast followed his lead and the audience cooled down as theatre employees extinguished the blaze. "You showed marvellous pluck to go on after the incident and I highly congratulate you," commented De Warfaz after the play was over. He awarded it the winning trophy in the regional and *Barretts* went on to win the award for the best play in English at the Final. One of the players who kept her head, Gay Scrivener, won Lady Tweedsmuir's memento for the best performance by a woman and eventually became a professional actress.

Then there was the panic in 1947 when Lt. Commander Robert Wall, the leading man in the Ottawa Drama League's presentation of Noel Coward's *Blithe Spirit*, was fogbound in Newfoundland. Would he make it in time for his group's performance at the London Final? For a while, the local press treated the Wall story like a cliffhanger – much to the satisfaction of the local festival committee, who anticipated that the Grand Theatre would have Standing Room Only when the Drama League performed their play. Assistant director Michael Meiklejohn hurriedly studied the role in case Wall failed to appear. Weather charts were worriedly examined. Finally, the Lt. Commander arrived in London at noon on the day of the performance, just in time for the dress rehearsal. Reporters panted to hear the amateur actor's story. Probably astonished at the attention, Wall happily obliged. Well, flights to Montreal from St. John's had been cancelled because of the fog. It was too late to make the trip by ship or train. No flights were possible to Ireland, where Wall could have shuttled back across the Atlantic to New York. Aircraft were even grounded at Fort Pepperel air base, but, acting on a hunch, Wall decided to hop a train to Gander. The trip took twelve hours and when he arrived, the airport there was as murky as that in St. John's. The only plane scheduled to arrive that day was from Germany, but he was told it had been diverted to Sydney, Nova Scotia. Just as he was leaving to find himself a hotel room, the plane appeared through the fog. Wall managed to get a seat on the aircraft and flew south to New York. From there, he caught a plane to Toronto and then to London. It was a perfect suspense story for Festival and Wall was briefly the hero of the week. Unfortunately for the hovering reporters, *Blithe Spirit* earned no prizes.

As the DDF grew older, however, even tales of missing actors, difficult journeys, lost properties and rustics who sounded like the Barrymores became commonplace at festivals which had seen them all. The DDF's last competitive festival in Winnipeg in 1970 did turn up a distinctive group story when it was discovered the Penthouse Players – who were scheduled to present a production of *Teahouse of the August Moon* – were prisoners from the Manitoba penitentiary at Stony Mountain. In a way, their story was as illuminating a glimpse of community theatre and its growth as the tale of the Progressive Arts Club back in 1936.

The group was apparently self-motivated. In other words, the prisoners themselves recognized their need for self-expression and contacted speech and drama lecturer Harold Turner at the University of Manitoba in 1964 to ask whether he would help them stage a play. "It was a frightening experience," the teacher told the press in Winnipeg. "The faces of the men were completely blank. I wondered how I would ever make a group out of them." Twenty-two inmates joined the drama club and in 1970 ("penitentiary sentences being as they can be") some of the originals were still around. According to Turner, a few prisoners even delayed their release on parole so productions could be staged without casting disruptions. The members of the club wanted to enter the 1969 Manitoba Regional but did not have a play ready in time. They began rehearsing early for the 1970 festival, however, and Turner himself took the group's request to Warden Ted Harris. "The warden gave his blessing," Turner recalled, "then the administration came up with the 75-dollar entry fee and ten dollars for costumes rented to supplement those the men made for themselves."

The warden also ironed out other problems. Two small boys needed for the cast were found when the prison's recreation officer, Joe Petzold, suggested that his young sons might be suitable. The female roles were played by local amateur actresses Marian Neild, Sheila Maurer and Janice Turner who had been asked to participate in a previous prison production of *Arsenic and Old Lace*. There had already been a significant breakthrough before *Teahouse of the August Moon* went to Winnipeg. Warden Harris had decided to permit families of prisoners to attend a performance of the club's play.

Who were the male actors of *Teahouse* and why were they at Stony Mountain? "I know their names," Turner told reporters, "but I've never asked what they are in prison for. All I know about that is that they are from the Big House, not the less-restrictive farm annex. I also know that many of them want to try for professional jobs when they are released. I think they are good enough to land them."

2.   "And look what the DDF did for me!"

In the late 1960's, a devout researcher within the Dominion Drama Festival rummaged among the corporation's dozens of programs and compiled a list of 400 names of individuals who climbed the professional ladder after appearing in a DDF Final. The catalogue included actors, actresses, directors, playwrights, designers, stage managers, producers, sound technicians and covered the years between 1933 and 1965. Supporters of the DDF were delighted with the study. All of this clearly proved what the organization had been saying all along – that the DDF was a path to professional success for theatrical aspirants within the ranks of Canadian amateurism.

While agreeing that a vast number of professionals now earning a living in theatre, films and television once did appear in a DDF playoff or Final, though, critics of the corporation insist that many of them had done some work in repertory

281

or radio before their drama festival appearance. And even if they had been virtual greenhorns, argue others, what proof is there that sheer talent might not have boosted them to the top of their chosen field, anyway?

One thing seems certain. Early DDF festivals were one of the few outlets for Canadians interested in the theatre, whether they wanted to become professionals or not. There is also evidence that the festivals often acted as springboards, which cut corners for many ambitious individuals. Adjudicators such as Harley Granville-Barker and Michel St. Denis auditioned several promising young Canadians and recommended their entry into English or French theatre schools. Later, CBC talent scouts made a point of attending the Finals, though spotters from New York or London never seemed to be around. The DDF itself argues that even after more professional outlets opened up in Canada, the adrenalin of a festival must have given young performers or stage technicians – especially those from small centres – the courage to try for a professional career. If they happened to land an award, of course, the organization confidently expected the trophy-holder to aim for higher things. Many did.

The sensation of the 1951 Final, for example, was a young actor named John Colicos, who won thunderous applause for his winning role as Best Actor in the University of Toronto Alumnae Drama Club's production of *In Good King Charles' Golden Days*. Joan Miller – who later starred in London's West End – was the hit of the 1934 Final in Ottawa when she was awarded a clock by Lady Bessborough for her performance in *Elizabeth the Queen*. Bill Walker of Regina earned two Best Actor awards in 1947 and 1950 then moved on to a successful career in radio and television. Even though he won no awards, a waiter named Percy Rodriguez who played Brutus Jones in the Negro Theatre Guild of Montreal's production of *Emperor Jones* was an electrifying personality at the 1949 Toronto Final. Not long after the festival, Rodriguez quit his job, found professional acting work and eventually became a success on Broadway. Rodriguez has put it on record that his DDF experience helped him make up his mind.

"The John Colicoses, the Anna Camerons, the Kate

Reids, the William Hutts, all of us cut our teeth on the DDF and were grateful for the chance," David Gardner has admitted. "Where else could I have got the chance to play a lead in *Uncle Vanya?* What professional company was there in Canada to do this production and to risk the part on an unknown clot like me?" Actor Leo Ciceri (who would become one of the Stratford Festival's most celebrated stars before his untimely death in 1970) certainly cut his teeth on a meaty role in *Amphitryon 38*, staged by the Montreal Repertory Theatre at the 1947 DDF Final. And the career of radio and television actor-producer Andrew Allan may have been influenced by his 1935 appearance in a winning Hart House production of *His Widow's Husband*. Actress Judith Evelyn — then a beginner, though already a part-time CBC radio recruit — appeared in a Hart House production of *The Magnaminous Lover* in the Final of 1936. Actor Alan King has said that his appearance in A. M. D. Fairbairn's *Ebb Tide* at the Victoria regional playoff of 1933 reinforced his decision to become a professional actor. The itch to tread the boards became so persistent after the festival that King finally got himself a job as a guard on a Canadian National Railway train and worked his way to Toronto. He landed his first parts in CBC radio dramas (invaluable outlets for theatre aspirants) through another DDF supporter, Edgar Stone of Hart House.

Eventually, the DDF executive became aware of the fact that many festival participants were hitting the professional big-time. The honour-roll was impressive to recite at talks to interested groups or prospective donors: Eric House. Terry Tweed. John Coghill. Amelia Hall. Frank Shuster. Johnny Wayne. Lorne Greene. Gratien Gelinas. Adrian Pecknold. Douglas Rain. Chris Wiggins. Sammy Sales. Paul Buissoneau. Jane Mallett. John Vernon. Ted Fellows. William Needles. Gabrielle Roy. Paul Soles.

One name not included on the list was that of Yousuf Karsh, probably because the DDF was uncertain as to whether or not the name of a photographer would clash with all those thespians, directors and playwrights. In many ways, however, Karsh of Ottawa's international success as a portrait photographer is one of the most stunning illustrations of how association with the Dominion Drama Festival could influence all kinds of careers. A Jewish-Armenian immigrant who first studied in Boston, Mass. then came to Canada in 1925, Karsh headed for Ottawa in 1932 "because" as he has recalled, "it was the capital of the country and I felt I would get chances there to photograph important personalities." The photographer had little money but towering ambitions at the time. Through professional contacts he managed to do some work at the 1932 Imperial Economic Conference then, a few months later, he met Solange Gauthier, an actress and director with the Ottawa Little Theatre. The two were married in 1939 but by that year, Yousef Karsh was well on his way to becoming the photographer of the great he had always dreamed of being.

The trick was turned by sheer luck and also by the fact that the earnest young immigrant – who spoke fractured English and gave little appearance of being good at anything – had extraordinary talent. Solange introduced him to influential members of the Ottawa Drama League such as Michael Meiklejohn, John Aylen and Henry Osborne, and even got him a part in a Little Theatre play. It was a production of *See Naples and Die*. Karsh portrayed one of two chess players who sit wordlessly on stage throughout the play, concentrating on their game. He has remembered that members of the audience in the front row occasionally broke into laughter when he made a move. To the initiated, it was obvious that the "actor" had never played chess in his life. At the end of the play, the chess partners shoot a general who is standing on a balcony. Karsh's amateur colleague became so excited during the big scene, he fired his shot into his pants pocket.

The theatre fascinated Karsh, not for the opportunity to act, but for the chance to study lighting. His early photographic experience involved the use of natural light but at the Ottawa Little Theatre he suddenly became aware of how spots could be manipulated to create character and mood. During rehearsals he would slip into the playhouse with his camera to try out ideas. Finally, when those connected with the theatre realized how fascinated the Armenian was with photography, they asked him to record performances on a paying basis. This job led to Karsh's friendship with Viscount Duncannon, Lord Bessborough's heir, who spent his Christmas vacations acting in Ottawa and Montreal. One of the best-known photographs of the young Duncannon, in fact, was made by Karsh during rehearsals of *Romeo and Juliet* in December, 1933. The picture shows the slim, nineteen-year-old Viscount poised between the wrought-iron gates of Juliet's tomb. Julia MacBrien, who played Juliet to Duncannon's Romeo, lies on a dais in the foreground.

Lord Bessborough took a personal interest in Yousuf Karsh and his experiments with lighting and film. At Little Theatre rehearsals the usually aloof Governor General would sit beside the young immigrant and offer advice. "Listen to the actor," he would tell him. "Now, when they set a scene which you consider photographic, make a note of the lines and the way the scene has been lit. Then, after rehearsal, go to the actor and ask him if you can make a photograph. The actor will catch the mood of the moment immediately and the lighting people will co-operate." Karsh's early photographs turned out so well that Bessborough decided to name him official photographer of the fledgling Dominion Drama Festival. Not only did the newcomer to Ottawa record some of the first plays to be presented at the festivals, he was also asked to photograph the DDF's founding fathers. He gained entry to Government House and his recollections confirm that the early years of the DDF were clearly no picnic for those who created it. During one Government House visit, Karsh has remembered, he encountered Vincent Massey and Henry Osborne pacing the halls, their arms linked fraternally. As Karsh approached them, Massey shook his head and said somewhat wistfully to Osborne: "We are the victims of our own intelligence."

Eric Duncannon also liked what Karsh was doing in the photographic field. His work was flattering and there was no doubt the Armenian's pictures showed theatrical flair. In 1933, after the production of *Romeo and Juliet*, Karsh decided to test his friendly relationship with Duncannon and asked him whether he could talk Lord and Lady Bessborough into coming to his studio for a photographic sitting. Duncannon agreed to help and later, Karsh was informed the Governor General and his wife would be pleased to come. "It was a poor little studio," Karsh has remembered. "It was furnished with orange crates covered with cloth. Anyone with any avoirdupois could wreck them, so we had to be very careful. When the Bessboroughs arrived for the sitting, protocol demanded that

I would have to photograph the King's representative first. I did so, then I found myself saying in my terrible English, 'Your Excellency, would you *recline* with my secretary in the office while I photograph your wife?'' Bessborough impassively left the room.

The Bessborough photographs were the first step in Karsh's determined ambition to record the most celebrated faces of his time on film. Unfortunately, when the shots were developed, he found to his horror that he had been so excited about the assignment he had fuzzed his focus. The Bessboroughs were humbly informed of the error and later turned up for another, more successful sitting.

In the meantime, Karsh was becoming as well-known a figure around Ottawa as members of the diplomatic and society set. As official DDF photographer, he was invited to all of the receptions during festival week. He was a friend of ambassadors, cabinet ministers, titled ladies and gentlemen who moved in Bessborough circles. Osborne and Massey accepted him into their group, William Lyon Mackenzie King knew him on a first-name basis. The friendships paid off. In 1943, Karsh wrote to Mackenzie King and asked whether the Prime Minister would grant him an appointment "to discuss my future as a photographer." Mackenzie King happily agreed. Karsh came straight to the point in the Prime Minister's office. He wanted to visit London so he could photograph some of the great people in Europe. Could Mackenzie King help?

Well aware of Karsh's connection with the Dominion Drama Festival, the Prime Minister immediately suggested the best person to contact in London was the Canadian High commissioner himself, Vincent Massey. He said he would back Karsh's request with a personal note. "When I arrived in London," Karsh has recalled, "I went to Vincent Massey's office at Canada House. Of course he remembered me from the days of the DDF and we talked about that for a while. Then I handed him the Prime Minister's letter of recommendation, told him why I had come to London and gave him a list of personages I would like to photograph. The names were pretty impressive, but Massey looked it over without flinching. Then he said he would put some as second choice and he would augment the list with other names as well. Some international figures, he thought." Massey then summoned Canada House press attaché Campbell Moodie and instructed him to contact all of the celebrated individuals on the list. "Except for the Royal family," he added. "Leave that to me."

Karsh had another stroke of luck during his 1943 visit to London. He encountered Leonard Brockington, long a DDF supporter, who was working in England as advisor on Commonwealth affairs to the British Minister of Information. Brockington was as well-acquainted with men and women of distinction as Vincent Massey. "It was during the war, of course," Karsh later remembered during an interview, "and bombs falling or no bombs falling, Brock would hold court. Great personages – men of letters or the theatre principally – would visit with him and stay until two or three in the morning. So Brock would telephone me and say, Yousuf, get out of your pyjamas and come on over."

Through Massey and Brockington, admits Karsh, he was able to photograph sixty world figures in sixty days. "The two men would do my homework for me," he has recalled. "They would say, now who are you photographing this coming week and I would say Noel Coward, George Bernard Shaw, King George VI, Admiral Sir Reginald Portal. Then they would say, well what do you know about Admiral Portal? When I admitted I knew very little, they would sit me down between them and tell me about the man so I would understand his personality. By the time the appointment for the sitting came around, I would be highly informed about my subject. By then, of course, I also knew a great deal about lighting. Many times when I was photographing men like Bertrand Russell, Augustus John, Winston Churchill, H. G. Wells, I would remember those early days in the Ottawa Little Theatre and how a miracle unfolded before my eyes."

3.   "The play's the thing,
       but where are the Canadian playwrights?"

If Canadian unity through the melding of the two founding cultures was always a top priority goal for the Dominion Drama Festival, the establishment of a truly national theatre had to rank high on the list of DDF aims as well. The trouble was that the corporation seemed to find it difficult to come to grips with precisely what it meant by a "national theatre." "I've yet to discover what the phrase national theatre really means," commented Col. Henry Osborne at the DDF's first post-war Final in 1947. "It is a phrase that is current of late. To some it means a building, to some a movement. I understand that there are to be discussions here this week about it all and perhaps we shall have some enlightenment. All we can say about a national theatre at the moment is that it represents an aspiration," he added. He felt that nothing that might bear this title could be built from the top. It must have "a natural growth founded on the love and understanding of the theatre, which the Drama Festival is trying to promote. Some people have a passion for organization. But organization will not produce a national theatre in the real sense of the expression."

It was clear from the first days of the DDF, however, that those who formed its executive believed the encouragement of Canadian-written plays could spark a movement that would lead to a national drama and then to the building of a bricks-and-mortar national theatre. Plays written by Canadians which managed to reach the finals were always elaborately publicized and the Sir Barry Jackson Challenge Trophy (donated in 1934) was handed out with as much DDF pride as the Bessborough plaque itself. But it was clear from a study of the plays that did come to the regional playoffs and the finals that amateur groups around the Dominion were not overly enthusiastic about the idea of presenting an unknown drama and perhaps jeopardizing their chances of winning the prestigious top trophy or even the best play in English or French awards. By staging a play that had been a success in London or New York, too, amateurs identified themselves with success.

There were not many Canadian plays around in the 1930's, forties and fifties and even into the 1960's for amateurs to choose from even if they wished, anyway. There were the stodgy verse-plays of Charles Heavysege and Marjorie Pickthall (Pickthall's untheatrical *The Woodcarver's Wife* enjoyed a mild boom among amateur groups in the 1930's), there was Merrill Denison's *Brothers in Arms* and some plays by Duncan Campbell Scott of the Ottawa Drama League.

288

When compiling a list of suggested plays to send out to groups in 1934, Vincent Massey and Henry Osborne could come up with just nine plays written by Canadian authors: the Marjorie Pickthall verse epic *Brothers in Arms* and *From Their Own Place* by Merrill Denison, A. M. D. Fairbairn's *Pacific Coast Tragedy* and *Ebb Tide, Madame Verité at Bath* by George A. Palmer, *Behind the Beyond* by Stephen Leacock, *The Second Lie* from the Hart House Theatre Collection published by Macmillan and Co., and Duncan Campbell Scott's *Pierre*. There were no French plays by Canadians on the list at all.

A glance at the plays entered in the first DDF festival of 1933 shows the kinds of authors preferred by amateur groups at the time: O'Neill, Barrie, Clemence Dane, Shaw, Masefield, Synge, W. W. Jacobs, Shakespeare, Rupert Brooke. Two Canadian plays survived regional adjudication and were invited to the Ottawa Final: Mazo de la Roche's *Low Life* presented by the Trinity Players of Montreal and *Jim Barber's Spite Fence*, written and produced by Lillian B. Thomas and presented by the Winnipeg Little Theatre Members' Night Committee. Neither won a prize. The festival of 1934 reflected the same pattern of thought among the amateurs: O'Neill, Galsworthy, Sacha Guitry, Maurice Maeterlinck, Barrie, Maxwell Anderson. But the Galt Collegiate Institute Staff Players Club turned up at the Final with Merrill Denison's *Brothers in Arms, and the* Montreal Repertory Theatre presented *All on a Summer's Day*, written and directed by Martha Allan, a lady who had little to lose by gambling on a Canadian product. Her play won the first Sir Barry Jackson Challenge Trophy, but – and this would recur often in the years to come – the DDF's executive's hundred dollars to the author of the best Canadian play presented at any of the regional festivals went to Captain Alexander Ramsay of Banff for his drama *Coercion*.

A real breakthrough for Canadian playwrights seemed to come in 1936, however, when the London Little Theatre presented *Twenty-five Cents* written by W. Eric Harris and directed by Catharine Brickenden. The play not only won the Bessborough Trophy but the Sir Barry Jackson award and the DDF's hundred-dollar cheque as well. Could this unprecedented event open the floodgates for Canadian theatrical writing? "I'd seen the play in Sarnia," Catharine Brickenden has recalled. "I must admit it was pretty grim stuff, but it really *had* something. I staged the thing and everyone hated it. But I took it to the regionals anyway, and to my surprise it won and we were invited to the Final. Well, I had no idea that any Canadian play would win anything except the Sir Barry Jackson Trophy. You can imagine how I felt when Harley Granville-Barker announced we had not only collected the Jackson award but the Bessborough Trophy as well!'

Maybe this really was the breakthrough. In 1937, Irish-born Torontonian John Coulter won the Bessborough, the Jackson and the DDF's hundred dollars with a one-act play staged by the T. Eaton Co.'s Toronto Masquers called *The House in the Quiet Glen*. Paradoxically, though, the play was set in Northern Ireland and a sensitive Coulter hastily promised a reporter that his next dramatic effort would be written about Canada.

Ten years later, Coulter was to write:

> Canadian theatre? what is it? If only playwrights, actors and producers north of Niagara would turn their eyes from Broadway and look around them at a place called Canada! There is inviting subject-matter for plays in prairie droughts and crop-failure, in mining disasters, in the poverty of slum dwellers of city streets or country shacks. But accurate reporting of misfortune or disaster or accident is not enough to make a play. And, indeed, what is dark and grievous in the actual circumstances of life has no rightful place on the stage till it is transmuted by art into the very different category of the tragic experience. True comedy can be as serious as tragedy. A hundred grand plays are waiting for Canadians who will write them. But if there were a great Canadian play, would Canadians bother to stage it – any more than they bother now to stage that first Canadian grand opera, Healey Willan's latest and major work, *Deirdre of the Sorrows?* Cover it up, good friends; cover it decently up with Canadian dust and let it lie. Some day the Americans or English will do it and tell us

not to be ashamed and then, having their word for it, we will tardily take the duster and disinter a work once made in Canada.

DDF governor Mona Coxwell said somewhat the same kind of things to a reporter in 1947. Miss Coxwell had backed the Canadian Playwright Series published by her employers, Samuel French, and she said the success expected of these plays by Canadian authors had never been achieved. Some, however, had been republished four or five times and had been well received by amateur groups in the United States and Britain. A great deal of the blame for the rejection of Canadian drama in Canada, she said, lay with local amateur theatrical producers. "If sufficient people in Canada wanted Canadian drama, I can't believe that our writers would fail them."

Despite the success of Coulter and Harris in the mid-1930's, however – and also despite what the DDF itself thought to be prestigious and material encouragement – amateur groups continued to stick to what some critics were already dubbing "the colonial tradition" and staging Irwin Shaw, Galsworthy, Thornton Wilder, Noel Coward, Franz Molnar. Clearly aware that the festivals were top-heavy with foreign plays, the DDF executive itself occasionally kicked around the idea of staging an all-Canadian play festival but motions were never carried or even seconded. The executive noted some signs of Canadian playwriting activity in 1938 when Jean Sweet of Saint John (for her play *Small Potatoes*) and J. H. Thurrot of Fredericton (for *La Tour*) split the DDF's hundred dollars, but their plays were not invited to the Final in Winnipeg. Arthur Prévost's *Maldonne*, staged by the French section of the MRT was rated highly enough to reach the Final and win the Jackson trophy.

The following year in London, *Divinity in Montreal* by Janet Alexandra McPhee, presented by the Sixteen-Thirty Club and directed by Herbert Whittaker won the Sir Barry Jackson award for "the best play written by a Canadian." The DDF executive gave its hundred dollars to Gwendolyn Pharis of Lamont, Alberta for writing a sombre drama called *Still Stands the House*, which apparently did not rate an invitation to the Final. Maybe it was a good thing, reasoned the committee,

291

to spread the encouragement around. Even after the Second World War, however, amateur groups were cautious about choosing Canadian plays to perform at DDF festivals. While the corporation's executive was debating hotly over the establishment of "a national theatre", just two Canadian entries — Paul Gury's *Maria Chapdelaine* and that old perennial, Merrill Denison's *Brothers in Arms* — reached the 1947 Final In London.

Mourned John Coulter: "I hear about the intense activity of amateur theatre in almost every region of every province in the Dominion. I have letters and programs on my desk recording the sub-regional and regional eliminating rounds of the Dominion Drama Festival. At first reading they are depressing. On this evidence so far as Canadian theatre is concerned, nothing has happened in the world since 1920. I look again at the list of chosen plays for the 1947 Final. They are so often farcical slapstick or, much worse, those same dreary old phoney-genteel concoctions, the would-be glossily clever plays that aim at sophisticated laughter but achieve only embarrassment and boredom for all but morons. Plays by half-wits for half-wits about half-wits!"

Coulter gloomily reviewed the Canadian plays that had been entered in the regions that first DDF year after the war. Marjorie Pickthall's *The Woodcarver's Wife* was still stoically making the rounds and so was Gwendolyn Pharis' *Still Stands the House*. Anne Flavelle of Saskatoon had authored a play called *Bobbie Pulls Up Her Socks* and a Mrs. Clements of Regina had written a piece that sounded about as Canadian as chop-suey: *The House of T'ien Yee*. A. M. D. Fairbairn's *Ebbtide* was still being tried by groups, perhaps because of its popularity in the nineteen-thirties and so was that old-timer, George A. Palmer's *Madame Verité at Bath*. Coulter found in 1947 that there was one new Canadian playwright worth watching, Robertson Davies of Peterborough, Ontario, who had written a play called *Overlaid*. Although the piece had been entered in the Eastern Ontario Drama Festival, the adjudicator had chosen Noel Coward's *Blithe Spirit* to represent the region in London.

The Toronto Final of 1949 featured just two Canadian plays: William Digby's *Over the Boiler Room* and that fellow Robertson Davies' *Fortune My Foe*. "In all the regional festivals across the country this year, only ten Canadian plays were entered," wrote Toronto Telegram book editor James Scott in an article which reviewed the bleak outlook for Canadian playwrights at the time. Of these, Scott pointed out, not one had yet been published. The editor continued that he felt this state of affairs was alarming. "I don't believe any country can long continue to have a vigorous theatre when it has to derive most of its material from outside."

Scott had interviewed regional adjudicator Robert Speaight "who was looking somewhat weary" after his cross-country marathon. The adjudicator was asked about the ten Canadian plays he had seen and picked the best five: Robertson Davies' *Fortune My Foe*, Elsie Park Gowan's *Breeches from Bond Street*, E. Paluscio-Morin's *La Voix Dans Les Chênes*, William Digby's *Over the Boiler Room* and Robert Orchard's *The White Man and the Mountain*. In the same article, Scott mentioned three other Canadian playwrights who actually seemed to be making progress with their work: Gratien Gelinas, Robert Fontaine and Morley Callaghan. Callaghan's play *To Tell the Truth* had been produced at Toronto's Museum Theatre by Dora Mavor Moore's New Play Society the previous winter and had also played for a week at the Royal Alexandra. In 1949, the drama was apparently headed for Broadway.

All right, so there were just two Canadian plays entered in the 1949 Final (a sampling of other authors represented: Ibsen, Racine, Krasna, Tennessee Williams, O'Neill, Shakespeare, Hellman) but that year the DDF was able to point with pride to the fact that the Scottish Community Drama Association had invited the DDF to pick a one-act Canadian play to present at the Edinburgh Festival. After some consultation among the DDF's High Command it was decided to scratch up the expense money and send Robertson's Davies' *Eros at Breakfast* to Scotland. The play had won the author the corporation's hundred-dollar award in regional competition the previous year.

But was all this effort really encouraging Canadians to write for the theatre? Critics of the DDF who look back on the corporation's work now muse that it might not have hurt the Canadian playwright but that it did little to spur him on, either. "Oh sure, they gave awards and patted local playwrights on the back," complains writer John Palmer. "But they also condemned everything that was really new. They weren't encouraging fresh Canadian drama. They were encouraging people to copy English or American plays. The DDF and its adjudicators always reflected colonial attitudes toward the theatre. I mean, what can you think of an organization that would give a Sir Barry Jackson Award for a production of a Canadian play?"

Even so, the DDF continued to initiate projects that it seriously believed were furthering the age of awakening for the Canadian playwright. Herbert Whittaker, who had become drama critic for *The Globe and Mail* in Toronto and was a member of the DDF executive, began plugging hard for an all-Canadian play festival as early as the 1950's. His arguments were met with polite attention, though his DDF colleagues clearly believed any such festival would cause a dull thud at the box-office. In 1960, however, the DDF policy-makers finally agreed that Canadian plays should be featured exclusively at the corporation's Final in Centennial Year, 1967.

"Our motto for the 1967 Final is All-Canadian plays!" wrote DDF executive-director Richard MacDonald to an organization supporter after the meeting. "Personally, I've never been in favour of this idea but I am in favour of encouraging Canadian playwrights as much as possible in getting as many Canadian plays to be done so that perhaps in 1967 we might wind up with three or four Canadian plays. However, our executive did approve of eight plays written by Canadians to be invited to the Final and their plan for the manner in which this should be arrived at was never fully developed. I doubt whether the plan will ever follow through as I do not think the regions will agree to it."

MacDonald was right about regional reactions. "Executive meetings were being moved around the country so that regional representatives could attend," Don McGibbon has remembered in an interview. "The all-Canadian play festival was approved at one get-together then shot down at the next. It really depended on where the meeting was held." While the 1967 idea was being kicked around, the DDF was still pointing with pride to the Canadian playwrights who had carried off top honours at past Finals. In 1953, French-Canadian dramatist Marcel Dubé clinched the Calvert Trophy for *Zone*. Patricia Joudry's *Teach Me How to Cry* won the top trophy at the 1956 Sherbrooke Final, a DDF spectacular which also spotlighted the work of French-Canadian writer Jacques Languirand. In 1960, the DDF "discovered" playwright James Reaney and showered him and the University Alumnae Dramatic Club of Toronto with four awards for his play *The Kildeer*. Even though it was in miniscule proportion to imported material, the exposure of native writing continued through the 1960's. Gil Harchoux-Vuillaume's *La Quintrala* was presented in Charlottetown in 1964. Jacques Duchesne's *Les Nouveaux-Dieux* was invited to the Brockville Final of 1965. John Burgess' *A Stranger Unto My Brethren* appeared at the Victoria Final of 1966.

Then Centennial Year was on the horizon and the DDF executive could report it had gained the somewhat reluctant approval of all regions to stage an all-Canadian Festival. London, Ontario, had issued an invitation to host the 1967 Final but backed out when it seemed certain the DDF was going ahead with its mad idea. Another thing that was upsetting many regions was that because the Final would feature Canadian plays only, the playoffs would have to go native as well. But where to find the darned plays? The DDF's national office swung into helpful action. Money had been pried out of the Province of Ontario Council for the Arts and super-volunteer Vida Peene had already begun tracking down published and unpublished Canadian plays written in English that groups could choose to produce. The two volumes of plays (the second was a supplement because manuscripts kept coming in after the first list was printed), yielded 240 titles, each complete with a synopsis, the number of characters and information about where the play could be found. DDF governor Guy Beaulne was asked if he would compile a companion French-Canadian catalogue and he worked industriously at it for a time until it began to interfere with his duties at the Quebec Ministry of Cultural Affairs The list never did appear in time for the 1967 Final (which, incidentally, Beaulne adjudicated) but the project was later taken over by former board member the Honourable Justice Edouard Rinfret as a private project.

Centennial Year's Final was held in St. John's, Newfoundland, a city which snapped at the chance after London's refusal because St. John's wanted the still-prestigious DDF to open its new Arts and Cultural Centre. But Newfoundland was a long way off for some groups across the country. How about chartering a ship? The good ship DDF could start off at the Lakehead, reasoned Richard MacDonald, collected competing groups along the way then sail on to the festival site. There was much excited twittering about the plan at executive meetings, but after some sober discussion it was decided it would be more sensible – though less romantic – to apply for special travel grants from the Canada Council. Sober discussion also produced more doubts about the St. John's venture. "Everyone was scared stiff," Don McGibbon has frankly admitted. "Not because of the quality of the groups but because of what might come out of the writing."

President John F. Brook's message in the program that year reflects no such trepidation, however. "The 1967 Dominion Drama Festival finals mark the culmination of our Centennial celebrations. This has been a brilliant year in the history of the festival for, throughout our fourteen regional competitions, 62 Canadian plays have been presented of which 29 were premieres. The Festival will continue to champion Canadian plays in all of its projects for it is dedicated to the establishment of the truly national theatre, centred around the playwright."

Six full-length plays were staged in St. John's and – luckily for the DDF executive's jangled nerves – all were sold out a month in advance. Two of the productions, Lister Sinclair's *The Blood is Strong* and Donald Harron's *The Broken Jug*, had been picked out of Vida Peene's painstakingly-compiled catalogues. The other four plays were Martin Hunter's *Out Flew the Web and Floated Wide*, Tom Cahill's *Tomorrow Will be Sunday*, *Gilliam* by Peter Wilson, R. T. Logie and Myles Murchison and French-Canadian Robert Gurik's *Le Pendu*. Gurik's play dominated the festival by winning the top trophy, the CBC's $2,000 prize for the best Canadian presentation (although all the plays in that year *were* Canadian), an award of $1,000 donated by the Canadian Association of Broadcasters, the Sir Barry Jackson Challenge Trophy, the Henry Osborne Challenge Trophy

296

and the Province of Quebec's scholarship of $3,000.

Had the DDF's 1967 effort sparked a stampede toward a truly national theatre at last? There was no attempt to suggest yet another all-Canadian festival the following year, but of the six plays presented at the Windsor Final three turned out to be Canadian: Jean Barbeau's *Et Coetera*, John Herbert's *Fortune and Men's Eyes* and Pierre Voyer's *Les Enfants de Voiture*. That was surely a breakthrough, wasn't it? The other three plays presented were standard festival fare: William Naughton's *All in Good Time*, William Wycherley's *The Country Wife* and Peter Weiss's *The Persecution and Assassination of Jean-Paul Marat*. As for the mutterings about breakthrough, Canadian play-watchers noted that fifty-eight productions had been entered throughout the zones and just fourteen had been written by Canadians. The majority of the fourteen had come from French-Canadian areas. English-speaking regions, it seemed, were generally sticking to well-known writers such as Agatha Christie, Tennessee Williams, Enid Bagnold, John Osborne, Luigi Pirandello, William Ingel, Neil Simon, Arthur Miller.

The 1969 festival looked even sadder as far as the much-publicized DDF dream of a national drama was concerned. Fifty-three plays were entered in the regions and a mere ten were Canadian-written. Of the six plays presented at the Kelowna Final, two were Canadian: Antonin Artaud's *We Are Not Yet Born* and Robert Gurik's *Les Louis d'Or*. At the DDF's last competitive Final held in Winnipeg the following year, the Canadian picture looked even drearier. Robert Tembeck's *Survivants* was the only Canadian-written entry presented.

"During the last 25 years, most of our theatrical effort has gone into the equipment, including buildings and the training of a corps of actors, directors, designers and technicians," wrote playwright Jack Gray in a chapter of *Read Canadian* published in 1972, continuing:

> This necessary first stage of achievement now makes it possible for Canadians in most major centres to enjoy some, usually highly-accomplished professional theatre. But the establishment of this base, with its attendant colonial bias in its repertoire, its

narrowly-based audience and its limited ability to accommodate the growing number of young people anxious to be part of the Canadian theatre has already begun to spark the growth of a series of alternate theatres of varying accomplishment, vitality and commitment. Strangely, it is this alternate theatre that has plunged most enthusiastically into new plays by Canadians, with some theatres devoting their whole effort to such work. Only now is such work beginning to be published. Those interested in the new drama should keep their eyes on this theatre and its writers, from whom we can hope to hear much more.

"Nationalism has to be the real spur for the Canadian playwright," Tom Hendry has stated. "It's beginning to happen now." Robertson Davies has said something similar. "The time had to be right for audiences to accept the Canadian writer. Unfortunately they were not ready during the years of the DDF. It was nobody's fault, really." Director David Gardner has added: "But I feel the DDF has to be given credit for doing much when practically nobody else was doing anything. Its efforts led to the establishment of the Playwrights' Co-op. I hope out of that will come a Samuel French for the Canadian writer. I know the Canada Council has now taken up the cause."

Yet another answer to the question of whether the DDF's well-intentioned efforts to encourage Canadian playwrights (including its parade of awards, its publicity for winners, its setting up Canadian Play committees) were in vain, has come from Professor Alvin Shaw of New Brunswick, a past-president of the corporation. "I think the 1967 all-Canadian festival was a tragic mistake. The groups around Canada did Canadian plays because they had to. They searched for material and they did plays they were not sold on. But there's no point in putting on Canadian productions just for the sake of it." Then he added something that echoed Col. Henry Osborne's sentiments back in 1947: "The whole thing has to come to the surface naturally. I know we'll have more and more Canadian theatre. But we can't force it."

4.   "And in this corner, the professionals."

The powerful founders of the Dominion Drama Festival were quite adamant about the character and purpose of the organization when they drafted its first set of regulations in 1932. The DDF was for amateur competition only and the adjudicators would not look kindly on performers or other participants – except for directors – who were connected professionally with the theatre or were simply taking a holiday away from it. At an executive meeting in April, 1936, however, the DDF executive backed away from this stance. "We feel it is far from beneficial to adopt rigid rules about this," the crackle-dry minutes of the meeting read. "We appreciate persons of experience should be elements of strength for an organization." Pressed for a more personal statement at Governor's Court, an unruffled Henry Osborne scanned the 1935 Royal Charter and informed doubting supporters of DDF amateurism that there was nothing in it that discouraged professional participation.

The attitude of the DDF in the 1930's clearly assumed that Canadians who were then striving to make a full-time living from acting, directing or designing would stumble over themselves to get into a DDF playoff or Final. Actually, some did in the beginning, notably young thespians who were already getting a foot into the doors of CBC Radio. But after the Second World War, when Toronto companies such as Dora Mavor Moore's New Play Society, the Jupiter Players then, later, the Crest of Toronto, Canadian Players, the Stratford Festival, the Everyman Theatre of Vancouver and the London Theatre Company in Newfoundland sprang into life, English-speaking professional interest in the DDF began to wane. (The DDF has always insisted that if and when professional companies folded, amateurs always organized to satisfy a theatre-hungry community.) "Although for years professionals have been entreated to compete in DDF festivals, most do not," commented a Province of Ontario Council for the Arts study entitled *The Awkward Stage* in 1968. "When asked about competing, half replied 'not applicable,' obviously believing the Dominion Drama Festival to be, by definition, amateur."

In many ways, this standoffishness was both embar-

299

rassing and a private relief to the DDF's policy-makers. Professional competitors – as Henry Osborne had decreed – were officially welcome, yet weaker amateur groups in the regions resented high-powered entrants with more polish than their own. Torn between these opposing points of view, the national executive sat pat and prayed the problem would simply go away. Not only did it remain, many professionals dropped their aloof attitude and became openly critical of the DDF's "expensive goal of self-perpetuation." Amateur dramatics, some argued heatedly, were in the same recreational league as gardening or golf. Professional theatre was for real and had nothing to do with the community theatre. Support for the DDF – personal or financial – was much like aiding the survival of a bird-watching society. And if public funds were involved, money that should be used to build a healthy professional drama was being diverted into helping part-time actors pretend they were as electrifying as Irving or Bernhardt.

Complaints and hostility from sections of the professional camp always puzzled and hurt members of the DDF work force – and continued to sting supporters of Theatre Canada. Co-operation between amateurs and professionals was essential in the building of a truly national drama, it was argued, and the Dominion Drama Festival recognized this long before professionalism began to sprout any muscle. For one thing, the DDF allied itself with the professionally-oriented Canadian Theatre Centre not long after it was formed as an arm of the International Theatre Institute in 1956, to help achieve this very end. Two DDF governors at that time, Dorothy Somerset of British Columbia and Emrys Jones of Saskatchewan were at the CTC's first meeting. For another thing, the DDF showed that the amateur organization helped the CTC with several key surveys, aided in sorting out its internal organization and even donated office space and services when the Centre's headquarters burned in 1964. How could the professionals continue to be so bitter about the DDF's "single-minded and self-perpetuating" philosophies and goals?

Besides, the DDF was a significant bridge between amateurism and professionalism. After all, as those lists of successful names proved, talented people had to start somewhere.

And community theatre helped build audiences. "Help build audiences!" Emrys Jones (no longer a DDF governor) has publicly snorted. "On the contrary, the incompetence of amateur groups alienates rather than attracts the public to the theatre. Once an individual is exposed to the public masturbations of rank amateurs, he hesitates ever to be dragged to a live performance again." The bridge? "Okay, at one time the DDF was the only way people could work in a theatre," Tom Hendry once admitted in an interview. "Now, if anyone seriously interested in the drama wants to learn and work, he can go to Toronto or Montreal. The alternate theatre is booming. I don't dig this idea that he is helped by nourishing his Little Theatre activities out in the mid-west somewhere. If he really wants to do something, he must pack up and go to places where the theatre is happening. It's simply like having to go somewhere else to attend medical school."

"If the DDF executive had forgotten regional resent-, ment and encouraged as many professional groups as possible to enter the festivals in the early nineteen-fifties, the bridge might automatically have been forged," Herbert Whittaker has mused. "Now I feel the DDF has levelled off into an amateur thing and you can't ever mix them." Emrys Jones has agreed: "I don't think there is any connection between amateur and professional theatre at all. I can't conceive of any bridge."

But the DDF could and Theatre Canada still can. Both the Moscow Art Theatre under Stanislavsky and the Abbey Theatre in Dublin had amateur beginnings, the organization has pointed out. In fact, both theatres were still amateur when they gained world attention and became professional only because of economic necessity. In Canada, the professional Manitoba Theatre Centre grew directly out of the amateur Winnipeg Little Theatre and the semi-professional Theatre 77 in 1957. Theatre London in Ontario is sprouting toward regional theatre status with its roots firmly embedded in the 39-year-old amateur London Little Theatre.

"Because the amateur movement in theatre in Canada is still well established and widespread, there are a number of cities which have a nucleus audience capable of being rapidly expanded, and a population large enough to provide, during the theatre's early years, sufficient ticket sales to sustain the theatre," wrote DDF critic Tom Hendry in a 1965 issue of the *Tulane Drama Review*. Because of these audiences, the DDF has nodded, it feels the Neptune Theatre in Halifax managed to get going under Leon Major's directorship in 1963. Because of audiences created by both amateur enthusiasts and theatre addicts exposed to DDF regionals and Finals, the professional Vancouver Playhouse gained support when it was established in 1964. The same argument, claims the organization, could apply to regional theatres begun in the sixties, such as Theatre Calgary, Edmonton's Citadel Theatre and the Globe Theatre of Saskatchewan. Even the drama festivals at Charlottetown, Lennoxville and Niagara-on-the-Lake benefited from the audiences developed. The DDF backs its argument that there is often only a flimsy membrane between serious amateur and professional theatre with a writer's opinion in a 1936 edition of the Ottawa *Citizen:* "Artistic and human importance of any theatre has nothing to do with whether it is amateur or professional."

While labelling amateur theatre as relevant to a national drama as "a game of bingo," though, Brian Doherty, founder of Niagara's Shaw Festival told a somewhat shocked western Canada Theatre Conference in 1947: "The only important function that the amateur theatre can and should discharge in relation to the two main theatre problems in Canada is to discover and give early encouragement and training to local talent of potential professional calibre and to facilitate the progress of such talent to semi-professional and professional theatre groups, operating on a higher level."

Staunch supporters of DDF ideals question Doherty's basic philosophies but thump back that this is precisely what the organization set out to do. So what is all this carping about self-perpetuation and the absence of bridges? In 1965, with the advice and financial backing of the Province of Ontario Council for the Arts and the Canada Council (then later, the Quebec Ministry of Cultural Affairs), the DDF began a professional training program which dispatched such theatre experts as George Luscombe of Toronto, Andrew Allen, David Gardner, Yves Gelinas to "the grass roots" drama groups throughout Canada. Names later added to the list of instructors include Peter Boretski, Hugh Webster, Gay Scrivener, Bruno Gerussi, Marigold Charlesworth, Herbert Whittaker, Paul Buissoneau, Dennis Sweeting, Adrian Pecknold.

"The number of professionals employed over the six-year period of the plan is 105," reported a 1972 Theatre Canada bulletin. "The workshops have covered every phase of theatre. Training received has been passed on by now to at least ten times the original number. In our opinion, the money obtained from the granting bodies has been spent wisely and well. It has encouraged Canadian playwrights, educated new directors at the community level, encouraged ethnic groups, assisted in the establishment of regional professional theatres and most important has enabled this organization to build a vast, knowledgeable theatre audience all across Canada."

In the face of snarls from professional critics, the DDF-turned-Theatre-Canada has fought back with other statistics to help underline its claim that community theatre is still as much the lifeblood of true Canadian drama as it was in Bessborough's day. According to Samuel French Ltd., Canada in 1972 boasted 500 active Little Theatre groups, 10 amateur children's theatre groups, 1,238 high school drama groups, 120 university drama groups, 200 college drama groups, 100 fraternal drama groups and an uncountable number of church drama groups. It is estimated the groups boast a total of 31,000 active members and that their productions reach an audience of 2,790,000 or approximately one-tenth of the Canadian population. In that year, the latest count of professional or semi-professional companies totalled between fifty and sixty, a spectacular increase during the nineteen-fifties and sixties which the DDF itself publicly applauds. "The professionals," spokesmen for the amateur organization have insisted, while still pledging total co-operation, "simply can't see the woods for the trees."

CHAPTER 10

Change

1.   **"We've got to keep moving with the times."**

Mini-typhoons of threatened changes were constantly gusting through the upper regions of the Dominion Drama Festival but major moves of any kind within the corporation—traditionally committed as it was to its quota of representation from across the country—were accomplished as sluggishly as those of a galleon trapped in the doldrums. Not that the members of the DDF executive refused to consider the possibility of shifts in policy and organizational structure. From the time that Col. Henry Osborne assumed the mantle of leadership from Lord Bessborough and Vincent Massey, there was recurring talk of expansion or contraction, revision of function and an overhaul of image. When changes eventually did become official, many of the revolutionaries and reformers within the corporation had already turned their backs in despair. "You have a vision," one dropout of the 1960's, Herbert Whittaker, has complained. "But until the animal itself heaves and turns over, the dream lies dormant."

Extension of the DDF's work as merely an organizer of one-act play festivals was discussed as early as 1936. But it was not until 1949 that the executive of the year decided to add an educational theatre conference to the Final. And it was not until 1951 that a still-doubting committee voted – under repeated pressure from visiting adjudicators – to confine competition in the Final to three-act plays. The first idealistic Committee of the Future was organized as far back as 1952 "to study possible future developments of the festival" but the executive committee was still listening to ideas from successive chairmen until 1964 and even later.

The 1952 Committee of the Future was chaired by Dorothy Somerset, professor of Drama – the University of British Columbia – a dogged DDF volunteer who was one of the corporation's rare workers who also had theatrical expertise. Miss Somerset seems to have been handed an airy mandate to discover feasible new directions for the DDF and decided to pursue it by mailing out a series of questionnaires to the various regions. The regions dragged their heels. At a 1953 executive meeting, the chairman reported sadly that replies had been sparse but the committee shrugged, smiled cheerfully and encouraged Miss Somerset to "carry on, regardless." After all, the future was a long way off and there was always another meeting to continue with the discussion. Some suggestions from the early Committee of the Future did filter through but it took years for any of them to be implemented. The fragmented survey showed that groups around the nation stressed "the need for training in the theatre" and wondered whether a "conservatory or central school could be established to give courses for experienced Canadian directors in the regions." Drama groups also wanted "a special DDF director-instructor to teach and assist" and reaffirmed that always-present ideal that "the DDF should promote a national theatre."

The Committee of the Future was later chaired by Roy A. Stewart (who discovered that the regions wanted the DDF to implement some kind of zoning and the use of Canadian adjudicators), Herbert Whittaker and Col. Yves Bourassa. The Bourassa report – which incorporated many of the ideas of former chairmen – was read at a 1964 Governors' Court in Charlottetown. It recommended, among other things, that the DDF become a multi-bodied, single-headed organization working in the fields of Canadian playwriting, professional theatre, community theatre and educational theatre. It created a flurry at the Charlottetown get-together, then settled with a gentle thud. Bourassa himself has complained angrily that the report was "watered down" by an executive then led by Vida Peene. But even so, it is easy to see why the policy-makers of the DDF

305

were somewhat intimidated by the flood of unusual and expensive ideas suddenly unleashed at the meeting. For one thing, the report strongly recommended that "festivals for the sake of festivals" in the regions should be discouraged. It also recommended that the DDF set up model programs of conferences, seminars and workshops throughout the year at regional level, with professional leaders, instructors and panelists supplied by the central office. "The climax of this season of learning," the report suggested, "should be a national conference possibly in Toronto, Montreal or Stratford where the delegates could see two or three excellent productions in addition to taking part in panel discussions, papers, group analysis of various problems of theatre." It was all mind-boggling for those still influenced by the Osborne-Jamieson way of doing things.

Bourassa's committee also recommended an all-Canadian play festival for Centennial year, bringing together seven *professional* companies (two of them French) which would be helped by the DDF to commission new plays by a Canadian author. The 1967 "Showcase Festival" would be non-competitive and last fourteen days instead of a week. It was suggested the showcase be held in Montreal but that others should also be organized in Toronto, Winnipeg, Vancouver, Halifax "or any other city that can afford them." In 1964, of course, the DDF was already girding its loins for an all-Canadian festival in 1967 and president Vida Peene's desk was buried under an avalanche of scripts submitted for inclusion in her Canadian play catalogue. But all-out professionalism within the amateur-oriented DDF? Non-competitiveness? A thrust into educational and training areas? A *discouragement* of regional festivals? As Bourassa has since stated with a cynical laugh: "We were called the Committee of the *Far* Future at Charlottetown."

But chairmen such as Whittaker and Bourassa had hit a nerve when they asked the DDF executive point blank: "We all know what Bessborough did in 1932 and why he did it. But if a group of Canadians truly representative of theatre came together today, what kind of organization would they create?" The question haunted DDF presidents John Brook, Don McGibbon and Alvin Shaw as the 1960's wore on. One thing that did come out of the 1964 report was the DDF's professional training program – an idea that had been part of Dorothy Somerset's submission twelve years before. But the future of the corporation itself continued to nag policy-makers even as they wrangled interminably over shaky finances, the nature of awards (Whittaker had long argued that group awards be abolished at the Final and individual awards retained but this was not done until 1969), the search for adjudicators and so on. There was no doubt the overall quality of productions at the festivals was declining as more professional opportunities in Canada drained off Little Theatre talent. So could it be, the DDF executive agonized, that the corporation had finished the job begun by Lord Bessborough? Had it destroyed itself by its own success? And if so, should it continue to exist?

The first real indication that the DDF had finally decided to come to realistic grips with the problem of its future was in October, 1969 when Professor Alvin Shaw of the University of New Brunswick – a jolly-faced DDF president who always looked as though he would prefer to avoid serious issues than face them – confronted an executive meeting in Winnipeg with some harsh home truths. Known now as the "Design for Tomorrow", the speech was as different from anything Vincent Massey or Henry Osborne would have said or thought about the DDF as a communist manifesto from a Tory homily. Could Massey ever have imagined, for example, that the extravagantly-publicized Dominion Drama Festival of the 1930's had lost so much of its public impact? "I was startled this summer," Shaw told the meeting, "to be congratulated on being the president of the Canadian Drama Festival, the Canadian Drama Society, the Canadian Drama Association, the Canadian Drama League, but only once as president of the Dominion Drama Festival. Is there any public awareness of us?" There were murmurs and shuffles in the room. "Are we really the dreary, dying festival as has been suggested, perhaps not in those words but in that substance over the years?" asked Shaw. "And do you wish me to preside at the demise of the DDF? I think it is really that serious. I, for one, certainly have no intention of living in the twilight of the gods!"

Twilight of the gods! That must have struck a chord for many of those present. Bessborough. Tweedsmuir. Alexander.

Michel St. Denis. Park Jamieson. Harley Granville-Barker. Massey. The aides de camp and the exciting balls at the armouries. Was this where it all was to end? "Perhaps we should abandon the Festival," Shaw went on. "Or perhaps we should be adventurous. Daring. Perhaps we should take a bold step and reshape the organization to give us a viable future."

Alvin Shaw's Winnipeg speech received thunderous applause. Of course that was the answer. Be bold! The founders, after all, were bold and adventurous in 1932. They understood the temper of the times and did something about fulfilling a need without shilly-shallying. And what was it Alvin had said? That the DDF was one of the few organizations still chartered under Section 12 of the British North America Act? The president's suggestions that fourteen short-term study groups be set up in the regions to explore such questions as bylaws, financing, playwriting, international involvement, education and so on, met with instant approval. So did another idea:

> I am suggesting that we not only keep the charter, but find a special purpose for the Dominion Drama Festival. One suggestion has been that we might, in co-operation with the National Arts Centre, develop a museum of Canadian theatre history where the charter of this festival would be a primary exhibit. Some special status, then, should be found for the present organization. Then, going beyond this, we must establish by incorporation, a new organization for which my officers suggest the name of Theatre Canada.

So there it was at last. It need not end at all. Perhaps it was only the beginning! The only problem now was how to shape the new organization so that as Shaw warned, "we will not continue to do anything more than drag on to a slow but inevitable death."

Riding high on renewed hopes, executive officers set to work with the study group plan. Chairmen were found in the regions and subject assignments, terms of reference and so on were quickly dispatched with attached pleas that if they wanted Theatre Canada to live, they had better get cracking as swiftly as possible. The response was so co-operative, the executive was able to dump the bundle of fourteen reports into vice-president Ted Fielder's lap early in 1970 with the request that he boil them down into some compact form. Fielder himself was clearly aglow with boldness, adventure and the heady new spirit of innovation was sweeping through the hoary DDF. In a foreword to what he dubbed "The Sixty-six Points," he penned some sentences that, compared with the noble phrases of Lord Bessborough's early outline of the Dominion Drama Festival, bear little resemblance to the original concept of the organization at all: "Art Needs Exposure. Theatre Needs Audiences. Audience Requires Quality. Quality Must be Achieved. Achievement Requires Study, Practice, Application. And Today – it must all be Relevant." And: "A complete frontal attack must be made on all the needs of that art form known as theatre. To keep biting at its heels may well be a waste of time." And: "There are those who participate in DDF today who do it for fun, for experience, for social advantage, for involvement, for an audience, for a career start, for art, for money, to write, act, sell tickets, forget work, forget home, forget everything, advance Canadianism, express social goals, etc. etc. etc. And all of those hopes, desires, needs, demand a pretty versatile forum in which to come together and bring forth worthy results."

The sixty-six points themselves crammed six pages. Some of them echoed what past DDF "radicals" and anti-establishment critics had been thumping for years. Some were obviously overly-idealistic. Others were new. Together, if accepted by the DDF, they would cost a king's ransom to implement. Among them:

Develop audience understanding. Broaden interest areas. Establish community need for local, regional, touring, national and international theatre. Serve both paid and unpaid theatre. Organize competitive festivals. Organize non-competitive festivals. Train adjudicators. Involve youth, purposefully. Translate plays. Commission plays for playwrights. Act as a magnet or focal point for money. Provide summer schools at locations across the country. Contribute

309

theatre conferences, workshops, discussions, backstage tours, summer recreation projects. Establish a theatre museum. Establish a theatre design centre available to groups, architects, communities, educators and others. Institute annual awards for professional theatre such as Oscars, Emmy or Pulitzers. Develop original play centre concept fully. Encourage, promote and support tours of regional theatres into local communities and continue to develop and provide audiences for them.

If Yves Bourassa's 1964 Committee of the Future report had been called far-out, what was Fielder's?

Alvin Shaw's officers were not sure. But they had commissioned the studies and the report and that was that. Perhaps the whole idea should be handed over to a bunch of individuals who had strong theatrical experience. Money, of course, was the usual problem but by then the floundering DDF had found other friends in need. When approached for funds so the corporation could arrange a professional seminar on the future of the DDF in April, 1970, Rothmans Pall Mall of Canada agreed to hand over the cash. Optimistically, the executive sent out invitations to such professional identities at David Gardner of the Vancouver Playhouse, Yves Gelinas of the Comédie Canadienne, William Wylie of Stratford, Ontario, Jim Garrard of the Theatre Passe-Muraille, Toronto, David Peacock of the National Theatre School, writer and artist Alan Jarvis.

The Rothmans brains trust pulled no punches when it got down to dissecting the ailing body of the Dominion Drama Festival. After agreeing that many members of the panel had a "personal fondness and affection" for the corporation and that the DDF had been essential to the development of theatre in Canada, it went on to agree that "its aims have become diffused in recent years." There were several reasons for this, it was decided. For one, "the traditional forms of theatre are fast becoming obsolete, yet there is resistance to change within the DDF from the conservative, often reactionary element which dominates in certain areas." For another, "there is constant war, often more confusion than conflict, between the amateur

310

and the professional." The group also believed that artists had far surpassed the organization in sophistication and that "the joy of amateurship" is seemingly lacking, while there is continual striving for professional status. It stated quite flatly that "the national body has attempted to impose severe limitations on the theatrical presentations from the different regions and this has been a real problem, particularly in Quebec."

Part of the Rothmans report reads: "The question 'is there a real need for the DDF' has been posed bluntly by Professor Alvin Shaw, president of the DDF. All present agreed that there was, provided that the organization could open up to become a showcase for theatrical activity of all forms, provided that it could agree to return autonomy to the regions and be content to act as national co-ordinator of regional policies and provided that it could provide real services rather than espouse noble but now impracticable aims." The group came to other conclusions, notably that there should be merger discussions with the Canadian Theatre Centre (a move to "umbrella" the functions of both Theatre Canada and the CTC that was bitterly regarded as a "take-over attempt" by CTC personnel until the organization disbanded in 1972) and that all regions should decide for themselves whether they wanted to hold festivals, an echo of Bourassa's space-age suggestion in 1964. Finally, the brains-trusters shook a warning finger at the proposed new organization: "Theatre Canada is a name not to be used unwisely. After a comprehensive reorganization (as recommended in this report), the name Theatre Canada would be appropriate."

Now up to its eyebrows in surveys, reports, suggestions and sundry finger-waggings, the DDF packed its bags and flew off to its last competitive Final in Winnipeg. It was May 1970, thirty-seven years since Vere Brabazon Ponsonby, the 9th Earl of Bessborough, proudly took his seat in the Ottawa Little Theatre to watch the results of his infant Dominion Drama Festival. The Winnipeg Final still featured some of the familiar high-jinks of other years but change hung thickly in the air. For some it might have been a sad and nostalgic occasion but – sure as always that everything would come out all right – the majority of DDF supporters swallowed the lumps in their throats and clung to the fact that Theatre Canada was about

311

to rise from the ashes. At Governors' Court held at the Fort Garry Hotel on May 22, 1970, it was all made official. A motion was made, seconded and carried that "all necessary steps be taken to create a new corporation under the Canada Corporations Act, with the title Theatre Canada."

In the meantime, Alvin Shaw and his colleagues were still struggling with the question of how to slice through the extravagant verbiage of all those reports and recommendations and form a clear-cut image of what Theatre Canada was all about. One definite point was decided in Winnipeg: that the new organization would hold a non-competitive "showcase" festival the following year at the National Arts Centre in Ottawa which would have no limitations as far as "professional, amateur, classical, avant-garde, experimental, French and English" were concerned. As for the role of Theatre Canada, the executive took another despairing look at the mass of information and ideas already pulled together then voted to find someone who could co-ordinate the material and conduct yet another nation-wide survey. The man picked by Alvin Shaw and administrator John Hill for the task was Philip Spensley, an English-born Montreal director and actor then working at Stratford, Ontario, on a Tyrone Guthrie award. Spensley – a nervous man who has been known to come close to tears when his ideals are questioned – has admitted he was "terribly surprised" to land the assignment. Once he agreed to do the job, Canada Council travel grants were diverted from income to pay the new researcher's expenses and he was waved on his way.

The Spensley reports (interim, initial, final and amended) ran to twenty-nine pages each and caused storms in Theatre Canada's executive meetings as fierce as those which raged in Lady Madge Tupper's day. The arguments ranged from criticism of the number of governors recommended to serve on the new board, to Spensley's (and the Rothmans Report) "umbrella" ideas concerning affiliation with other organizations. His suggestion that Theatre Canada should be "based on two pillars, the DDF speaking for amateurs, the CTC speaking for professionals" was challenged by governor Guy Beaulne, who insisted that the Association Canadienne de Théâtre Amateur (L'ACTA), not the DDF, spoke for French-Canadian amateurs, and that Theatre Canada should be based on *three* pillars, not two. At yet another meeting it was stated that unlike Theatre Canada, L'ACTA was founded on constitutional reality and that it did not accept the multi-cultural aspects of the new organization, anyway. Heresy! After rows, hair-tearing and walkouts, a final, amended Spensley report was accepted at an executive committee meeting in February 1971. After that, the material was condensed into a policy paper which was still being debated at Theatre Canada's 1972 festival in Saskatoon.

A meeting of what is now known in Theatre Canada legend as The Group of Six probably came to grips as well as any other get-together with what Spensley was striving to recommend for the organization. The group included John Hill, David Peacock, Professor Norma Springford of Sir George Williams University, Guy Beaulne, David Barnet, director of the Manitoba Theatre School and John Hirsch of the Manitoba Theatre Centre – who sent his regrets at the last moment. Spensley presented a digest of his suggestions, prefaced with the paragraph:

> There is a fantastic amount of theatre activity in this country. There is little done to communicate this fact. Activity is often at cross-purposes. Professionals, amateurs, educators and the new experimentalists do not talk to each other. It would seem evident that Canada has a cultural need to identify itself. It is the duty of all theatre lovers to abandon the barriers and to seek a common meeting ground through communication and exchange. The real need is to recognize it as fact not fancy. We must do it now.

The digest was considered and discussed, then the group endorsed its points with the observation that they were much the same as those presented in the Rothmans Report of 1970. This, they felt, was highly significant. Theatre Canada should certainly exist, provided it stuck to fourteen goals as recommended in the Spensley study:

> To make information available. To stop duplicating activity on a national level. To dictate priorities. To

build strong independent regional theatre, but not in cultural isolation. To train animateurs. To encourage professionals, amateurs and educators to meet regularly. To improve management. To interest groups in being civic-minded. To organize creative workshops. To encourage playwriting by production. To run a national festival of theatrical activities somewhere between Edinburgh and Woodstock. To encourage ethnic drama. To explode myths. To open doors.

Somewhere between Edinburgh and Woodstock! It seemed like a tall order (and officers of Theatre Canada did not hesitate to say so at future meetings) but then, the Word was to be adventurous and bold. No one wanted to witness the twilight of the gods. In the spring of 1971, Theatre Canada's first non-competitive "showcase" festival was held in Ottawa, where Bessborough's dream first began. The Governor General would have been stunned to watch the bustling goings-on. The showcase included a production every evening in the National Arts Centre (the bricks and mortar that some early DDF supporters felt was the answer to a national theatre in Canada), and the performances included a mimodrama, a puppet ballet and a Yiddish play. There were late-afternoon shows in the Centre's studio and 11 a.m. happenings in the salon. Just in case Theatre Canada had missed something in launching its bustling new image, there was also "peripheral theatre" in parks and streets around the national capital. Now would the public become aware of what the organization was all about?

A pleased Alvin Shaw, in his last year of a stirring two-year presidency, set the new tone of Theatre Canada in a message printed in the 1971 program:

> Theatre is people. Theatre belongs not to a special class of cultural elite, but to us all, whatever our ambitions, delights or fears. Whether we become involved, or whether we fail to partake, depends more upon an influence than upon a native desire. Theatre Canada '71 is a reflection of theatre from

across Canada. It is about the people of Canada. It is played by the people of Canada. It is hoped that through the influence of this festival you will become more involved in, or aware of, the arts in our country.

Was that what Lord Bessborough meant in his festival program message of 1933? "The spirit of a nation, if it is to find full expression, must include a national drama."

"Well, we've dropped the word drama from our name, you know," Theatre Canada's new president, Helen Smith, told a reporter in 1972. "We feel the word is too rigid. We want to develop other areas in our festival of theatre – music, dance, everything. But I do think the 'showcase' festivals of 1971 and '72 prove we've hit the right format. Where is the organization going now? Well, right now we're concentrating on the job of making this current concept work. As for the future, we're still trying to find focus."

315

2.   So what happened to all those people in Saskatoon?

Early in August, 1972, Dr. Harry Hay sat at his desk in Saskatoon and stared at a sheet of figures which told the story of how Theatre Canada's big bash fared in his city that previous May. To begin with, the optometrist noted with a self-congratulatory smile, the sale of tickets and programs had earned $11,703 for the Showcase Festival, $1,303 more than was budgeted. So he had been dubbed a disagreeable ogre in his battle to control costs, had he? The week had turned out so well, in fact, that he had returned $750 to the Saskatchewan Arts Board (which had come through with an extra $5,000 thanks to some determined arm-twisting from Theatre Canada's Ottawa office) and $750 to the City of Saskatoon. "This will have a good effect when future affairs of this kind are needing help," Dr. Hay commented happily to a reporter. Theatre Canada had also been paid its guarantee – less $750 for "unforeseen expenses."

He turned to a page which listed ticket-sale breakdowns for the week and his smile grew broader. Oh, there was no doubt that planning at the local level paid off. Just as he had told the people from Theatre Canada's national office, French plays left Saskatoon audiences absolutely cold. Look at the figures for Monday night's staging of *La Nuit des Assassins*. Just $83 worth of tickets sold! And *Fragments* from Le Théâtre Français d'Edmonton. Sixty-one dollars! Even worse, Les Feux-Chalins' presentation of *La Sagouine* chalked up a mere $58 at the box-office.

But take a look at the Feehan High School's production of *Saskatchewan I'm Coming Home*. Sure, he had heard those ana, ana, amateurs, no, *anamateurs* had torn the thing to pieces. But Saskatoon really turned out for that one. *One thousand, five hundred and fifty-three bucks!* And the local Gateway Players' show, *Hadrian the Seventh*, had syphoned in $1,678. No point in adding up the income from all the children's plays he had scheduled – much to the annoyance of a whole slew of doubters, incidentally. Together with the productions from Saskatoon they had pulled the whole enterprise into the black. And even with all that idealistic talk about showcase productions from across the country and people learning from each other, there wasn't much point in putting on a festival if it floundered under a deficit.

Well, mused Dr. Hay, there had been rows and disagreements he supposed but by golly, it had been fun as well. By the time Saturday night had come around and he was having a drink at Jeannie Walter's party he had begun to feel something of what Festival was all about. He wondered how Helen Smith and John MacPherson were going with their ambitious plans to get Theatre Canada rolling smoothly. He thought about Jeanne Sabourin and Yvon Dufour. French Canadians were tough to understand at first but everyone was quite chummy by the end of festival week. He wondered about those kids who came from all over Canada. The people from Moncton and St. Catharines. The boys and girls from Medicine Hat who put on *The Ecstasy of Rita Joe*. Did they still want to be part of the theatre? Or had they forgotten all about Saskatoon by now?

Across the country in Ottawa, the national staff of Theatre Canada was gleaning news of participants in their 1972 Showcase Festival. The Dei Gelosie Compagnie of St. Catharines, which had presented a Commedia del Arte show ($247 worth of tickets sold) had disbanded. During the summer, the company applied for grants from the Canada Council but were told this was possible only if the group became fully professional and cut its ties with Brock University. "A great idea," commented company director Warren Hartman, who is a drama teacher at Brock. "But absolutely impossible at this time."

In the meantime, continued Hartman's report, three members of the festival group had confidently pulled up stakes and gone off to seek recognition in the professional theatre world of Toronto. Pamela Warr was working with the Smile Company which tours local hospitals. Elizabeth Fajta had allied herself with the active Toronto Dance Theatre. John Blackwood had found himself some set-design assignments with the Canadian Opera Company after the Saskatoon festival and his reputation was already filtering into the United States. "Me?" added Hartman. "Well, I'm up to my ears in teaching at the moment, but I want to become involved in Theatre Canada festivals again, perhaps as an animateur."

Dorothy Jones, director of *Rita Joe*, was writing from Medicine Hat that "I would not say the festival as such has helped our group. But the production we did, the experiences it provided and the resulting interest it evoked certainly did." Conscious of its efforts to develop meaningful new goals, Theatre Canada's national office took note of Mrs. Jones's comment that "the major profit for my group came from the workshops prior to the festival when we had a chance to meet and work with playwright George Ryga. It was a fascinating and unique experience for us all and it was made possible by a Theatre Canada-Canada Council grant." But was the festival a boost for aspiring professionals? "Well, we have a number of converts to the theatre now," wrote the Medicine Hat director. "Some on a professional basis, I hope."

The post-festival story of Viola Léger, solo performer in the controversial French-language production of *La Sagouine* was certainly upbeat enough for Theatre Canada supporters to illustrate that the organization's work still had purpose. Mlle. Léger had been a relatively unknown drama teacher in New Brunswick before Eugène Gallant of Moncton University directed her in the challenging monologue concerning "a woman of the sea" by Acadian author Antonine Maillet. *La Sagouine* was one of the financial flops of the Saskatoon Showcase but its artistic success rippled clear across the country. In October 1972, it played to standing-room audiences at the prestigious Rideau Vert in Montreal. In November, it was invited to Paris by the Canadian Cultural Centre. It was booked for a cross-country tour during January to March, 1972, then invited back to Le Rideau Vert for a further 33 performances. A clearly excited Theatre Canada was already working behind the scenes at the end of 1972 to send Viola Léger and *La Sagouine* to represent Canada at the International Amateur Theatre Association's Monaco festival in August, 1973. Amateur? "There seems no doubt," admits Eugène Gallant, "that Viola Léger is inevitably headed toward professionalism."

Interestingly, the professionals who had been invited to Saskatoon seemed to have cashed in on the Showcase Festival as much as the amateurs. The Vellemens' Canadian Puppet Festivals of Toronto, which packed in hundreds of children during the week had been granted financial aid from the Canada Council and the Department of External Affairs to export their animated dolls to an international festival in France. After the festival, the Vellemens were off on a tour of theatres and cultural centres in five European countries. "Congratulations!" enthused a Theatre Canada bulletin. "It's the first international tour ever for Canadian puppets!" Company One, another professional group which came to Saskatoon from Victoria, travelled on from Saskatchewan to Belleville, Ontario then to Montreal, meeting new admirers all the way. "As a result of our contact with other groups at the festival," wrote Susan Stephen of the company, "French-speaking Marie Cadieux (who performed in *La Nuit des Assassins*) was able to see our work. She has now joined the company." Contacts generated by the festival, in fact, added Miss Stephen were invaluable to the group. After Company One's 1972 national exposure, it began mounting new productions and planning an ambitious 1973 national tour, the only professional theatre company to do so.

What, no carpers? "Well, personally, I was disappointed at the general calibre of performances in Saskatoon," commented Warren Harman of Brock University. "It was certainly no real show-case of theatre, though there's no doubt the workshops and the chance to meet other people interested in the theatre was terrific." Wrote Mme Claire Ifrane somewhat sparsely from the Université de Moncton: "The department's development is taking place as planned and this is quite apart from our experience of staging *La Nuit des Assassins* at the festival." But, she added, "the festival provided an occasion for this department to make itself known and to strengthen our standing in the eyes of the university adminis-tration."

Still, enthusiasm for the 1972 Theatre Canada Showcase seemed to outweigh any lacklustre response or criticism. "An unfor-gettable experience," decided George T. Wilson of Ottawa's Sir Robert Borden High School, which presented a production of Arthur Kopits' *Chamber Music* at the festival. "All of us have become more discriminating and aware. Personally, we have formed a more lucid understanding and acceptance of our cultural differences." Reported Ian Nelson, chairman of Saskatoon's Gateway Players: "The festival definitely increased interest in our group and inspired all of us to work harder and more imaginatively." Theatre Canada itself noted the significance of a request from the Gateway group for a grant to employ an artistic director and that the company is searching for its own theatre. Added Nelson in his report: "There's no doubt there is more theatrical activity in Saskatoon since Theatre Canada came here. A new group called the 25th St. House has appeared. The Saskatoon Summer Players staged two productions

319

instead of one after the 1972 festival. Our own company did a summer show for the first time, a Canadian play called *The Hunt* by Ron Marten. And Gateway has decided to set up a system of co-operation with other groups around the province to swap costumes and other services.''

Then there was a letter from Danielle Fortosky of the Feehan High School in Saskatoon which had presented the financially successful *Saskatchewan I'm Coming Home*. Had that searing session with Theatre Canada's animateurs discouraged the group? Well, reported Danielle, Larry Biblow who played the lead in the show landed a spot in a touring rock band not long after the Saskatoon bash. Holly Ann Knott, the female lead of *I'm Coming Home*, played a major role in a local production of *Man of La Mancha*. Danielle herself won a CBC bursary and was brought to Toronto after the festival to mingle with local professionals.

One part of her report would surely have had Lord Bessborough, Vincent Massey and Col. Henry Osborne nodding knowingly if they could have read it. Perhaps it even helps bring Theatre Canada's new direction into focus. "The Feehan High School Theatre Guild went to the community for assistance in producing *Saskatchewan I'm Coming Home* and as a result, more than 200 individuals – children and adults – became involved in the production. Speaking to these people afterwards, they have always expressed enthusiasm in remembering the experience of Theatre Canada. Certainly a bond was established between the community, the school and the amateur theatre.''

Selected Bibliography

Booth, Michael. "Pioneer Entertainment: Theatrical Taste in the Early Canadian West." *Canadian Literature,* Spring, 1960.

Charlesworth, Hector. *Candid Chronicles.* Toronto: Macmillan, 1925.

Cowan, John. *Canada's Governors-General.* Toronto: York Publishing Co., 1952.

Dominion Drama Festival, 1905–1967. Correspondence, files, documents, scrapbooks, microfilms, accounting records, memoranda, in the National Archives of Canada.

Edwards, Murray D. *A Stage in Our Past.* University of Toronto Press, 1968.

Encyclopedia Canadiana, Theatre Section. Ottawa: Canadiana Company, 1962.

Freedley, George and **Reeves, John A.** *A History of the Theatre.* New York: Crown Publishers Ltd., 1968.

Firth, Edith G. *The Town of York, 1815–1834.* University of Toronto Press, 1966.

Graham, Franklin. *Histrionic Montreal.* Montreal: John Lovel and Son, 1902.

Hartnoll, Phyllis. *Oxford Companion to the Theatre.* London: Oxford University Press, 1967.

Harvey, Ruth. *Curtain Time.* Boston: Houghton Mifflin, 1949.

Lee, Betty. "Other actors, other times." *The Globe Magazine,* February 21, 1970.

Lescarbot, Marc. *The Theatre of Neptune in New France.* Translated by Harriet Tabor. Boston: Richardson, 1927.

Massey, Vincent. *What's Past is Prologue.* Toronto: Macmillan, 1963.
Ontario Theatre Study Report. *The Awkward Stage.* Toronto: Methuen, 1969.
Parkhill, Francis. *The Dominion Drama Festival, its history and influence.* Thesis.
Rhys, Horton. *A Theatrical Trip for a Wager.* Vancouver: Alcuin Society, 1966.
Scott, Robert. *Amateur Theatre in Toronto.* Thesis.
Speaight, Robert. *The Property Basket.* London: Collins and Harvill Press, 1970.
Tait, Michael. *Studies in the Theatre and Drama of English Canada.* Thesis.
Theatre Canada. Minutes of meetings, 1969–1971.
Willis-O'Connor, Col. W. *Inside Government House.* As told to Madge MacBeth. Toronto: Ryerson Press, 1954.
York Pioneers and Historical Society. Annual Report, 13–15, 1930. *Toronto Theatres in the Old Days.*

Personal and taped interviews

Beaulne, Guy, Quebec City.
Bessborough, Countess of, London, England.
Bourassa, Yves, Montreal.
Brickenden, Catharine, London.
Coxwell, Mona, Toronto.
Cook, Michael, St. John's.
Davies, Robertson, Toronto.
Gardner, David, Toronto.
Gray, Jack, Toronto.
Hendry, Thomas, Toronto.
Hersenhoren, Jeannie, Toronto.
Hope-Wallace, Philip, London, England.
Jamieson, Park, Sarnia.
Jones, Emrys, Saskatoon.
Karsh, Yousuf, Ottawa.

Legault, Pierre, Montreal.
MacDonald, Richard, Edmonton.
MacPherson, John, Antigonish.
McGibbon, Donald, Toronto.
McGibbon, Pauline, Toronto.
Melanson, Laurier, Fredericton.
Ongley, David, Toronto.
Palmer, John, Toronto.
Peene, Vida, Toronto.
Ramsay, Beatrice, Regina.
Rinfret, Edouard, Montreal.
Sabbath, Lawrence, Montreal.
Shaw, Alvin, Fredericton.
Smith, Helen, Victoria.
Spensley, Philip, Montreal.
Stone, Edgar, Toronto.
Wetmore, Donald, Halifax.
Whittaker, Herbert, Toronto.

Index

Acadius, 46, 47
Adams, Maude, 62
Adaskin, John, 185
Adjudicators, 109, 110, 213-247
Aikens, Carroll, 81, 82, 101
Ainley, Richard, 237, 239
Alberta Drama Festival, 79
Alexander of Tunis, Lord, 185
Allan, Andrew, 31, 283
Allan, Martha, 95, 96, 103, 106, 132, 134, 164, 277, 289
Allard, T. J., 203, 204
All on a Summer's Day, 289
Allport, Mr., 49
American Company of Comedians, 45
Les Anciens Du Gesu, 162
Anderson, Mrs. A. H., 115
Anglin, Margaret, 67
Archer, Thomas, 106, 258
Artaud, Antonin, 297
Aster, J. de B., 147
Awards, 104, 258-269

Aylen, John A., 123, 124, 132, 134, 181
Aylward, Alan, 31
Azevedo, Don Joseph, 46

Babel, 30
Baker, Mrs., 48
Band, Charles, 188, 190
Barbeau, Jean, 297
Bayefsky, Aba, 194
Beaches Library Drama League (Toronto), 111, 112, 116
Beaufort, Ernest, 69, 72
Beaulne, Guy, 171, 204, 243, 295
Beaulne, Jean-Pierre, 28
Beaux Arts Society (Victoria), 277
Behind the Beyond, 289
Bellamy, Cecil, 236, 237
Bennett, E. G. Sterndale, 79, 95, 102, 108, 109, 111, 120, 259
Bennett, R. B., 86

Béraud, Jean, 243
Bernard, John, 49
Bernhardt, Sarah, 62
Bessborough, Lady, 84, 98, 123, 161
Bessborough, Lord (see Ponsonby, Vere Brabazon)
Bessborough Trophy, 104, 105, 263-265
Bishop, Howard B., 157
Blake, Charlie, 35, 36
Blakeney, Allan, 19
The Blood Is Strong, 296
Blue, Wilson, 69
Bohemian Company of Players (Winnipeg), 74
Booth, John Wilkes, 55
Booth, Michael, 55
Sir Robert Borden High School (Ottawa), 30
Bourassa, Lt. Col. Yves, 140-142, 173, 200-204, 206, 235, 305, 306
Brain, Arthur, 95
Breeches from Bond Street, 293
Brickenden, Catharine, 95, 104, 127, 192, 223, 289
British Columbia Drama Festival, 82, 144
Brockington, Leonard, 287
The Broken Jug, 296
Bronfman, Samuel, 200-202
Brook, Bubby, 238
Brook, John F., 142, 296
Brooks, Charles, 223
Brothers in Arms, 162, 289, 292
Brown, Frederick, 50
Browne, N. H., 150, 151
Bruce, Katharine, 277

Buchan, John, 127, 128, 220
Buchanan, Donald W., 125
Bullock-Webster, Major L., 102, 144-148
Burgess, John, 295
Bury the Dead, 34, 37
Button, Henry, 215

Cabana, Msgr. Georges, 158
Cahill, Tom, 297
Callaghan, Morley, 293
Calvert Distillers, 136, 137, 155-161, 191-202, 260-264 passim, 267
Calvert Trophies, 260-267
Campbell, Colin, 134
Campbell, Mrs. Patrick, 66
Campbell, Mrs. W. D., 156
Canada Council, 200, 202, 205, 267
Canadian Association of Broadcasters, 203-207
Canadian Broadcasting Corporation, 31, 269
Canadian Drama Award, 148
Canadian Puppet Festivals, 31, 318
Canadian Theatre Centre, 300, 311
Caplan, Rupert, 78
Caple, Mrs. K., 210, 211
Carter, Alex Scott, 104, 265
Le Caveau (Ottawa), 164, 167, 168
Centre d'Essai des Auteurs Dramatiques (Montreal), 21
Cercle Dramatique des Etudiants de Laval, 162
Cercle Molière, (Winnipeg),

165, 167, 169, 173, 175
Ceyatano's Spanish Circus, 50
Chalmers, Floyd, 191
Chamber Music, 30
Charlesworth, Hector, 60, 61, 65, 66, 72-75, 227, 228
Ciceri, Leo, 283
Le Cid, 44
Citadel Theatre (Edmonton), 31
The Citizen, 46, 47
Clark, Barrett H., 225, 226
Clive Dramatic Society, 276
Coercion, 289
Colicos, John, 282
Colman, George, 46
Colonial Theatre (Victoria), 55
Comédie Nouvelle (Ottawa), 169-170
Committee of the Future, 304-310
Community Players (Toronto), 78
Community Players (Winnipeg), 78
Compagnie de Montréal, 173
Compagnons de St. Laurent, 168-170
Company One (Victoria), 30, 319
Conservatoire Lasalle (Montreal), 169
Conservatoire National de Musique de Québec, 162
Considine, Leo, 277
Constantineau, Mr. Justice, 127, 167
Copeau, Jacques, 224
Corbett, E. A., 127
Corbin, John, 72

Couldock, Charles, 53
Coulter, John, 165, 186, 290-292
The Countess of Salisbury, 48
Cours François Rozet (Montreal), 170
Court Players (Toronto), 78
Coxwell, Mona, 115, 187, 225, 251, 291
Craig, John, 83, 94
Crerar, Caroline, 95
Cromarty, W. D., 134
Cromie, Donald, 137, 138
Crystal Palace Opera House (Montreal), 61

Dalhousie Musical and Dramatic Society, 34, 37
Daoust, Sylvia, 198
David, Athanase, 97
Davies, Dorothy, 243
Davies, Robertson, 153, 189, 190, 261-265 *passim*, 292, 298
Davies, W. Rupert, 96, 108
Dean, James, 243
De Champ, St. Elme, 113, 163
Delaute, J. F., 194
De l'Autre Côté du Mur, 171
De Montigny, Louvigny, 128
Denison, Merrill, 101, 162, 289
Dennistoun, Beck, 107
Devine, Major, 69, 74
De Warfaz, George, 279
Dickens, Charles, 54
Dickens Fellowship Players (Toronto), 65, 77
Digby, William, 292
The Disintegration of James Cherry, 36

Divinity in Montreal, 228, 291
Dodson, J. E., 68
Doherty, Brian, 228, 277, 302
Donn, Basil, 78, 82
Douglas, T. C., 151
Drao Players, 270
Dubé, Marcel, 171, 295
Duchesne, Jacques, 295
Duffy, V. G., 276
Dufour, Yvon, 21, 24-26, 30, 31, 38, 39
Duncannon, Viscount Eric, 84, 93, 106-108, 123, 125, 284, 285
Dyba, Ken, 31-33

Eaton, Robert Y., 133
Margaret Eaton Associate Players (Toronto), 74
Margaret Eaton School of Literature and Expression, 65
Ebb Tide, 289
Ecole de Musique et de Déclamation de l'Université d'Ottawa, 164
The Ecstasy of Rita Joe, 32-34, 318
Edmonton Amateur Dramatic Club, 74
Edmonton Little Theatre Association, 79
Edwards, Gwillym, 127
Embassy Players (Vancouver), 275
Les Enfants de Voiture, 175, 297
L'Equipe, 168
Eros at Breakfast, 293, 294
Et Coetera, 297
Evelyn, Judith, 283

Fairbairn, A. M. D., 289
Father Malachy's Miracle, 228, 277
Feehan High School (Saskatoon), 20-23, 321
Ferguson, George V., 83
Fergusson, Brenda, 275
Fergusson, C. Bruce, 45, 48
Feux-Chalins (Moncton), 30
Fielder, Ted, 310
Flavelle, Sir Joseph, 178
Fletcher, Robert, 46
Fontaine, Robert, 293
The Fool's Jewel, 34
Forbes-Robertson, Sir Johnston, 61, 62
Forsyth, Bertram, 81
Fortune and Men's Eyes, 271, 297
Fortune My Foe, 292
Frank's Hotel (York), 52
From Their Own Place, 289
Frontenac, Louis de Buade, Compte de, 45

Gallant, Eugène, 30, 318
Gardner, David, 206, 243-247, 283, 298
Garrick Club (Hamilton), 65, 68, 70
Gascon, Jean, 170, 206
Gateway Players (Saskatoon), 40, 319, 320
Gauthier, Solange, 284
Gelber, Arthur, 185
Gelinas, Gratien, 293
Gianelli, Adèle M., 248
Gill, Robert, 243
Gilliam, 296

Gilstorf, Eve, 25, 38
Vaughan Glaser Company, 81
Globe Theatre (Regina), 21
Glover, Guy, 278
Gomery, Percy, 101-103,
144-147
Gordon, Sir Charles, 94, 97,
133, 177, 178
Gordon, K. W., 258, 259
Goring, Marius, 243
Gowan, Elsie Park, 293
Graham, Mrs. A. G., 275
Graham, Franklin, 49, 50, 55,
58
Graham, George E., 134
Grand Central Dime Museum
(Montreal), 61
Grand Opera House (Toronto),
54
Granville-Barker, Harley, 128,
164, 220-224
Gray, Jack, 297
Greene, Lorne, 225
Ben Greet Company, 77
Grein, J. T., 124, 125, 214,
216, 217
Grey, Lord Albert Henry
George, 65-75 *passim*
Earl Grey Musical and
Dramatic Competitions,
65-75
Group of Six, 314
Gurik, Robert, 175, 296
Gury, Paul, 272
Guthrie, Tyrone, 102

Hadrian the Seventh, 40
Hahn, Emmanuel, 260
Hamilton, Mary, 157

Hanbury-Williams, Sir John,
68
Harchoux-Vuillaume, Gil, 295
Harman, Warren, 319
Harris, W. Eric, 289
Harron, Donald, 296
Hart House Theatre (Toronto),
77, 78, 81, 82, 111, 113, 125
Hartman, Warren, 317
Harton, Hall, 48
Harvey, Rupert, 105, 113, 117,
118, 122, 124, 125, 163,
213-217, 236, 241
Harvey, W. Eric, 223
Haskins, Robert, 276
Hay, Dr. Harry, 18-21, 23, 32,
35, 36, 38-41, 316, 317
Heavysege, Charles, 288
Hébert, Louis Philippe, 67
Hendry, Tom, 253, 298, 300,
301
Herbert, John, 271, 297
Her Majesty's Theatre
(Montreal), 61
Hersenhoren, Jeannie, 212
Hill, John, 209, 210
His Majesty's Theatre
(Toronto), 78
Hoffman, Guy, 170
Holmes, John W., 270
Holroy, Frank, 80
Hope-Wallace, Philip, 169,
224, 229, 237, 240-242
Horne, Cleve, 260
The House in the Quiet Glen,
165, 290
Hunt, Hugh, 230, 232
The Hunt, 320
Hunter, Martin, 296

Ifrane, Claire, 319
Innes, Capt. W. C., 102, 103
Les Insolités, 173
Irving, Sir Henry, 60

Jackson, Sir Barry, 79, 122
Sir Barry Jackson Trophy, 259,
    267, 289-291, 294, 296
James, Rev. F. E. H., 157
Jamieson, D. Park, 95, 101,
    112, 133-137, 140, 150-152,
    187, 188, 191, 194, 196,
    253, 259, 262
Jane Shore, 45
The Jealous Wife, 46
Jefferis, Nella, 77, 127
Jim Barber's Spite Fence, 111,
    116, 289
John, Evan, 230
Jones, Dorothy, 33, 34, 317,
    318
Jones, Emrys M., 134, 168,
    229, 242, 300
Joudry, Patricia, 173, 295
Jousse, Eugène, 243

Karsh, Yousuf, 283-287
Kean, Charles, 51
Kean, Edmund, 50, 51
Kemble, Charles, 51
Kemble, Fanny, 51
Kerlin, Donald, 191
The Kildeer, 295
King, Alan, 283
King, Thomas C., 55
King, William Lyon
    Mackenzie, 86, 116,
    286
Kramer, Ken, 21, 22, 31

Lamont, Gwendolyn Pharis,
    292
Languirand, Jacques, 173
LaRoche, Roland, 21-23, 31
Lascelles, Allan F., 86, 89,
    92, 145
Latour, Rev. Conrad, 127, 134
Laurence, Colin, 279
Leacock, Stephen, 289
Lefèvre, Pierre, 170, 236
Legault, Rev. Emile, 168-170,
    190
Lemain, Beaudry, 97, 133
Lescarbot, Marc, 43, 44
Letourneau, Jacques, 170
Letourneau, Yves, 170
Levesque, Rev. Georges-Henri,
    202
Lieven, Prince Paul, 165-167
Littlewood, S. R., 135, 227,
    228, 241, 242, 276, 277
Logie, R. T., 296
London Drama League, 112
London Dramatic Club,
    65, 73, 74
London Little Theatre, 223,
    289
London Theatre Company,
    (Newfoundland), 299
Long, Rev. Ernest, 156-158
Loring, Frances, 198, 260
Les Louis d'Or, 297
Low Life, 289

MacBrien, Maj.-Gen. J. H.,
    108
MacBrien, Julia, 108
McConnell, J. W., 177
MacDonald, Alan, 149

MacDonald, Richard,
135-138, 171, 172, 190,
191, 193, 199, 200-203, 205,
206, 229-236, 239, 253, 254,
294, 296
McDowell Company, 58
McGibbon, Donald W., 141,
143, 204-209, 294, 296
McGibbon, Pauline, 140, 141,
185, 192, 193, 196
McIntyre, Barbara, 20
Mackay, F. F., 70, 71
Mackay, J. Ewart, 140
Mackenzie King, William
Lyon, 86, 116, 286
McLaughlin, Col. R. S., 179,
180
McNiven, Justice, D. A., 138
Macphail, Sir Andrew, 94
McPhee, Janet Alexandra,
228, 291
MacPherson, John, 20, 25,
29, 37-39
Madame Verité at Bath, 292
Major, Leon, 243, 302
The Man Born to be Hanged,
111, 116, 118
Manitoba Drama League, 83
Manitoba Theatre Centre,
301
Mansion House Theatre
(Montreal), 50
Maria Chapdelaine, 292
Marks Brothers, 58
Marquis, Col. G. E., 118, 163
Marten, Ron, 320
Martin, Ross, 195
Mason, Lawrence, 104, 110,
112, 121, 122

Masquers Club (Toronto),
165
Masquers Club (Winnipeg),
116, 118, 119
Massey, Lionel, 158-160, 195
Massey, Raymond, 81
Massey, Vincent, 76, 78, 81,
82, 85-94, 96, 97, 99,
101-105, 108-114, 118, 119,
122, 123-128, 131-133, 138,
144, 150, 151, 155-161,
177-180, 184, 188, 189,
194, 202, 203, 215, 255,
262, 265, 266, 286, 287
Massey Award, 267
Massey Foundation, 180
Matthews, Charles, 51, 53
Maurer, Sheila, 281
Mavor, Dora, 67, 77, 185
Medicine Hat College, 32, 33
Meighan's Ballroom (York),
52
Meikeljohn, Michael, 279
Meikle, Jack, 115
Mendel, Fred, 203
Miller, Joan, 282
Mills, Hugh O., 127
Mills, John, 49
Mitchell, Betty, 243
Mitchell, Langdon, 69
Mitchell, Roy, 78
Molson, Col. Herbert, 178
Molson, John, 50
Montreal Repertory Theatre,
82, 95, 106, 117, 118,
162, 277
Montreal Theatre, 49
Monument Nationale
(Montreal), 61

Moore, Dora Mavor, 67, 77, 185
Morgan, Basil, 77
Morgan-Powell, S., 102, 104, 107, 149, 150
Morley, Malcolm, 217-219, 225
Morris, Clara, 53
Morris, Frank, 226
Morrison, Charlotte, 54, 59
Mount Allison University Drama Club, 267
Mulcahy, Sean, 31-34
Murchison, Myles, 296
Myers, Lillian D., 85

Nanaimo Dramatic Academy, 275
National Theatre School, 211
Negro Theatre Guild (Montreal), 282
Neild, Marian, 281
Nelson, Ian, 319
Neptune Theatre (Halifax), 302
New Grand Theatre (Halifax), 47, 48
New Market Theatre (Montreal), 50
New Play Society (Toronto), 185
Nickinson, John, 53
No Name Theatre (Winnipeg), 23, 24
Noseworthy, Joseph, 197
Les Nouveaux-Dieux, 295
Nova-Scotia Gazette, 45, 46
La Nuit des Assassins, 24, 30, 316, 319

The Old Trouper, 223
Olivier, Sir Laurence, 254
Ongley, David, 131, 137-140, 155-161, 172, 188, 190-193, 196, 198-200, 255
On the Way to Carberry, 23, 24
Orchard, Robert, 293
Ormsby, Mr., 48, 49
Osborne, Col. Henry, 79, 93, 97, 100-105, 108-115, 119, 122-124, 126, 127, 131, 132, 134, 146, 147, 150, 161, 163, 165, 166, 177-183, 184, 185, 213-225 passim, 250, 251, 253, 298
Ottawa Drama League, 76, 79, 84, 96, 102, 108, 116
Ottawa Dramatic Club, 68
Ottawa Little Theatre, 106, 113-115
Ottawa Players Club, 65, 74
Ottawa Thespians, 71
Out Flew the Web and Floated Wide, 296
Overlaid, 292
Over the Boiler Room, 292
Oxenford, Lynn, 233, 234

Pacific Coast Tragedy, 289
Palmer, George A., 292
Palmer, John, 272, 294
Paluscio-Morin, E., 293
Peacock, David, 243
Peene, Vida, 141-143, 202, 212, 270, 271, 295
Pelletier, Denise, 170
Pelletier, Gérard, 19

Pelletier, Gilles, 170
Pelletier, Jean, 142, 173, 206
Le Pendu, 196
Penthouse Players, 280, 281
Percival, W. P., 163
Perlin, John C., 210
Pharis, Gwendolyn, 291
Phelps, F. N., 140, 192, 193
Pickthall, Marjorie, 162, 288
Pigott, Leslie, 82
Players Club (Toronto), 76, 78
Players Club (U.B.C.), 76
Players Guild (Hamilton), 112
Playwrights Co-op, 298
Ponsonby, Vere Brabazon,
    Ninth Earl of Bess-
    borough, 83-97 *passim*,
    106, 107, 113, 114, 117,
    122, 123, 125-127, 132, 144,
    146, 161, 177, 213, 250,
    254, 262, 263, 274, 275,
    285, 286
Pope, Donald J., 152
Port Arthur Mummers, 238
Pott, Herbert, 145
Powell, Charles Stuart, 48
Power, Tyrone, Sr., 55
The Present Times, 46
Prigmore, Seth, 49
Princess Theatre (Toronto), 61
Progressive Arts Club
    (Vancouver), 277, 278
Provost, Guy, 170
Pyper, Nancy, 216

La Quintrala, 295

Rampe d'Ottawa, 162
Ramsay, Capt. Alexander, 289

Ramsay, Bea, 28, 39
Reaney, James, 295
Redfern, Sir Shuldham, 148
Reid, William, 152
The Release of Allan Danvers,
    69
Renaissance Théâtrale
    (Montreal), 164
Richmond Hill Curtain Club,
    267
Rickett's Equestrian
    and Comedy Co.
    (Philadelphia), 48
Rideau Vert, 168, 169, 318
Rinfret, Edouard, 173, 254,
    295
Riggs, Kate Douglas Wiggin,
    69
Rittenhouse, Charles, 150
Road companies, 57-63
Robertson, James L., 82
Robinson, Rogers, 80
John Beverley Robinson
    Amateur Players
    (Toronto), 72
Roche, Mazo de la, 289
Rocks, 121
Rodriguez, Percy, 282
Rosay, Françoise, 172
Rothmans Pall Mall of
    Canada, 310, 311
Roux, Jean-Louis, 170
Rowland, A. H., 167
Roy, James A., 103
Royal Alexandra Theatre
    (Toronto), 61
Royal Lyceum (Toronto), 53
Royal Opera House
    (Toronto), 53

Ruben, Jose, 170
Ryga, George, 31-33

Sabourin, Jeanne, 24, 25
La Sagouine, 319
St. Alban's Dramatic Club
   (Winnipeg), 74
St. Denis, Michel, 164, 165,
   170, 174, 206, 224, 225, 229
St. Francis Xavier Performing
   Group (Antigonish), 30
St. John Theatre Guild,
   83, 223
St. Laurent, Louis, 136, 156,
   157, 195, 197
St. Mary's Dramatic Class
   (Halifax), 68, 70
St. Valliere, Bishop Joseph
   de, 45
Sandwell, Bernard K., 64, 72,
   101, 112, 113
Sarnia Drama Club, 111, 112,
   133
Saskatchewan Arts Board,
   19, 151
Saskatchewan I'm Coming
   Home, 20-23, 316, 320
Saskatchewan Little Theatre,
   83
Schneckenburger, M. M.,
   155, 192, 196, 199,
   200, 201
Scott, Duncan Campbell,
   79, 289
Scott, James, 293
Scott, Mary Jane, 16, 17,
   29, 30
Scrivener, Gay, 279
Sears, Harold, 19

Shaw, Alvin J., 142, 143, 209,
   211, 212, 298, 307, 308,
   311, 314
Shaw, Irwin, 34
Shea's Theatre (Toronto), 61
Shiller, Leyden, 69
Simcoe Little Theatre, 142
Simpson, Charles W., 78
Sinclair, Lister, 296
Sinclair, Moray, 153
Sinclair, Walter, 81
Sixteen-Thirty Club
   (Montreal), 291
Skillan, George, 227, 276
Skinner, Dr. Alan, 135,
   151-153, 188
Small Potatoes, 291
Smith, Helen, 15-17, 20, 25,
   26, 28-30, 36-39, 41, 315
Somerset, Dorothy, 137, 300,
   304, 307
Southam, H. S., 134, 180, 181
Speaight, Robert, 150, 153,
   169, 186, 229, 231, 232,
   237, 241, 255
Spensley, Philip, 26-29, 39,
   41, 312, 313
Stannard, J. H., 115
Stephen, Susan, 319
Stewart, C. D., 141, 142
Stewart, Roy A., 140-142, 193,
   202, 253, 305
Still Stands the House, 291
Stone, Edgar, 82, 85, 86, 96,
   102, 111, 125, 138, 139,
   141, 184, 216
A Stranger Unto My Brethren,
   295
Strollers Club (Winnipeg), 74

Strolling Players
   (Vancouver), 279
Stuart, Robert, 229
Studio Players (Toronto), 78
Sullivan, Barry, 55
Sully, B. A., 210
Summers Stock Company, 58
Surveyer, Edouard Fabre,
   94, 96
The Suspicious Husband, 46
Suter, Graham, 231
Sweet, Jean, 291

Tale Theatre, 30
Tavernier Company, 59, 60
Teach Me How to Cry, 173, 295
Tec-Voc Travellers
   (Winnipeg), 34
Tembeck, Robert, 175
Terry, Ellen, 60
Theatre Calgary, 31
Le Théâtre de la Mandragore,
   175
Le Théâtre du Nouveau
   Monde, 170
Theatre of Action (Toronto),
   277
*Theatre of Neptune in
   New France*, 43, 44
Theatre Arts Guild (Halifax),
   82
Theatre Canada
   incorporated, 311-312
   Saskatoon Festival (1972),
   15-41, 316-320
Theatre Canada Magazine,
   190, 204
Théâtre Française (Montreal),
   61

Theatre Guild (St. John),
   83, 223
Theatre Guild of Canada, 81
Theatre Project (Saskatoon),
   267
Theatre Royal (Montreal),
   50
Théâtre 1 (Montreal), 175
Theatre Upstairs (Toronto),
   267
Thomas, Lillian B., 111, 116,
   289
Thorndike, Dame Sybil, 128
Thurrot, J. H., 291
Tirol, Marcel, 128
Tomorrow Will Be Sunday, 296
Toronto Associate Players, 73
Toronto Conservatory, 77
Toronto Garrison Dramatic
   Company, 65, 68
Toronto Opera House, 61
Toronto Opera House
   Company, 54
La Tour, 291
Tremblay, Mrs. Antonio, 115
Trinity Players (Montreal), 82
Trinity Players (Toronto), 78
Trophies (*see* Awards)
Trotter, Zee Pauline, 79
Troupe de l'Echiquier
   (Sherbrooke), 267
Troupe de l'Université de
   Moncton, 24, 30
Troupe Universitaire de la
   Laurentienne (Sudbury),
   175
Tupper, Lady Margaret, 83,
   95, 104, 112, 119, 126, 132,
   134, 225, 263, 264

Turner, Harold, 280, 281
Turner, Janice, 281
Tweedsmuir, Lord, 127, 128, 220
Twenty-five Cents, 233, 289

Union Dramatique de Québec, 118, 162
University Alumnae Dramatic Club (Toronto), 266
University College Alumnae Association (Toronto), 78
University Dramatic Club (Montreal), 65, 68
University of New Brunswick, 36

Vachon, Denis, 170
Van Cortland, Ida, 59, 60
Vancouver Little Theatre, 78, 119
Vancouver Playhouse, 302
Vanier, Georges, 201
Victoria College Players Club (Toronto), 76
Victoria Theatre, 56
The Virgin Unmasked, 45
Voaden, Herman, 82, 121
La Voix dans les Chênes, 293
Voyer, Pierre, 175, 297

Wade, Allan, 128, 164, 214, 217, 219
Walker, Bill, 282
C. P. Walker's Theatre (Winnipeg), 61
Wall, Lt. Commdr. Robert, 279

Walters, Jean, 26, 41
Watkins, William B., 195, 197
We Are Not Yet Born, 297
Wells, Dalton, 140, 141
West, Richard, 239
Western Ontario Drama Festival, 109
Western Ontario Drama League, 101
White, Dorothy, 79, 96, 114, 134, 138, 192, 236, 264
The White Man and the Mountain, 293
Whittaker, Herbert, 165, 166, 228, 259-265 *passim*, 291, 294, 301, 304, 305
Williams, Evelyn, 230-235
Wilson, George T., 319
Wilson, Murray, 191, 193
Wilson, Peter, 296
Winnipeg Dramatic Club, 68
Winnipeg Little Theatre, 94, 116
Winnipeg Thespians, 74
Wray, Maxwell, 237
Wrede, Gerda, 234-235
Wyle, Florence, 198, 260, 261

Xavierian Players (Antigonish), 267

Young, Roly, 250

Zone, 171, 295